THOSE WHO TRESPASS AGAINST US

TONI O'KEEFFE

BASED ON THE LIFE OF WALTER O'KEEFFE (1930- XXXX)

This book is based on the life of Walter O'Keeffe.
To protect the privacy of those still living, and, the families of those now deceased,
many of the names, places and events have been altered.

TRAFFORD
USA • Canada • UK • Ireland

Note for Librarians: A cataloguing record for this book is available from Library and Archives Canada at www.collectionscanada.ca/amicus/index-e.html
ISBN 1-4251-0457-6

Printed in Victoria, BC, Canada. Printed on paper with minimum 30% recycled fibre.
Trafford's print shop runs on "green energy" from solar, wind and other environmentally-friendly power sources.

TRAFFORD
PUBLISHING
Offices in Canada, USA, Ireland and UK

Book sales for North America and international:
Trafford Publishing, 6E–2333 Government St.,
Victoria, BC V8T 4P4 CANADA
phone 250 383 6864 (toll-free 1 888 232 4444)
fax 250 383 6804; email to orders@trafford.com
Book sales in Europe:
Trafford Publishing (UK) Limited, 9 Park End Street, 2nd Floor
Oxford, UK OX1 1HH UNITED KINGDOM
phone +44 (0)1865 722 113 (local rate 0845 230 9601)
facsimile +44 (0)1865 722 868; info.uk@trafford.com
Order online at:
trafford.com/06-2214

10 9 8 7 6 5

For Dad

In loving memory of Bessie, Eileen, Billy, Jim, and Sean.

One

MARCH 1939

This day, I woke long before the sun began to crack through the blackened sky over Polrone. I was damp and chilled from the pee that had soaked up the back of the tattered jumper I had fallen asleep in. My eight-year-old belly ached and the cutting chill that filled our house brought out a mass of shivering goose pimples that covered my arms and legs. The small thatched roof cottage that had always been my home was silent. The scents of our dirty clothing and unwashed bodies fought with the smell of rotting spuds and two full chamber pots. Soiled rags stained with blood, were tangled amongst the wrinkled sheets that lay on the floor beside the iron bed where my father Edmund had died two days ago.

I held my knees tightly to my stomach, shivering, aching, and wet. My belly churned and gurgled as it pushed around the foul stuff that was making me sick. I ached both from hunger and worry. What would happen to us? I closed my eyes and tried to imagine the familiar and calming warmth of a fire burning in the hearth. Still my body shook. I struggled to imagine the smell of made coffee and rhubarb cake warming on the hob, and strained to hear the sound of my father puttin' about in the yard and the clicking of hooves as he hooked up and readied his coal wagon to make the trip to Piltown.

They're not dead and I'm not cold. I'm just dreamin'. I'm gonna' wake now and mother's going to put me on the pot. My eyes opened but nothing had changed. The house was cold, dirty and it stank. This was real. My parents, Edmund and Bridgett, were dead; and this was the day my Dad would be put in to the ground. And damn, I'd peed myself again.

The breath rose from my two brothers, Sean and Jim, as they lay in the bed with me, the two of them coiled up stiff. All of us dirty, pale, and thin. Crawling over the arms and legs that shared my cot, I could feel the dampness of the pee that had soaked in around my brothers. Jees' they're gonna' be mad at me. Maybe not, maybe Jim peed too. I rubbed my hands over his spot on our mattress to see if he had also wet himself. Crap only me.

Holding on to my belly, I stumbled off the bed and hurried to make my way to the chamber pot that was almost overflowing. Made it! Just as I sat my arse down on the cold porcelain pan my inners exploded and splashed back against my bum. My butt burnt inside and out. My dirty bare feet vibrated as I tried to hold steady. My eyes were strained and tightly closed as I held my breath and tried to balance myself over the pot. Finally, the rumblings inside me stopped, and I let out the mouthful of air I had been holding.

Carefully, I rose from my squatting position so that I wouldn't dribble or tip anything on to the floor. With nothing to dry my bum I reached between my legs and pulled the back of my woolen pullover forward to dry off my inner thighs. I stepped back from the pot, picked it up and carried it out of the room leaving a path of drippings behind me. I set the filthy white and blue porcelain container down on the aged wooden sideboard that had once been the place where my Mum had prepared our family meals and where she had set her baking to cool. The sideboard was now piled with rotting spud peelings, dirty tin plates and some dried rosemary that would not likely see its way into a stew any time soon. I lifted the iron latch on the heavy wooden door that led to the outside.

A piercing chill rushed in and stabbed me in a hundred places as it entered the pores of my flesh. Although severe, the clean fresh air was a welcomed contrast to the foul odors that filled the house. I hauled the pot to the grassy ditch behind our home where our family routinely left our "doings." I dumped the pot on to the grass and watched the yellow sickly liquid flow down towards the base of the trench. The grass here grew tall and dark green. Animals loved the grass from this part of the yard. My Dad had said that the earth feeds us and in a way, this is how we feed the earth. I always laughed about it.

The sky was dark but I was able to see silhouettes of the outbuildings that were home to the donkeys, greyhounds, rare birds and other livestock that had earned my Dad ribbons in almost every fair in County Cork, and many in County Killkenny. Against the darkness I could make out the two clothes wires that my Dad had run between the barn and the shed, one for drying clothes and the other for the birds he kept and took to fair. This morning, the wires were lined with rows of canaries, finch, piccolos, and other fowl that waited and called out for the seed that would not be thrown their way today.

The high wet grass was cool against my naked legs. It tickled as blades of grass and streams of dew worked their way between my toes and licked the dirt from my skin. The scents—of moisture on the air, of dill, thyme, and dried hay, and even the smell of donkey and horse manure, were pleasing. "That's the smell of life," my Dad would say. "Water, plants growing, hay drying, animals pooping are all part of this amazing cycle of life." He loved it and I loved it. I closed my eyes and took in several deep breaths. I had always enjoyed the peacefulness of morning. But today the peacefulness of my surroundings did not calm me. I felt uneasy and anxious.

From behind one of the outbuildings "Prowler," our dirty, tan-coloured dog, slowly made his way towards me. Prowler had been part of our family for as long back as I could remember. We didn't know what type of dog he was. Dad said he was a little bit of everything. Today the normally lively dog walked slowly. His head and jowls hung low and his tail drooped and dragged behind him. "I wonder if he knows?" I thought to myself. "I bet he does 'cause dogs can sense these things." Even while my Dad lay ill and dying, we could tell that Prowler was concerned and stayed by father's bed. On the day that my Dad died, Prowler had started to howl hours before father passed away. When Dad finally passed on, the dog fell silent.

Prowler plopped himself down on the damp grass next to me. He laid his chin in my lap, then proceeded to slowly and affectionately clean my dirty fingers with his tongue. Holding on to my companion I felt the burrs hidden deep in his coat. I thought that maybe I should pull them out, but not today. I held him for several minutes before I rose and headed back towards the house. The dog did not move but let out a heavy sigh. He lay there on the damp ground with his jowls turned down, his brow creased and his dark brown eyes looking quite human, as if he was experiencing great sorrow. He was.

As I headed back towards our whitewashed cottage I could see the multiple shades of pink and orange that were just beginning to creep up over the meadows in Polrone and beyond to Mooncoin. The colours melted together and crowned the crest of the sun as it began to peak out from beneath the River Suir. Now my belly began to rumble again, this time from hunger alone. It could only be from hunger as there was nothing left inside me to come out.

Back inside nothing had changed. My two sisters, Bessie and Eileen, were snuggled close together in my parents' bed. My brother, Billy, lay in a small cot next to the bed I shared with Sean and Jim. None of them stirred. They were frozen asleep, too cold to move. We looked like a family. All of us with our thick, wavy, raven, hair, an obvious gap between our front teeth and our olive skin. Black Irish is what they said we were. Different than our red haired freckled cousins. Since our Dad had passed away two days earlier, the six of us had stayed in the house alone. There had been some talk of who might take care of us but for now, we were on our own.

I pulled on a gray jumper my mother had made me more than two years earlier. It was much too small, but I didn't care, I only cared about lookin' my best when I went to say my final goodbye to my Dad. I slid on a pair of under-shorts, a pair of gray woolen trousers, woolen gray socks, and scrunched my toes into my black leather boots. Still, none of the others woke.

We O'Keeffe children were not expected at the burial in Mooncoin but I was goin'. We had all been there when Dad was taken from our house. My sisters crying', Sean, Billy, Jim and I just stood back, out of the way, as the grown-ups prepared to take my Dad. At the time, it hadn't hit me that he was never coming back.

Our father was a huge man. When they did take him from our house it was quite an operation. There wasn't a coffin big enough to fit him so one was built around him, right there inside our house. Before the carpenter who built the thing nailed down the lid my Uncle Jim tried to put Dad's boots on him. With his boots on he was still too big for the burial box so Uncle Jim just tossed the boots to the floor. I didn't like that, my Dad going into the ground with no boots.

When they were ready to take him away, ten men gathered around to lift him up and move him out. They quickly realized that this box and my father, were not leaving through the front door. This group of men, who were all very close to my Dad, set the coffin down on the floor and scratched their heads, rubbed their chins, studied the width and the length of the box, to con-template how they would get him out of there. My Dad would have loved this. What a comedy! One of the fellows even suggested that they take Dad out of the box first and drag him through the door and then take the box apart to get it outside.

Eventually, John Commerford suggested that they try and pass the casket through the window. With five men inside and five outside that's what they did, and it worked. They lifted and tilted, turned the box this way and that way, trying to get him out of the house. I'm surprised he didn't fall right out of there. They grunted and groaned, their faces red and sweaty, cussing as they hauled him away. When they finally got Dad to the funeral wagon they were all exhausted.

Meanwhile, the driver of the funeral cart had just sat through this entire ordeal, reading from the bible, never once looking up at the comedy taking place around him. Dressed in black, thin, and with pale white skin, he looked like death himself. Three of the men pushed Dad and his coffin all the way to the back of the funeral wagon and covered him up with a horse blanket. Without making eye contact with anyone, the driver drew his fingers to his lips and sounded off a short whistle and the horses started to move. Dad's body was taken up to Mooncoin to the home of his band mate Frank Long, and laid out so family and friends could say their final farewells, and I planned to be there.

I found my Dad's comb and carefully raked my tangled black curls to one side. Standing in front of my father's small grooming mirror, I could see that my hair was still sticking up so worked up a good spit, spat into my palms and ran my fingers over my hair to make sure it was neatly in place.

As I left the house I stumbled over my Dad's boots, still lying where they had been tossed. My stomach tightened when I realized that I would never again watch him struggle to pull those dirty well-worn rubbers off his feet. It stank when he pulled them off. "Tis a good smell," he'd say. "That's the smell that feeds this family." These boots that took him everywhere—He should be wearing them today; it's not right, I thought as I bent down to straighten them up so they were at least side-by-side, standing tall.

Heading out to the yard I turned to see if Prowler was in eyeshot. He was still curled up on the ground where I'd left him. Normally the dog would have run up to the gate and made a scene until he was allowed to come along. Today, he just lay there.

As I headed down New Road I looked out towards the Phelan family cottage to see if there were any signs of life. Maybe they'd be heading up to Mooncoin in their wagon and pick me up along the way, but I didn't see anyone up and about.

The Phelans had been our neighbors for years. Josie Phelan and I were the same age and the best of friends. Josie with her beautiful blonde hair and pale skin was quite the contrast to my olive skin, dark eyes, and black hair. We were a grand little couple and often met down by the banks of the River Suir to putter with nature. We'd watch the black beetles wiggle through the mud, were fascinated by the bees and could watch them moving about for hours. We'd race along the tall grassy banks of the Suir trying to keep up with the swans as they gracefully drifted with the flow of the water. One of our favorite past times was to go on walks and count up all the different life forms we could find: rabbits, dragonflies, trout jumping up from the river to catch flies, owls, worms, spiders, frogs, and even the odd fox were all a part of this magical place that was our home. People thought it was odd for two young folk to be so caught up with nature—plants, insects and such. Nonetheless, Josie and I enjoyed sharing our time with each other. In my mind we were more than friends. One day I might even marry her, if she'd have me.

Carrying on past the Phelans, I walked alongside the dirt road picking and nibbling on pieces of hawthorn, bluebell stems, and other greenery to fill my belly. We had never been hungry when our parents were alive. Now that was all I thought about—food. Violets, primrose buds, anything I knew the animals would eat, I picked and gnawed on. I jumped the ditch and cut in through Mrs. Murphy's yard. I walked along the path beside the old graystone Murphy house and followed the Murphy property until I came to the large iron-gate at the edge of the garden. This was a beautiful home with a garden full of apple trees, colourful flowers, and a wonderful place for any bird, bee, or bug to live. Later in the fall, I'd come back to shake the Murphy's Sheep Snout apples. If the seeds rattled inside the apple that was a sure sign that they were ripe and ready to eat. But today the trees were barren.

On the other side of the large iron-gate was the ancient Polrone graveyard. This was my favorite place. I had started exploring the old burial ground when I was barely three years old. The abandoned graveyard was a magnificent place to come and dream about the past and the future. When the cemetery in the Mooncoin churchyard had been put into use many years earlier, this beautiful monument to Irelands warriors and clansman was forgotten. Rich green ivy embraced the archway to the burial yard and crept its way around every ancient headstone. Celtic crosses, the old stone-walls, and the beautiful ancient ruins of a cathedral, made this spot mysterious, yet comforting. Wild purple and blue violets grew amongst the ivy and looked like tiny peeping eyes keeping watch over each resting place in the yard. This was my playground. No one ever came here. But today there would be no time to play and no time to dream.

I made my way to the main road that led to Mooncoin. I had been lost in my thoughts and hadn't noticed the rain clouds that had now moved in behind the rising sun. I felt the first few droplets fall from the clouds overhead so I pulled the lapels of my small jacket together and quickened my pace. The rest of the world was now beginning to wake and smells of breads and meats cooking filled the air. Every once in a while, a rabbit would scurry in and out of the ditch. Each time I saw one I imagined how good it would taste. I wondered if I could cook a rabbit by myself. Father used to do it; it didn't look so hard. I wonder if you cook the guts and all?…could make something with the tails I supposed. Again, here I was thinking about food.

Looking out towards the River Suir, I could see the fishing boats heading out like my Dad's once had. I'd usually be there at the end of the day to watch him come back in. When he wasn't fishing, hauling coal, or tending the animals, my Dad would take my brothers, sisters, and me down to the river when the tide was low. He, in his tall black rubber boots and rolled up sleeves, would search the river's edge for the perfect rock.

When he found it he'd give us a whistle and wait for us to gather 'round. When he knew he had our attention and we were all staring down at the rock he'd flip it over to reveal the lively squirming eels that were hiding and thrashing about. I laughed my arse off each time he did it. We would giggle and squeal as we picked up the eels and threw them into a bucket.

After taunting our sisters with the squirmy worm-like creatures, we would head for home and take the bucket to our Mum. She would cook up the entire lot in a huge pan of butter. It was disgusting watching those eels getting cooked up while they were still alive. But oh, they smelt good. As gruesome as it was, this memory of life with my parents was a happy one.

Again I quickened my pace and held the collar on my jacket tightly around my neck to stop the droplets of rain from running down my back. The sun that had barely had a chance to wake had now completely disappeared behind the coal colored clouds and the rain began to spit down harder upon me. I began to run to beat the downpour before it completely drenched me all the way through.

"What would happen after today?" My belly began to cramp. "Where would we live? Could we stay in our house?" I started to break a sweat across my brow? "Would we still be hungry tomorrow and the day after that?" My insides began to burn. "Would anybody come to take care of us? Maybe we could mange on our own?" I ran into the bush before my gut exploded once again. I had barely got my shorts down when the burning liquid burst out. After it had stopped I just sat. Relieved that I had not soiled my clothes, I thought of nothing, dreamt of nothing and for a moment felt nothing, only relieved.

Two

THE FUNERAL

After walking for what seemed like miles drenched through to my under-shorts, I finally walked up the path to Frank Long's cottage. Like all the others around it, the cottage was white turned gray, framed in with a stone fence, and a wire gate that didn't sit quite right on its hinges. The cottage's thatched roof was in need of repair and the chimney that was pumping out black smoke was a few stones short of falling in on itself. Jesus I was hungry; maybe they'll be serving up biscuits or cake. The red wooden door was held open by a well-worn milking stool. Two large tabby cats, one on top and one underneath, covered the seat and legs of the stool with a mess of colourful fur. I stopped to stroke the cat sitting on top of the stool. Soft and warm he was. He rolled on to his back to have me scratch his belly. "These damn cats," I thought, "they got it made—lots of cuddling, lots of food and they never have to worry about a thing."

I moved into the cottage. Through the long black skirts and pipe smoke, I could see father's casket lying open in the center of the room. The smoke danced in the air and swirled about each time someone raised an arm or coughed. I had not expected to see my Dad's body again. I thought it was all done and over and now the last task was to place him in the ground. I was strangely pleased to see the coffin cover open. The large tabby followed me in and was rubbing up the side of my leg, his long soft tail caressing my calf. We had always had cats at our house. When my Mum was sick and dying, I'd crawl into bed with her, our big cat Tinker tucked under my arm. I'd have to pretend Tinker and I were both sick, just so we could get into the sick bed with her. She'd pull me close and let me snuggle into her and we'd share one of the jam filled biscuits that always seemed to be on her bedside table. With Tinker nestled in my arms, my Mum would caress my face and stroke my hair and most often I would fall asleep. The poor cat...I even fed her cod liver oil to make it look like she really was sick and needed to be in that bed with us. God I loved that safe wonderful feeling of being that close to my mother. Funny that I would be remembering this now, just before my father is about to go into the ground. Those two cats, warm and comforting, reminded me of home.

No one much noticed that I had entered the house. The whiskey was flowing and good songs sung poorly were being belted out. As most of the men were already well into the drink I figured they must have either been at it all night or been up darn early. Most of the people in the house were older men who had been friends of my Dad, some cousins and a few elderly aunts. They were all pretty much dressed the same. Men in white shirts, brown woolen trousers, woolen jackets and caps, pipes hanging out the sides of their mouths, a drink in one hand and a chair or a wall in the other holding them up. The women were in long black skirts and shawls, some holding rosary beads, all of them holding on to hankies. The odd laugh could be heard as a joke or tale was told about my Dad, Edmund, but mostly it was bad singing and tears and a few old women reciting Hail Marys.

"Come on Franky, give us a tune...how 'bout "Rose of Mooncoin?" someone called out.

"Nope' I won't, 'cause I wouldn't be doing the song no justice. Little Ned, God rest his soul, was the singer in this band and I ain't taking 'is place today." Little Ned was the pet-name that had been given to my Dad because he was so big.

"Come on Franky, it wouldn't be right to send 'im into the ground without singin' "Rose of Mooncoin" one last time."

"Alright, alright." Frank Long pulled himself up from his place, straighten his jacket, poured back what was left in his cup and stumbled a bit before he was steady on his feet. "I'll be asking the angels to forgive me if I don't sing it just as well as our dear old Ned."

Frank began to spew out "The Rose of Mooncoin" and shattered what was once a beautiful piece of music. Being that they were all too drunk to tell the difference, the tears started flowing from all ends of the room. "The Rose of Mooncoin" always got this kind of reaction from our townsfolk no matter how good or bad it was being sung. Men draped their arms around one another, women wrapped in black shawls wailed and wiped their runny eyes and noses. This was the Irish, this is what we did. I had seen it before in the pubs and in the homes of others who had lost their loved ones.

I pushed through the crowd of mourners, thieving a bread crust and piece of cheese that had been abandoned on a tin plate. I quickly ate up the morsels I had found, wiped my hands on the front of my jacket, and walked up to the open casket. I wasn't scared. Seeing a dead body, especially my father's, didn't frighten me at all. Even if the dearly departed could rise from the dead and haunt us, my Dad would never scare me or hurt me.

I pulled over a wooden chair and knelt on it so I could look in. I just stared at him. I don't know for how long but I just stared. My Dad didn't look like he was sleeping. He looked dead. "Why do they always tell children dead people are sleeping? They're just dead, anyone can tell that," I thought.

I leaned in closer to take a good look. When I did, the smell of the coal dust that had seeped into his clothing reached my nose. That smell had been a welcome and reassuring sign that our father was home safe from another long day delivering coal to the many homes and businesses throughout Counties Cork and Killkenny. I raised my hand and touched my father's cheek. His face was cold and stiff and my finger left a dent on his skin. I stood there for what seemed like a long time remembering every feature of his face. His thick light brown hair, his sculpted cheekbones, his long jaw.

Staring at my father's once strapping frame, I remembered sitting on the banks of the Suir watching as he'd hoist in a net and pull in a salmon. He would raise his strong arm and whack the fish with a fish knocker. There was always a delay from the time he hit the fish to the time the sound of the knocker reached the shore where I sat. My Dad had been so many things, was so talented, so alive, so much fun, and so loving. Now he was dead, just dead. It didn't make a lot of sense. Even dead he looked strong and handsome. But I knew "he" wasn't in there. My Dad was gone, his sprit sent to look out for my Mum and my brother Eammon.

I let out a heavy sigh and rested my chin on the edge of the coffin almost breathing right into his face. I wanted him to get up and come home with me, but I knew that wouldn't happen. I wanted him to grab me and pull me in there with him and never let me go. I wanted to go with him and be with him and my Mum.

"Well, let's get on with it. We best be off," called out one of the men. I was quickly drawn back to the present when the lid to the casket was shut. As it came down, I could still see the tiny imprint my finger had left on my Dad's cheek. This gave me some comfort, knowing that a part of me was going with him. I liked that I had left my mark on him, and him on me.

"Wattie O'Keeffe, what are ya' doing here boy?" called out my Uncle Jim. "Who brung ya' here lad?"

"I brung myself."

"Who told ya' you could come?"

"I told myself."

"Well, I'll be whistling jigs to a fencepost trying to get ya' to head home, so ya' may as well go on and get in the hearse."

"What did he mean?" I thought. "This is my father and he would have wanted me to come. Why did he ask me who told me I could come?" This was the first time it hit me that it would be other adults making decisions about my life, adults who really did not understand me or my siblings. This realization scared me to death.

As I was leaving the cottage, I caught sight of an abandoned tin cup of yellow liquid resting on the edge of the wooden table. I grabbed it and drank it down quickly. I didn't care if it was beer or any other type of liquor. I was parched and dying for anything wet to moisten my lips. "Thank you God!" It was lemonade, still cold and wonderfully sweet. I rubbed my tongue over my mouth to make sure not one drop of the delicious liquid missed making it to my tummy. I placed the tin back down and hurried out the door.

Again, it took ten pallbearers to lift the coffin and slide it through the open window. Four large black horses strapped to the hearse stood waiting to receive their next patron and shuttled him off to the Mooncoin Cemetery. I jumped into the back of the hearse with a group of relatives that were still unaware of, or ignoring, my presence. A line of other friends and family gathered behind the wagon to follow it to the churchyard.

Rain pounded down on the small thatched roofed cottages in the tiny town of Mooncoin. It was usually like this during the month of March. I was thankful to be inside the hearse. Sore from the long walk and boots that did not quite fit, my feet were throbbing. I loosened the leather laces, stared out into the wet streets, and appreciated the bit of rest.

The wet cobblestone roads were an untidy clutter of garbage, pee pots, soaking woodpiles, blackened coal buckets, and dirty children. A stream of mud and animal droppings made its way to the poorest end of town, where families had surrendered to the elements and no longer attempted to keep the rain from seeping in under their doorways. Black smoke rose from the simple homes that burnt coal in their charred chimneys. Inside, families waited out the chill, the damp, and the boredom. They watched for the dirty wet drizzles that would find their way through the straw bale roofs that were meant to keep the rain out, but didn't.

When it rained this hard and for this long, it was impossible to escape the pungent odor of burning coal combined with the stench of pee buckets whose contents had been tossed into the streets, and the wet garbage piles that had become living quarters for the town's rodents. Our home, in Polrone, had been a pleasant contrast to the dismal huts the funeral procession passed by on the way to the cemetery. My parents had kept a tidy home and farm; all of us were well-fed and well-dressed.

The heavy hooves of the horses as they hit the rain drenched cobblestones, and the huge iron wheels on the hearse as they turned, made a distinct and repetitive slapping sound. The familiar noise drew people to their windows to watch the hearse go by. After only a few minutes, the hearse arrived in front of the churchyard. "Hardly enough time to rest," I thought. The horses knew were to stop—they had taken this trip a hundred times before. The driver did not even have to pull back on the reins.

Still, very few people had acknowledged my presence. My feet were still throbbing when I jumped down from the hearse. Like everyone else, I made my way towards the gray-stone church building. As I drew near the entrance I could hear a choir singing a sad gloomy hymn. At least they could sing.

A long line of people filtered into the church to attend the service before my father would be laid to rest in the churchyard. Once inside, I moved towards the front pews. Through the corner of my eye I could see the priest getting dressed in his black robe, preparing to ring the funeral bell. The church filled up as the choir continued to sing melancholy hymns. The sight of the priest caused me to tremble. I began to sweat. "If I look directly upon 'im, I might be next," I thought. "Damn my stomach was in knots." In his black robe, this man frightened the hell out of me. I don't know why I was afraid of these men of the church, maybe it was because they were held in the highest regard. To me, they were one step away from God.

Near the front of the old stone cathedral, I caught the glance of my godfather, Jack Fitzgerald. Jack had always been a caring, friendly, and easy man to get along with. I liked him. Jack and my Dad had been friends for years. Jack was also one of the men who struggled to get my Dad's coffin through the window at our house. Jack and my Dad had played in the band together, fished together, and often helped each other with various jobs.

Jack motioned me to come to him. He had bushy unkempt red hair, rosy round cheeks, cracked yellow teeth, and was one of the kindest men I had ever known. I made my way towards him. Without saying a word he handed me a sixpence. He gazed with great concern into my eyes and looked like he wanted to say something but would start to cry if he did. Jees', he looked worried, and that made me nervous. He patted me on the butt and sent me back to my seat in the pew. "A sixpence! Jesus, that would buy a lot of sweets." I thought.

When the service ended I was surprised, since I had not really noticed that it had begun. I had been too busy looking about, watching the priest, gazing at the faces of strangers, and still trying to taste the lemonade on my lips. I followed the procession through the wet, green, cemetery yard to the edge of the freshly dug plot. The rain that had been pounding down only half an hour ago had now completely stopped. As the men prepared to lower father into the ground I tried to remember the day my mother was buried, but I could not remember a thing. I had stood here in this same spot only two years ago but could not remember it. We had been back to the cemetery yard many times to visit my Mum not knowing it would not be long before Father was laid to rest with her.

I wanted to remember these last few moments with my Dad's casket. I did not want to think back in a few years, and not remember this day. I focused on what was taking place around me. Staring at the casket, I remembered my finger imprinted on his cheek, the smell of coal, the fishing boats, the coal wagon, the birds, Prowler, the fairs, the Greyhounds, singing, bands, eels, tailored suits, all of it—and then watched as several men lowered my father's coffin into the ground. I knew I would never forget.

My Dad, Edmund O'Keeffe, was laid to rest at the age of 39 in the same grave as his wife, Bridgett, who had passed away two years earlier of pleurisy or some other disease. No one really knew for sure. My youngest brother, Eammon, who had perished at the age of ten months was also in there with them.

The funeral bell now rang out. Before my father's casket hit its final resting spot, I began to make my way back through the crowd and out of the churchyard. Once out on to the street I darted donkey carts, men on bikes, and other wagons, to make my way to the sweet shop. I felt rather proud walking into a shop with the ability to purchase and pay for something rather than coming in to look and smell. The bells dangling from the shop door jingled as I entered alerting the storekeeper that he had a customer. I was starving. The sweet smell of chocolate made me drunk with excitement. I opened my mouth as if the scents of the sweets in the shop could be tasted.

I pulled the sixpence from my pocket and placed it on the glass counter. Too short to reach any of the sweets on my own, and without saying a word, I pointed to the chocolates, lemon drops, and other treats I wanted until the shop owner told me I had spent the lot. I took the brown paper bag from the storekeeper and scurried out eager to devour my purchase. Finding a spot at the edge of the road with the churchyard still in view, I sat my arse down on the roadside. As I wolfed down my sweets, I gazed back at the cemetery and thought about the night father had first injured himself. Who would have known that a slip off a wagon would lead to his—death.

We had been on our way back from Piltown where my Dad often took his produce to market and entered various varieties in the fair. Once again, he had won several ribbons and sold a good deal of his produce, and for a good price. Like all trips back from Piltown, we pulled our wagon into Commerford's Pub where father was well-known to the locals. There was all sorts of 'tittle-tattle' that we were somehow related to the Commerford clan, but I wasn't sure how. The old man, John Commerford, was always really nice to us and our Dad.

During the evening, the patrons of the watering hole would send Fry's chocolate and ginger beer to the table where we sat in awe of our father and his ability to please his audience. All night we were treated kindly and amused. The longer we children were occupied and happy, the longer the patrons at the pub could rely on our father to keep them entertained. Some nights, there were so many sweets sent to the table that we had to throw the stuff under our chairs as our tummies could not tolerate another sickly-sweet piece.

At the end of this particular night, my Dad loaded us on to the wagon. As he hoisted himself up, having had one-too-many pints in him, he slipped and landed on the rusty axle, which left him with a large gash on his hip. For the first couple days after he hurt himself he managed to hobble about. But then, a ghastly infection set in and he could not move from his bed.

I stood by and watched as my two elder brothers and my sister Bessie used their fists to try and extract the poison and pus from our Dads hip.

"Don't worry Wattie. Your old Dad is going to be fine," my father told me. I guess he could see the concern in my face. "The doctor from Waterford will be coming 'round to fix me up and then I'll be jumping out of this here bed to take ya' boys eel huntin'."

As the weeks went by, father's hip turned green, then black. The wound oozed yellow stuff, and gave off a foul odor that we could smell throughout our small family cottage. The rags used to soak up the fluids from the wound were strewn on the floor of the room were father spent his final days. Sean jumped and rolled on our Dad's ailing body and made gagging sounds, pinching his nose as Bessie, Jim, and Billy worked on healing our father's hip. Six-year-old Sean had no idea that our father was so near death. The older ones and I knew our Dad was dying, yet none of us spoke about the likelihood of loosing him. We just carried on the way we always had.

A lady did come 'round to see Dad; I don't know if she was a nurse or a doctor. She tried to clean up his wound but even she knew there was no hope. She gave him some tablets, for the pain I think. She told us to keep him comfortable until his time, and we never saw her again. I could see the infection creeping down his leg like an ivy vein seeking something to grasp on to.

When the priest came 'round and dotted oil on my Dad's eyes, ears, nose, lips, and hands, I knew the end was near. *"Through this holy unction and His own most tender mercy may the Lord pardon thee whatever sins or faults thou hast committed quidquid deliquisti by sight, by hearing, smell, taste, touch, walking, carnal delectation."* I knew these words; they were the words spoken just before someone passed on. The next day, my father lost the battle with his wound and died.

"Splat!" A wagon rumbled by and spit up a pool of dirty water, soaking my already damp clothes and knocking me back to the present. Clutching my sweet bag, I let out a heavy sigh, stood, wiped the front of my jacket, and started back down the road to Polrone not knowing what the world would spit up at me next.

Three

AUNT MARY MOVES IN

I was exhausted and dying of thirst by the time I reached the pathway to our house. "Wattie O'Keeffe ya' filthy little beast, where have ya' been boy?" shouted my Aunt Mary from the front porch of our home. What's she doing here? I hate that fat cow.

"Ya' get yur' arse up here before I give ya' a tannin' to remember."

My brother Billy came hustling by me quickly carrying two buckets of "doings" on his way to the ditch. "She's moving in Wattie, her and Uncle Bill, and all the cousins. Father gave em' the house if they keep us." Billy just kept moving as if fear itself was chasing him.

I felt faint. I was stunned. She can't live here in mother's house? She's mean, smells bad, she yells, swears and she beats her kids. Our Aunt Mary was a terrible beast. My head dropped into my hands and I fell to my knees in disbelief that this pig of a woman was moving into our home. I thought now of the time she whacked my cousin Willy, her son, over the head with a broom. She whacked him so hard the handle broke in two over the top of his skull. She was always beating them up.

I then felt the agony of a thousand roots of my hair being pulled from my head. The force was so great that it launched me back to my feet. When I looked up, all I saw was the palm of a huge red wrinkled hand as it made its way to smack the side of my face. Again I was stunned as the ripple of her thrust made its way through my head. The force of her blow left my ear ringing with pain. Through the corner of my eye I could see Sean frozen and panicked sitting outside our front door. His nose had been bleeding and he had a large palm print on the side of his face.

"Ya' Ned O'Keeffe boys have been coddled too long. You're feeble, you're stupid and I won't have a buncha' pathetic pretty boys living under my roof. This is my house now and yur' damned lucky I'm going to let ya' stay here." She dragged me by the hair towards the door where Sean sat shaking in fear. "Ya' lot make me sick with yur' fancy clothes and yur' fancy shoes, it's wrong I tell ya'," she shrieked, as she stared her hideous face right into mine. "God is mysterious ya' know. He has given me the opportunity to rear ya' lot 'and make ya' appreciate what many other folk don't got." She pulled her face away from me, thank God as her breath was as foul as anything that was tossed in the ditch outback. "Its not right," she continued, "that we've been living just up the road 'bout near starving and you's down here are eating like kings."

None of us knew what she was rambling about. Our father had always worked hard after our Mum died to put food on the table for his family. He had also often left vegetables, eggs, and milk at his brother Bill's home, full-well knowing that Bill and Mary's kids were hard done by with their impoverished parents. It wasn't as if Mary or Bill couldn't go off fishing or grow a garden; they were just too lazy, too busy hating each other or drinking, to be bothered.

"She's mental," I whispered to Sean. "She needs to live in one of those places where they put crazy people."

"Mary, leave 'em boys alone now. Let 'em get settled." My Uncle Bill came out from behind the house, and just in time I thought. "Leave em' be Mary, they're not bad boys."

"No, but they're lazy boys who 'ave never been disciplined, and that's going to change under my watch. I expect the same from these young-'uns as I do from my own," she barked back to her husband.

Before he died, my Dad promised Uncle Bill that he and Mary could have our home and the animals if they continued to look after us. Bill and Mary had been living in a shack in Mooncoin with their nine children and were elated with the thought of moving into our house. Mary was not at all pleased that we were a part of the agreement. Although my Uncle Bill was a decent and caring man, he was a simple drunk and Mary was clearly the one in charge.

Mary was a heavy-set woman with small narrow eyes and a creased little mouth that always seemed to be frowning. She wore a scarf to hide the red, scaly, balding spot in her thinning, reddish-blond hair. When she removed the scarf, flakes would flutter from her head like snow. The red marks and veins on her cheeks were no doubt caused by all the yelling she did. I swear I could see the blood vessels exploding in her face each time she screamed at me. She had a body odor that was grossly unpleasant. She secreted the scent of rotting fish and cooked cabbage and most people, including her husband, found her hard to be around for any length of time, which explained the amount of time he spent away from the family drinking in the local pubs. She rarely bathed or laundered her clothing, so it did not take long for her repulsive scent to seep into the fabric of our home. Her odor lingered even when she was not there. She was an angry, ugly woman with a heavy, cold heart.

How were fifteen children and two adults possibly going to live in this house, our house? I hadn't a clue. But that was it, they moved in and there did not seem to be a lot we could do about it. Life changed quickly for all of us. Our once loving home had been turned into a place that was cold and frightening. Under Mary's guard the household chores fell to my brothers, our cousins, and me. Each day, before and after school, what ever she wanted us to do we did: haul water and wood, gather what was left of the garden, haul chamber pots, etc. Meals were never prepared nor was there any sort of food-stuff available for any of us to take to school; we were all left to fend for ourselves.

I do remember old John Commerford from the pub, coming 'round once. He pulled up in his cart and set a sack of potatoes and turnips at the gate of our house.

"Which one are ya' then?" he had asked me.

"I'm Walter, Edmunds Walter," I had replied.

"You're a good-looking lad Walter. Be well now," he replied and then he left.

Quickly, I filled the front of my jumper with spuds and as many turnips as I could, then ran to hide them. In a dark corner of our old shed, I dug a bit of a hole with my bare hands and covered up my stash. Mr. Commerford was a kind man and reminded me of my Dad, but he never came around after that.

By late April, only a month after father had passed away, most of our family's precious items—including my father's fishing boat, Mother's sewing wheel, vases, furnishings that had been hand made by my Dad, crockery, and even the animals—had been sold off to buy whiskey and a few staple items like flour and sugar.

Life at school was a welcome relief from the misery of home. Our teacher, Sister Theresa, was perhaps the kindest woman I had ever met next to my mother. Although she dressed in a traditional black and white gown, I could tell that she was a very thin woman as her long thin fingers, tiny wrists and frail arms were exposed daily as she wrote out numbers, letters, and prayers on the chalkboard. She was much more attractive than most nuns at the school. Maybe they didn't have a habit small enough for her tiny frame or she had too much hair under there, as occasionally two long curly brown ringlets would find their way loose and frame her petite, soft, white face. She was so young and quite beautiful, I often wondered why she became a nun and did not have a husband or a family of her own?

"Children, I think you've worked hard today, all week in fact, so I am going to let ya' out early," announced Sister Theresa. A burst of cheers swept through the classroom as thirty enthused youngsters began fantasizing about how we would spend this couple of extra hours in our day. "I'm letting ya' out early to work on a homework project." The cheers fell to a dull sigh.

"Before ya' make yur' way home to tend to yur' chores I would like ya' all to spend a wee bit of time exploring the living beauty that God has created for us here in Polrone and Mooncoin. I would like each of you to study a plant or a flower or a bird. Whatever ya' like, but it has to be something living. Then I want ya' to write down how you believe these living gifts to us from God contribute to our life here in Polrone."

From the narrow rows of tightly-packed, wooden desks hands flew up to ask a barrage of irrelevant questions. The assignment was really just an excuse to let us out early, yet the questions had to be asked I guess.

"Can I write about my dog, Sister, as he scares away the other animals that get after our sheep?" asked Nettie Hogan.

"Yes, Nettie, that would be fine."

"How long does this have to be Sister?" shouted out Brendan O'Connell in a gruff little voice.

"As long as it takes you to describe yur' living item, Brendan, That may be one line or it may be one page."

"Sister," a small female voice made its way through the rumblings of others in the class. "Can I write about you?"

"That would be lovely, Bronwyn, that would be just lovely. Alright now, gather yur' things and be off. I will see ya' all tomorrow."

With that, thirty pairs of hands and feet scurried about to grab books, lunch sacks, pencils, and woolen socks that had been removed during the day. I had nothing to collect. No shoes, no socks, no books, no lunch sack, or pencil.

Sean, Jim, and my cousins, Willy and Watt', waited by the back door for me. Watt's real name was Walter like mine. With two Walter O'Keeffes in the family they took to calling him Watt', and me Wattie. Like me, my brothers and cousins were in bare feet, dirty trousers that were too short, and all of us lacked the necessities other children brought along to school each day.

It was nearing the middle of May and the day was perfect for splashing about naked in the mud. We loved to do that. Just a few more weeks of school and we'd be off for the summer.

"Wattie," a familiar, soft voice called out from behind us. "Wattie O'Keeffe wait up!"

I turned and saw Josie Phelan running up the dirt road behind us. Sure she must be an angel. She truly took my breath away.

Josie ran to catch up with me and the other boys. The sun acting as a backlight, created a beautiful, golden outline that illuminated and traced her entire form. She glowed and she was beautiful. Her pale, blue dress hung just above her knees. She dragged her book sack behind her as she ran to catch up. One woolen sock had fallen almost to her ankle exposing her thin, bare leg while the other was still in place neatly turned down. A simple hairpin kept some of her tresses pinned to the side of her pale face and out of her eyes. The rest of her locks were a tangled mess. But God, she was beautiful.

"Go on ya' all. I'll catch up with ya' later," I announced to the other boys.

"Ya' going to go smooching are ya' Wattie?" asked Willy as he made kissing gestures and giggled.

"Shut up Willy. Get out of here," I snapped back.

The other boys continued to run up the road towards the river as I held back to wait for Josie. The sight of her made me sweat. I could feel the redness filling my neck, then move up to my cheeks, and finally cover my entire face. My hands were moist and I nervously kicked at the dirt with my bare toes until she—this angel—caught up to me.

"Wattie, what ya' going to write about?" asked Josie.

"Don't know, bees I suspect."

"That's a good one," Josie remarked. We fell silent for a moment and started to head slowly up the road. I was just a bit too nervous to look right at her. Josie stepped out in front of me and started to walk backwards looking right into my eyes. "Do ya' want to know what I'm going to write about, Wattie?"

"Sure, I suppose."

"I'm going to write about all the women of Polrone, and how hard they work to keep their families fed and tended to. Do ya' think that's stupid, Wattie?"

"Nah, that's good, just keep me Aunt Mary out of it, would ya' please?" We laughed and headed up the road. Once at the river's bank, we headed to our favorite spot and threw ourselves on to the ground. As we did, a wave of tiny, blue butterflies escaped from the grass—there must have been a hundred of them. We lay on our backs and gazed up into the soft, blue sky that was brushed with white streaks of thin cloud. The blue was almost the same colour as Josies dress. A multitude of colorful birds—jays, finch, meadowlarks, and a few gulls—created a kaleidoscope in the sky as they swooped back and forth in a variety of different formations. A slight wind drifted up from the river sweeping over our young faces. We lay motionless enjoying the sounds, scents, and companionship of the moment.

"Wattie?"

"Yes."

"Today, I am going ta' kiss ya'." The blood that had finally left my face quickly surged back through every part of my body.

"Oh," I said sort of stupid like. I was not able to move or take a breath. I watched a cloud pass over us and after a few seconds, I inhaled and in a timid, nervous whisper asked, "When will ya' be doing that?"

"Now, I suspect." She then rolled over and straddled herself on top of me. I still could not move. She was so close that her hair brushed against my cheeks and lips. She smelt sweet and clean. She pulled her hair back from her face and tucked it behind her ears. She just stared at me. Still, I could not move. My legs were stiff, my arms stuck by my sides, and I knew I was red all over. Slowly she moved in. I could not pucker up, even though I had practised for this moment; my lips were paralyzed. My first kiss and I couldn't move. I closed my eyes just as I felt her lips reach mine. Her mouth was soft and wet. It was warm and sweet. My body was tingling in all sorts of places. It was nice. It was as good as I expected it to be, except, I had frozen and not done my part, whatever that was.

When she pulled herself back up, I opened my eyes and saw her still positioned over me. She covered her mouth and began to snicker. I wondered, was she laughing because it was so bad?

Holding one arm on her hip, batting her eyes like girls do and in a voice much too sophisticated to be just eight years old, Josie asked, "Was that yur' first kiss, Walter O'Keeffe?"

"My first real girl one, I suppose," God that was a dumb thing to say. Why did I say that? She's gonna' think I've been kissing boys or something. Why did I say that?

Josie giggled again. "Me too," she proclaimed.

My first kiss—a moment I had always wondered about, fantasized about. Now, it had come and gone. But it was good. I decided I wouldn't tell the other boys. They would surely tease both Josie and me, so for now I resolved to keep this special moment, this secret, between just the two of us.

"Well, I'll have to marry ya' now Josie Phelan."

"I suppose ya' will, Wattie O'Keeffe."

"Help, Shit, Help!" I sat up quickly as the screams for help reached my ears. The yelling was coming from the river and the voices were familiar. Both Josie and I were startled to our feet. I started to run towards the water where I could see my brothers and cousins panicking and moving about.

"Watt's trapped," screamed Sean. "He went down in the mud and hasn't come up." Frantically, boys were going in and out of the water trying to find my cousin, Watt. I pulled off my trousers and jumped in with them. My eyes panned out over the top of the water, but I couldn't see a thing. Then, a few meters down from us I saw a mass of black hair moving down the river with the current. I climbed out of the water and ran down the bank to get in front of the floating object.

"It's 'im," I screamed. When I was far enough down the bank I jumped back in and swam upstream towards the floating mass of what I hoped was my cousin. The river was cold and fast. I held my eyes on the water in hopes that I would see Watt's head pop up. All I could see was the black hair coming down the river towards me. As it rushed by I grabbed it and was relieved that the mass of hair was attached to Watt's head.

I pulled him towards me and wrapped one arm around him while I swam with the other arm. The current pulled us downstream and I barely had the strength to keep us afloat. Ahead of us, I could see a nest of branches and other floating debris. Using my legs to guide me, I was able to get us to the mound and grab on. It took all the strength I had to pull both Watt and I out of the water and onto the bank where I collapsed. He wasn't breathing and had started to turn blue. I turned him onto his belly and started to push on his back like I had seen the men do when they pulled fellas out of the water. At seven years old, Watt was skinny and frail; at one point, I thought my arms would push right through him. The rest of the boys and a bunch of other kids were now gathered around us all screaming out his name.

After several attempts at lunging into his back, a huge amount of muddy-brown water came exploding out of Watt's mouth. He then began to shake as stuff continued to flow from his mouth and his nose. When he started to cough and cry, I knew he'd be alright.

"Jesus Christ Wattie, that was brilliant, screamed Willy. "Fuckin' brilliant." All the kids were patting Watt and I on the back. Everyone was excited and relieved. From the back of the crowd, Josie pushed her way through and handed me my trousers.

"Quite a day you've had Wattie O'Keeffe," she said. "You're a hero." I didn't think about what I had done or that I was a hero. I was still thinking about that kiss. I slipped on my trousers, helped my younger cousin up, and headed for home. Yes, it had been quite a day.

Four

MY MISERABLE LIFE

By early summer, most of the rare birds kept by my father had either died or been eaten by Mary and Bill. Our home looked nothing like it had when my parents had been alive and it was clear that Mary was becoming more intolerant of the responsibility, burden really, of having to keep my brothers, sisters, and I in the home.

When school was out for the summer it was hard to stay out of Mary's way. We would rise early to do our chores and then take Prowler down to the Suir to fish. Most days we caught nothing, which assured us a beating for not bringing home a meal. Each day ended the same with ten to fifteen children, depending on who was around, crawling into the one room we shared and taking a spot on the floor wherever we could. All of us dirty, hungry and afraid.

My potato and turnip stash were long gone. I had shared it with my brothers, Willy and Watt. We ate that stuff dirty and raw; we were starving. My brothers and I also managed to steal the odd cabbage from Mrs. Crowley's garden. We'd hide the stuff, usually in a ditch, and wait until we knew we wouldn't get caught eating. Four of us could gobble down a cabbage in seconds. It bothered me that we took cabbage from the Crowley farm, but I promised myself that I would pay her back one day when I could.

Jim, Billy, Sean, and I were heartbroken when that summer our beast of an aunt made arrangements for our two sisters, Bessie and Eileen, to be sent off. There was no discussion with us. We arrived home from fishing and were told that our two sisters had left, gone forever, no goodbyes, no last hug. They were just ripped from the family like animals being sent off to a work farm. Mary even sent off a couple of her own kids, telling them they had to fend for themselves. At least we had fond memories of our mother; these poor cousins of ours would never have that.

I continued to have bellyaches and continued to wet myself during the night. Fearing the wrath of my aunt, I'd take my undershorts and clothing to the river to rinse them off the best I could and then put them back on wet. My brothers and I got sicker and thinner. I had a constant fever and would often get the chills. Although I was starving, I had lost my appetite and felt weak and tired most of the time. My brothers, Jim in particular, were not doing any better. In addition to being physically sick, the family was sick with poverty. Uncle Bill had no work to speak of and spent most of his time at the pub.

When we went back to school in the fall it was a great relief. This year, however, we were transferred from the Catholic school in Polrone up to the public school in Mooncoin. I wasn't sure why, but Josie and many of the other children were moving up to the Mooncoin school as well, so we just accepted it.

It was now late in September. The dirt road we walked daily to and from school had begun to freeze up. The sun was setting earlier and the fog lingered most days, making the air heavy and hard to breathe for both Jim and I. We had both developed terrible coughs, were weak and always tired.

Sean had boots on his feet this day, as the Headmaster had given him a pair. With the front of our house now in view, I could see Mary wrestling with something. It was Prowler. Mary had a rope anchored tightly around his neck. She was dragging him along with one arm and beating him over the head with a piece of wood with the other. Prowler's back legs were thrashing about madly as the poor dog tried to back himself away from his attacker. When she got sight of us she pulled the dog along behind her and was marching in our direction. I could see that Prowler was choking.

"Keep this filthy animal out of my house," bellowed Mary as she tossed the end of the rope into my face. Quickly, I dropped to my knees to release the rope from around Prowler's neck and helped him steady himself. "This animal no longer lives here," my aunt continued. "I will cook 'im up into a stew and force ya' to eat 'im if he ever sets foot in my house again."

"But he 'as always lived in the house with us. Our Mum and Dad always let 'im."

"Well Walter, yur' Mother and Father are not in charge any more and this beast is not coming in to my house."

"But it's our house." I sobbed as I wrapped my arms around the dog that had been in our family for years. Sean and Jim were now huddled with me attempting to comfort our family companion.

Mary grabbed me by my hair and pulled me to my feet. Making a fist with her left hand she swung her arm around and punched me in the side of my head knocking me on to my back. Prowler pulled away from my two brothers, rushed to my side, and started to lick my face. I was stunned and could feel a trickle of warm fluid running down my jaw line. When I put my hand to my cheek, I felt blood from my ear streaming down my face. Dazed and in shock I tried to get up but fell over. Jim tried to catch me but was too late, and I hit the ground again. Mary moved in ready to whack me for a second time. Prowler put himself between her and I, started to growl, and showed his teeth. She stepped back.

"This is not yur' house," shrieked Mary. "This is our house and you're damned lucky I'm lettin' yas' stay here with us. And if ya' ever challenge me again, Wattie, I will send ya' into the afterlife to visit yur' parents." She turned to move back into the house, but stopped when she got sight of Sean sitting on the ground wearing the boots he had been given by the headmaster.

"And what 'ave ya' got on yur' feet, rat?" she demanded.

"Headmaster gave 'em to me."

"Is that right? Well, take 'em off. This goddamn dog of yur's has been barking all day, upsetting the neighbors. So until ya' get rid of 'im or get 'im to stop barking, ya' won't be wearing those boots. She bent down, ripped the boots from my brother's feet, and headed back into the house.

Pushing my luck and my aunt's patience, I blurted out "What neighbors were complaining? The only neighbors we got is the Phelans and the Crowley's and they love Prowler." Mary turned. The strained veins in her face, her clenched teeth and her bulging eyes told me she was about to blow. I knew I was in terrible trouble for questioning her, but it wasn't right taking away a boy's boots because the dog was barking; it was just stupid. She came towards me like a wild beast on stampede. I grabbed Sean and the two of us began to run. Prowler followed close behind. Mary was too fat to keep up with us and was out of breath before she reached the road.

Still cold, hungry, and shoeless, we kept running, heading towards Crowley Lane. Once we realized she had given up the chase, we slowed our pace. Down the narrow lane old Grandfather Walsh was sitting on a stump at the side of the ditch with a pipe hanging off the side of his mouth. The lane was covered with blackberry briars and the last of the year's yellow primroses. We searched the briars and the ditch for any bit of greenery to gnaw on but there was nothing.

Mr. Walsh was splitting rock; we never knew why, but he was always there breaking up rocks and loading them into sacks. Not knowing where to go or what to do, we sat with him and began smashing rocks, too. Mr. Walsh never said too much; he just sat and sang soft Irish tunes. Often, he would be found in the pub singing along with Father's band, but today, he sat whispering out soft Irish melodies while he crushed rock.

"How sweet 'tis to roam by the sunny Suir stream,
And hear the doves' coo' neath the morning's sunbeam,
Where the thrush and the robin their sweet notes combine,
On the banks of the Suir flows down by Mooncoin,
Flow on, lovely river, flow gently along.
By your waters so sweet sounds the larks merry song,
On your green banks I'll wander where first I did join,
With you, lovely Molly, the Rose of Mooncoin.

It was dark now. The fog was thick and the sounds of all life had fallen to sleep. We, and our loyal companion, quietly made our way through the fog and the cold back to the inescapable tragedy that was our home. That night Sean and I slept in one of the out buildings with Prowler nestled between us, fearing that if we went into the house we would both surely get a beating. My cough kept both of us up most of the night and neither of us slept very well, if at all.

In the morning, damp, cold, and hungry, we crawled out of the shed like dirty barnyard animals. Like all mornings, we headed to school, unfed and in the same rags we had been in for days. Today, I had to stop often on the way to school, to puke up. I was coughing up huge wads of phlegm and bile. Each time I coughed or puked my chest felt like it was breaking open. I was sick and I knew that whatever I had was getting worse. This frequent stopping made us late for school once again.

"Wattie and Sean O'Keeffe can you come to the front of the class please?" asked Miss Keely, the schoolroom teacher. Fearful that we would get expelled for continual tardiness or perhaps something else we had done, the two of us timidly moved to the front of the schoolroom.

The wood beneath our bare feet was cold and rough. I stumbled as a splinter entered my left heal. This was not the only affliction on my exposed feet. Blisters, boils and an infection between my toes caused my feet to swell and throb constantly. I continued to move to the front of the class with my head down, gazing out the side of my eyes to see if the other kids were snickering at us. Sean held my hand tightly, afraid of what might be in store for us.

"Why haven't ya' any shoes on yur' feet?" Miss Keely asked in a gentle and concerned voice.

"Our Aunt Mary took 'em cause the dog had been barking. She said this would teach us for having a bad dog," Sean announced.

Miss Keely had shown us the same compassion as Sister Theresa had. She was obviously concerned about the deteriorating state we were in and must have noticed the decline of our health. I knew we looked pale, were weak, and most often—all the time in fact—we came to school ill-dressed for the weather and with no food for lunch or snack time.

"Come to the back with me. I want to have a chat with yas'. She took us to the back room and knelt down in front of us. "Have ya' boys been havin' much to eat these days? You and yur' brothers all look a little bit scrawny."

"Ah, we find stuff," I told her. "Aunt Mary don't know how to cook and she's sick sometimes so we fend for ourselves."

"What kind of stuff have ya' been finding?"

"I don't know, green stuff, potatoes, sometimes we boil an onion if we find one." I said.

"Sean, how have ya' been getting all those bruises and cuts on yur' face?" Miss Keely asked. Neither of us knew what to say. We looked at each other, then looked to the ground. "Has yur' aunt been hitting ya'?"

"No Ma'am," Sean said in a nervous, trembling voice. "The donkey kicked me." Miss Keely took one of each of our hands in hers. It felt nice, her warm gentle hand holding mine.

"Nobody should be hitting ya' If they are, ya' can tell me and I can see that you're taken care of properly." Still scared to death of our aunt, we said nothing. Our silence and the terror in our eyes must have told the concerned teacher all she had to know. "Let me know if ya' need any help ya' hear?" She presented her words in such a caring, loving way that I almost told her about how our lives had changed since our parents had died, but decided I better not.

Although the young teacher believed that she was helping us, we would pay a price for her concern and kindness. We took our places with the others. I peered around the room and stared at my brothers and my cousins. God what does life have in store for any of us? My poor cousins—how they had suffered under the brutal hands of their mother all of these years. At least we had a mother who was kind, gentle, and took care of us, and a father who provided food, shelter, music, and laughter in our house. I guess you can't miss what you've never had.

At the end of the day we headed home as usual. We hated going home, since we never knew what to expect. I looked down the road and waited for Prowler to come running to meet us like he always did. That dog was the one comfort left from the home we had shared with our parents. What a loving friend that animal had been. Where is he, I thought? I put my fingers together, placed them between my lips, and blew out a sharp whistle to signal to our dog that we were on our way. Prowler did not come. How odd; he was always there to greet us.

"Prowler," Sean called out. Sean picked up his pace as he continued to call out for our loyal pet. "Prowler," he called out again. Still, no sign of the dog. I now picked up my pace and ran behind my brother. As we got closer to our house Mary came through the front door and charged at us. For a woman as sickly as she proclaimed to be she sure was able to muster up her strength and speed when she wanted too.

She was coming at us red-faced, at full speed and obviously angry as hell, waving her hands wildly in the air like the madwoman she was. Sean and I both stopped where we were and leaned into each other as she came at us. Her long dirty fingernails stabbed into my head as she took hold of my hair. God damn it, this stupid witch is going to pull every hair from my head before I grow into a man.

She had a hold of Sean in the same way and was dragging us both along side of her. She was moving so fast that neither of us could keep pace. I kept fumbling and falling, as did Sean, but each time we fell she would yank us back to our feet and continue to drag us along the dirt road like two squealing pigs being hauled off to slaughter. My knee was bleeding from falling and then being dragged. Sean was limping and hopping as if he had twisted an ankle or injured his foot. She was heading towards the river. My God this hurts, what had we done?

I had my hands placed tightly around hers in an effort to reduce the pulling of my hair. To shake me off, she pulled her arm upward, and I suddenly felt the burning sensation of hundreds of hairs being pulled right out of my scalp. I let out a yell that I am sure could be heard all the way up the Suir.

We reached the banks of the river where she finally released her grip. Looking down, I saw a handful of my black hair in her palm.

"So you're telling the Gardai that I'm not caring for ya'?" Oh Jesus, what was she talking about? We had not talked to the Gardai. "Well then, we best be getting rid of that dog as he's eatin' too much and takin' food off yur' plates. I told yas' yesterday that if this dog comes into my house one more time I would kill 'im. Well, he came in my house today."

Mary kicked Sean and I over to the bank of the river where there was a huge gunnysack only inches from where Sean and I were forced down to the ground. She picked up the sack, which was tied shut with a large rope. Inside, something was wrestling and moaning—it was Prowler.

"This is what I will do to the two of ya' and yur' brothers if ya' ever go to the Gardai and tell 'em that I'm not taking care of yas'." Her eyes were wild and almost popping from their sockets. Every blood vessel on her faced was bulging, struggling to pump the blood through her swollen, angry, hideous face.

Maybe she's gonna' die right here and now before she throws the sack into the river. "God, No!" I screamed out, which made her even angrier. She lifted the sack, spun it around and then slammed it down on top of me, striking me in the head. I tried to grab on to the rope that was tied around the sack to release Prowler. Mary was kicking me and trying to pull the sack back from me but I wouldn't let go. I could not let her do this. Sean grabbed hold of the sack and we both hung on. Then, she started to kick the sack itself.

"Ya' let go right now," she screamed, "or I'll kick this mangy mutt to near death and then let 'im die out here in the cold."

"Sean, let go," I screamed out. We both released our hold on the sack hoping she would stop kicking our dog. When we did, she threw the sack over her back and walked towards the river.

No, not prowler! I sobbed uncontrollably as I tried to fight back tears. My small body began to tremble. I placed both hands over my mouth to lock in the cries that wanted to burst out of me. My eyes were a well of tears and the mucus from my nose blew out with each heaving sob. I was sick to my stomach and thought I would throw up right then.

Maybe Prowler is gonna' chew his way out of the sack and bite the life right out of her. Maybe…I was confused. Why was this happening? Why was everything I loved being taken from me?

Mary lifted the sack and with all her strength threw it into the rushing river. "Bye bye ya' damn dog," she yelled, as the sack flew through the air and into the cold water below.

By this time, my cousins Willy and Watt and my brothers, had gathered at the river's edge. Sean and I were inconsolable. We had both collapsed to the ground and were sobbing into each other's arms. My two older brothers were stunned and not sure how to comfort us. The water was too deep and running too fast to be able to jump in after the sack. Even if we could retrieve the sack and the dog, Aunt Mary would surely kill us all.

Turning and shaking her pudgy, red, crooked finger at Jim and Billy, she hollered from the pit of her gut, "Don't ya' touch 'em or I'll toss the two of ya' right in there after that dog." Then she turned to Sean and I. "You will not eat or go to school for a week. And, you will not sleep in my house. That should teach ya' to keep yur' mouths shut."

Again she grabbed us by our collars and dragged us towards the house. I was chocking. Once inside our yard, Mary dragged us to one of the small outbuildings that our father had built for his livestock. First she tossed me inside and then threw Sean in on top of me. The way she screamed and swore at us was horrible. Neither our Mum or Dad had ever used the awful words she spat at us. "You'll remain here for the rest of the week, ya' two pathetic pieces of shit."

She then slammed the short wooden door, and I heard her set in the wooden latch to ensure we would not get out.

Mary left like a black cloud rolling across the sky, big, dangerous, and finally gone. In shock and weak from hunger, emotional turmoil, and continual beatings, we did not dispute being condemned to this prison. We were too upset and exhausted. Inside the shed, we collapsed and buried our faces into each other.

"Oh God, I hate her Wattie. I want her to die. I want Father to come home, Wattie. I hurt, make it stop," Sean sobbed uncontrollably, his tears painting little streams down his dirty face and neck. "God I hurt, Wattie. My stomach, it hurts so bad."

Sean began to heave. I held my younger brother as he threw up in the corner of the shed where we would be spending the next several nights. His entire body convulsed each time he lunged forward. Yellow bile from the pit of his stomach was all that came out, but the heaving did not stop. He was sick with despair, sick from hunger, and sick from living with this cruel, loveless creature that had stolen our home.

Sean finally collapsed from exhaustion. His stomach ached and his heart was forever broken. We had lost our parents, our sisters, our home, our happiness, and now Prowler. This brutal unkind act of hatred and revenge would scar us for the rest of our pathetic lives.

How could we ever love anything again after losing everything we had ever loved? Why was the world this cruel? Why would I risk loving anything ever again, knowing that at any moment someone or something could rip it from me? At the young ages of six and eight, we learnt that to love anything was dangerous and painful. At that moment, I was near void of any feelings. With both arms wrapped around my younger brother, I closed my eyes drunk with fatigue, and faded off into unconsciousness.

In my dreamworld, I saw my father coming down the River Suir in his fishing boat. I saw him pulling Prowler from the river and bringing him into the boat. My mother was there too. She looked sad. "Wattie, be strong now, be very strong. We are not far away," I heard my father's voice say. "Be very strong now."

Five

NEAR DEATH

"Wattie?" (pause) "Wattie, Sean?" a voice whispered through the shed door. Rays of light pierced through the cracks in the shed wall. It was Billy. "Wattie, I brought ya' some bread. Here, take it before she sees me." Billy pushed two slices of bread under the door and hurried off before he would be caught. Too tired to move, I just lay there and fell back to sleep. When I woke again, I found Sean sitting over me holding a slice.

"Wattie, someone brought us bread; I ate one, and here's one for you." Sean could have eaten them both before I woke. Even though he was starving, he had saved a slice for me. I could barely eat, but knew I had to. Am I dying? I wondered. Is that why I had seen my mother and father and Prowler in my dream? I was confused.

Sean passed the time poking about the old shed finding many old jars, tins, rusted tools, and the odd empty ail crock. The shed was full of bird droppings. Sean spent hours analyzing the colour of the poop and what the bird might have been eating to make their poop green, white, or brown. I just lay there and watched my younger brother explore the shed. Like me, Sean was connected to the natural world and loved plants and animals. Mostly, he loved birds.

I felt weaker than I had in a long time and my cough was getting worse. My throat was raw, my chest hurt and I continued to break into cold sweats and cough up mounds of phlegm. God, maybe I would die right here and never have to see that old cow Mary again, but if I died Sean would be heartbroken. No I can't do that to him. Not today, but I thought that I might be dead very soon.

Sean came running from the back of the shed. He had something in his hand. "Wattie, look what I found." He was holding a tiny bird's nest. At first, the nest appeared to be empty. Good, something to occupy him, I thought. "Wattie look at this, look."

Looking into the nest made of mud, hay, and string, I was surprised to see one little baby piccolo barely moving. Sean tenderly picked up the tiny bird and placed it in his palm. He lovingly stroked the head of the bird. "He has survived out here all on his own Wattie, with no Mamma' or Papa to care for 'im. They musta' died like our Mamma and Papa."

"Poor sweet baby bird," Sean whispered as he placed his lips to the head of the tiny creature. He paused and stared intensely at the little creature. Maybe the bird reminded him of himself. Then without warning, Sean grabbed the tiny bird by the neck, letting the nest fall to the ground, and snapped its neck killing the small animal instantly. "He's gonna' die anyway," Sean stated nonchalantly. I was stunned, definitely not expecting my little brother to do something like that.

"I'm not going to love anything ever again Wattie," Sean announced. "If ya' hate things instead of love things, it hurts less. I'm gonna' hate everything."

"Sean, you're stupid. Stop talking dumb-like. We should find a place and bury that poor little thing."

"We're not burying it Wattie," he screamed. "I'm putting 'im back in his nest and I'll put the nest back where it was. If his parents aren't dead, it will teach 'em a lesson for leaving a little bird all by itself. I hate birds, they're fucking stupid. I hate everything!"

"Sean, don't talk like that you're being an idiot." I had never heard him use that sort of language.

"Shut up, Wattie!"

"Sean, you're mad because Prowler died. Ya' don't hate everything," I told him.

"I hate you Wattie!" Sean yelled back at me.

"No ya' don't."

"I do. I hate ya' and Billy and Jim and Papa and Mamma."

"Stop it!" I cut him off in the middle of his attack. "Stop yur' crap right now or I'll break yur' head just like Aunt Mary would," I warned.

"I'll scrap ya' Wattie, right now.

"Shut Up!"

"Wattie," Billy whispered through the door of the shack. "Sister Theresa asked about ya' today. I saw her when I stopped by the convent school. I told her you weren't well, so she sent ya' this." Billy passed a piece of brown paper through the old wooden door.

"Thanks. Where's Jim, how come we haven't seen 'im?" I asked.

"He's real sick Wattie, coughing, sweating, stuff like that. He looks bad he does, real bad."

Jim had been ill and was coughing all the time just like me. As Jim and I had continued to get sicker and sicker, Mary had done nothing to comfort or nurse us back to health; in fact she barely noticed we were ill. "I gotta' go or she'll kill me," Billy said quickly, then ran off.

I was still lying on my side in pain but managed enough strength to pull myself over to the door where Billy had passed the brown paper through. I hurt everywhere. I propped myself up against the backside of the aged wooden door and set the brown package in my lap. I unwrapped the paper and found two icing-coated shortbread biscuits, one pink, one green. They looked almost too good to eat. After inhaling them for a while, I looked up at Sean. He was staring back towards me with his eyes glued to the biscuits. "Are ya' sure ya' hate me ya' little runt?" I asked.

After thinking about the question, Sean responded, "Nah I guess not." He then scurried over to my side.

"Which one ya' want?" I asked him. He pointed to the pink one. "Take it then." Sean picked up the biscuit and leaned up against me resting his head on my shoulder. I knew he didn't hate me.

We slowly ate the biscuits one small piece at a time making sure we savored each nibble. After the biscuits were gone, we licked the paper to make sure we hadn't missed one grain of sugar or icing.

"Now that the biscuits are gone, do ya' hate me?" I asked Sean.

"Maybe, I'm not sure," Sean replied. "I don't want to kill ya' or nothing, so I guess I don't hate ya'."

We were weak, tired, and dirty. My cough continued to worsen. Each time I coughed I thought my ribs were ripping apart. All I wanted to do was sleep. Although I had barely eaten a thing in the past few days, I was not hungry. Sean, on the other hand, was pulling grass through the cracks in the shed and eating it. He also nibbled on birdseed that he had found buried in the ground of the shed floor. He even ate the brown paper that the biscuits had been wrapped up in. I was freezing, then sweating, and could barely stay awake. I found solace only in sleep.

When I fell into the dream world I had the same dream over and over again. My parents were there. My father's strong, reassuring voice was telling me to stay strong, "Nothing is difficult for the brave and the faithful," he was telling me. My mother was cradling me and stroking my hair. I loved her gentle loving touch. It was good to be with them. But each dream ended the same, with Mary yelling at me with such force that the wind from her lungs blew the images of my parents into dust. The colours of them bled together until their images were no longer recognizable. Then, the mass of colour that had been them, blew into a twister that grew over my head and up into the clouds and they were gone.

The next morning, after spending three nights in the shed, our cousin Ely came out and told us that we were allowed out and able to return to school. She removed the wooden latch and helped us out. Emerging from the shed on my hands and knees I felt dizzy, and my eyes hurt as I looked towards the sun. Ely pulled two boiled potatoes from her apron and handed them to us. "Don't tell Mother," she said. Sean gobbled his potato down in seconds, but I could barely get mine in my gut and keep it down. We stumbled like zombies down the road towards the schoolhouse still dressed in the same filthy clothes we had been in for weeks.

"If they ask ya', tell 'em you and Sean have been coughing so ya' stayed home," Ely instructed us. "If ya' tell 'em Mother locked ya' up, she's sure to kill ya' both." At this point, for me, death was welcome. I wanted to go and be with my parents, and get away from this misery. The only thing keeping me alive, I'm sure, was the fear that my younger brother would be left behind under the cruel hands of that wretched woman.

Entering the schoolhouse I was stunned when I saw my brother Jim slouched over in his seat with his eyes closed. He looked dead. His skin was gray, his lips were white, and he was obviously very sick. Miss Keely's eyes watered up as she saw Sean and I enter the classroom. I felt sorry for her. She had been so kind to us. This was not her fault. How was she to know that Mary was the Devil?

Miss Keely said nothing to us, aware that her actions may have caused us this latest absence from school. All eyes in the classroom were on Sean and I. Why, I wondered, is everyone staring at me? I didn't like all these eyes on me;

it was embarrassing. I tried to dust the dirt from my clothing and tried to tidy my hair and push it out of my eyes.

Josie was frozen in her seat, her eyes also pooled with tears, and her hands held tightly over her mouth. As I took my seat behind Josie, she turned to me. "Wattie, are ya' okay? Ya' don't look too good." She placed a package, which was her lunch sack, on my desk. "Maybe ya' need to eat something Wattie," she whispered.

"I'm just tired Josie, that's all." I could barely get the words out to speak, I was exhausted and felt drunk. I had been drunk once before when Jim and I had snitched some dark ale, I didn't like the dizziness of it. I didn't know what day it was, or what year it was? How long had we been under Mary's guard? My head was spinning; I felt lightheaded, wobbly. What's wrong with me? I thought. Just let me go to sleep and not wake up…I'm happiest when I sleep…I don't need food…just let me sleep. The room buzzed and the light faded to dark.

"Wattie, wake up boy," I could feel a hand gently patting the side of my face, but I could barely open my eyes to respond. "Wattie, open yur' eyes. You'll be okay; we're going to get ya' help." Someone was holding a cup to my lips and I could taste something sweet. Tea, warm tea, Mmm…it's sweet. How come I can taste warm tea? The distant hum of voices far away buzzed in my ears. I swallowed the sweet liquid, and the sounds of voices drew closer. What's happening?

As the voices grew louder, I became aware that someone was holding me, and slowly, I woke from my drunken state. Gradually I came to and realized that I was lying in the arms of the headmaster, my legs flopped out on the floor next to my desk. Miss Keely was stroking my head as the headmaster was trying to bring me 'round. "Wattie drink this, you'll feel better," said the headmaster as he held the blue, enamel cup close to my mouth. I lifted my head feebly and wrapped my hands around the warm cup to sip down the liquid slowly. Eventually, Miss Keely and the headmaster gently raised me up so that I was seated on the floor. "We thought we'd lost ya' there boy. Ya' fell straight to the floor," announced the headmaster.

"Walter, you're not well," said Miss Keely in a concerned and tender voice. "You and yur' brother, Jim, we think ya' both have tuberculosis." I hadn't a clue what they were talking about, I was tired and confused. The headmaster put another cup of warm tea in my hand and told me to drink it slowly. I noticed two very official school authority types standing by the back door.

"These men are going to take you and Jim home," the headmaster explained. "We're going to arrange to get ya' to a hospital in Dublin." Miss Keely ran a cool cloth over my face. It felt so good. She took out a biscuit and placed it near my lips. I had a flashback to when my mother gave me biscuits as she was dying. Biscuits and death...hmm, "Am I dying?" I asked.

"Don't worry Walter. We're going to get ya' to a hospital where they will take good care of ya'," replied the teacher. Both Jim and I were helped outside and placed in what seemed to be a Gardai motor car. My ears began to buzz again and I drifted off. When I woke, the vehicle had stopped in front of our home. Both Jim and I sat in the auto covered with a wonderfully soft, woolen, blue blanket, while the authorities spoke with Mary at the front door.

Odd, this was my first ride in a motor car and it was not having any impact on me. I had always wondered what it would be like to ride in an auto. Now here I was, and I really didn't care. I was just scared to death of what Mary was going to do to us. "Damn, she is going to be pissed at us Jim. I'd run for it, but I'm too tired," I said.

"Me too," Jim replied, still with his eyes closed as he leaned against the vehicle door.

Looking back towards our house, I could see that Mary was now running out to the car. Oh crap, here she comes, I thought, but I could not move, so I slid down, covering my body with the blanket and pretended to be asleep. I knew she would beat the day-lights out of us, but was too tired to fight back, so all I could do was try to hide. The two school authorities and the Gardai were right behind her. God please, I couldn't stand another beating.

"Oh my poor boys," crooned Aunt Mary. "Come now, lets get ya' in the house and get ya' warmed up and fed."

"What the...hell?" Jim opened his eyes and sat up as if he had risen from the dead. We were stunned. We looked at each other in shock as our bitch of an aunt pretended to express any sort of affection towards us. This was insane. She was obviously afraid of the authorities, so she was putting on quite a show. She opened the door and kissed me on the forehead. Her sickening odor filled the vehicle in no time at all. God that woman stank! "Let me help ya' out there, Wattie. We'll get ya' both inside and fixed up, yes?" I said nothing.

"We'll be back tomorrow to pick 'em up and get 'em to the hospital in Dublin," one of the men announced. "Keep 'em warm, dry, and well-fed "til then. Also, make sure they get lots of fluids in 'em. Tea is best, with lots of sugar," they advised.

I was too weak to walk to the house and had to be helped in by Ely. As we left the auto, I could see Sean and Billy running down the road from school. "Can they come with us to the hospital, too?" I asked one of the men.

"No boy, but we will keep an eye on 'em." The man then looked directly at Mary as if he was giving her a warning. Mary kept her eyes glued to the ground as she helped Jim out of the vehicle trying to conceal her guilt.

That night, all of us ate rabbit, boiled potatoes, turnips, and tea. We were allowed to use clean, warm water for washing up, and Jim and I were given our parents' bed to sleep in. Although the mattress and bedding smelt sickly like Mary, I managed to fall off into a deep sleep and never woke even to pee.

Early the next morning, an ambulance arrived to take both Jim and I to the hospital in Dublin. We were both still sleeping when they arrived at our house and were wakened when a man dressed in white, gently shook us on our shoulders. "I'm going to take ya' up to Dublin now boy. You've nothing to worry about, ya' hear?" I said nothing and let him do what he had come to do.

He placed my dirty feet into a clean pair of long gray socks and put a cap on my head. Jim was done up the same way. Although we had washed up the night before, I still felt dirty and was full of sores. We were too exhausted to walk and had to be carried out to the ambulance. My cousins, as well as Billy and Sean, were standing around as they placed us in the car. Josie was there standing beside the ambulance looking concerned and very afraid. She was beautiful, my best friend, my angel. I was hoping we would not be gone long because I knew that I would miss her as much as I would miss my brothers.

"Wattie, they'll take good care of ya'. When ya' come back, we'll go down to the river and the graveyard and all. We will Wattie, we will." Josie grabbed my hand with both of hers and kissed the top of it. I could see that she was crying and concerned for me.

"Yes we will Josie. We'll do that when I come back," I replied in a feeble, weak voice. Josie turned and ran towards her home in the meadow next to ours. She didn't look back, not even once. When would we be coming back? I had no idea.

"Please let Billy and Sean come with us. Please," I begged the driver.

"Sorry boy, you two are the sickest. Don't worry. These two will be looked after."

I reached for my two brothers as I was placed in the ambulance. The attendant stopped long enough for me to hug each of them around the neck. Sean was crying and hung on tightly to Billy as I was loaded in the vehicle. They hugged on to Jim as well, then the four of us hugged, arms entwined around one another. I hoped that they would be okay; they looked scared. Did they think we would die and never come back? As we drove off, I peered out the back window and continued to hold up my arm to Sean and Billy as they stood at the gateway to our home. I didn't know when I would see either of them again. I also did not know that those last few minutes together was the last time the four us would ever be together again, alive.

Six

PEADMONT

The drive to Peadmont Sanatorium in Dublin was long. At least it seemed long. On the way, I fell in and out of consciousness. When I was awake, I peered out the window where the sights were strange and new to me. As we approached the city I could see row upon row of crimson, brick houses each one with a different colour door, a little iron balcony, and black stair railing. Some homes had names above the entrance, some had flowerpots on the steps, much fancier than the homes in Mooncoin.

The cobblestone roads were wider than I had ever seen and littered with more motor cars and buggies than I knew existed, each fighting for a bit of road space. There were crowds on each street corner, and shops upon shops like I had never seen. Why would ya' need so many shops, I thought. I had been to Waterford with my father, but it was nothing like this. And the lights, where were they coming from? There were lights all over. It was all very confusing. I saw groups of children leaning up against buildings, just standing there, some of them holding out little boxes.

"What are they doing, those children?" I asked the driver.

"Just beggars, don't need to mind yur'self with 'em."

The vehicle stopped for a few moments to let a row of buggies pass. I looked out and saw four children, two boys and two girls, huddled together against a white wall that was plastered with papers and posters I could not read. The children must have been from the same family 'cause they looked alike. All had unkempt dark hair, red runny noses, and filthy faces and limbs. Huddled together the way they were, I knew they were cold. Their stone-hard features were void of expression and they looked like they had given up on any chance of a decent life.

The youngest one, a girl, must have been only two or three years old. Her hair was a tangled mess, yet she had a little, red bow that held some of her hair together at the top of her head. The others, maybe five, six, and seven, were equally disheveled. The smallest boy had his tongue stuck out and was licking the snot dripping from his nose. None of them had laces in their worn out boots and the eldest had a piece of rope tied around his tattered trousers, to hold them up I supposed.

As a man raced past them, the two older ones held out their hands, but the man didn't even look at them. He never noticed that they were in need, or maybe he did and didn't care. I felt sad for these children. Did they have parents? I wondered.

The vehicle began to move again and I looked back and stared at those haunting faces. I guess they reminded me of our family and what had happened to us. How many other Irish families were suffering like us? Those fragile miserable faces, I will never forget them. We then turned a corner and suddenly, they were out of sight.

I awoke again as the ambulance slowed down. We were heading up the narrow lane to the sanatorium. "Wake up boys," the male driver called out, "wake up now."

"Jim, wake up. I think we're here." Jim had slept almost the entire trip waking only to nibble on the bread and cheese provided by the driver of the car. Jim pushed himself up from his slumber. He looked like a drunkard waking from a night out on the drink. "Where are we Wattie?" he mumbled.

"The hospital I think."

"Yur' at the Peadmont Sanatorium," announced the driver. "It's where we bring young 'uns like you who are sick." The vehicle stopped. The door was opened by a heavyset woman, a nurse, in stark white clothing—clothing so white it was blinding. The driver got out of the car and handed the woman an envelope. "Good evening to ya' Ma'am."

"Evening Patrick, must 'uv been a long day for ya'," she said, as she played about with two chairs on wheels.

"Ah' it was. I'll help ya' get these young uns' in then."

"Yur' a right mess aren't ya' boy," she said, her large chest hanging over me as she fumbled around to get me out.

"Yes Ma'am, I suppose," I answered uncertainly, still confused by what was going on.

"We'll clean ya' both up, get ya' well, and get ya' back home," she said. As she lifted me out of the vehicle, again my face was buried in her large bosom. I couldn't breathe, but I was too weak to struggle. Finally, she set me down on one of the waiting chairs and I filled my lungs with air.

"Name's Ms. Bridgett, but ya' can call me Bridie," she announced. "I expect ya' to be well-behaved while you're here, ya' understand now?"

I was scared, so I gave her a polite, "Yes, Ma'am." I just went along with all of it. What else was I going to do?

Patrick, the driver, assisted Jim into the other chair, and we were pushed up along the cobblestone path to the grand front entrance of this huge red brick sanatorium. There must have been ten, or maybe twelve, chimney stacks coming out of the roof at different spots. This place was enormous. As we entered the building an odd smell hit my nose, not unpleasant, just odd. "What's that I smell?" I asked.

"It's likely the disinfectant. We use it to clean everything in here. You'll get used to it," Bridie replied. As she spoke, her voice echoed down the long, green hallway. It was all so peculiar to me.

As she pushed me along I looked up, I looked down. There were people and things everywhere. The halls were lined with carts full of white, enamel pans and jugs. Chairs with wheels, like the ones Jim and I were in, were parked here and there. The hall ceiling was tall, and green. Even the fan had been painted green. Each doorway we passed was trimmed with thick, dark wood and protected by a large, white door, each of them shut.

"Alright, I'll get yur' charts set up," We arrived at a large reception office where Bridie started shuffling about bunches of paper and clipped them to some sort of board.

"Patrick," she ordered, "ya' head down to the kitchen now and make yur'self some tea while I process these two." I didn't know what that meant, "process" us. Again, I felt the nerves in my stomach tighten. But Bridie continued, "We'll clean ya' up, feed ya'; and get ya' to bed, then you'll see the doctor in the morning."

After we had answered a bunch of questions about where we lived, where we slept, and what we ate, Bridie called another nurse over to assist her. "This here is Nicolette. She'll be helping me clean yas' up." With Bridie pushing me, and Nicolette pushing Jim, we travelled along the hall to a large bathing room. This room was all gray with cement floors and walls. That smell, the one she said was disinfectant, was really strong in this room. Two large, round, tin tubs were ready to receive mine and my brothers aching bodies.

"Alright now, let's get ya' in," Bridie encouraged. With her assistance, I slowly got up and was making my way into the tub clothes and all. "No boy. You'll have to be taking 'em off. Ya' won't be seeing the likes of these tatterins' again."

Without waiting for consent, Bridie quickly began to strip me down until I was naked. I was too weak to protest and held my hands tightly over my privates as she lifted me into the hot tub. I scrunched my eyes shut as tight as I could. No woman, other than my mother, had ever seen me in the bare buff. "My God. Ya' can't weight more than three stone and a bit. There's nothing to ya', "Bridie exclaimed.

Meanwhile, Jim had been placed into the tub next to me, assisted by Nicolette. The heat felt wonderful. The steam entered my nostrils and I immediately began to sweat. It was good, and at least now, my naked body was covered by water. So maybe "being processed" wasn't so bad. Just as I had settled into the tub and had begun to relax, I was assaulted by a heavy brush being scraped over my flesh. "Ow!" I cried out, as I felt the layers of dirt begin to loosen. Bridie scrubbed me like a woman scrubbing out a stain on a washboard.

"Quit yur' fussin' now. You're filthy. We can't be putting ya' in a good, clean bed with all this filth on ya'." She continued to scrub, and it continued to hurt. She grabbed my arms and scrubbed them almost raw. She ran the brush across my back and then over the sores on my feet. "Ow!" I shrieked again, as one of the scabs on my foot was broke' open.

"Oh Jesus, ya' poor thing," she said in a concerned voice. "Yur' feet are a mess." She dropped the brush into the tub and pulled a soft rag from the side table. "I'll take it a little easier on ya'," she said as she gently washed between my toes and around the heal of my foot. Blood flowed from the scab that had just broken open and it was staining her wash cloth.

"You've got an infection in here," she said referring to my foot. "I'm going to push out the poison, then we'll bandage ya' up. Just take a deep breath." I did what she asked and took in a deep breath. She squeezed the sides of the wound with all the force she could muster up.

"It hurts," I cried out, as I braced myself by placing my two arms on the bottom of the tub and arching my back. The pain caused me to scream out and I started to cry. Bridie continued to apply pressure to the sides of the wound until I felt a huge burst like something had exploded in my foot. The force of the poison and blood coming out was so strong, that it shot out and splattered her white uniform.

"There ya' go. I know that hurt but now we've got it open and it can drain. With my leg held upright and my heal in her lap, she continued to squeeze the wound and I watched as the yellowy puss ran down the edge of my ankle. This is how my father had died, an infection in his leg. The poison coming from my foot looked just the same.

"Am I going to die?" I asked her.

"Not from this," she replied. When she finally had pushed most of the poison out of my foot, she carried on scrubbing the rest of me down.

"How long will we be here Ma'am?" I asked.

"Long as it takes, until you're well," she told me. Then she began to examine my head with some sort of instrument. "Hmm...lice, not unusual. I'm going to have to look under yur' privates to see if ya' got 'em there, too." I was scared, I had never had anyone look at my privates.

"Do ya' have to Ma'am?" I asked.

"Yes, if you've got lice down there, we've got to clean ya' up or you're going to get even sicker." In the next tub, Jim was going through the same sort of examination so I felt a bit relieved, sort of. "Raise yur' arms boy so I can have a look."

I scrunched up my face, closed my eyes, placed my arms over my head, and turned my head away in disgust. She lifted my willy and looked under it. "Yes, ya' got 'em down here, too. I'm going to put some liquid on ya' that'll help get rid of 'em." She rubbed and scrubbed and splashed my testicles, and then poured clean water from a pitcher over my entire body. "All done. That wasn't so bad, was it?"

What could I say? I pushed my wet hair out of my eyes and opened them. She grabbed a large drying rag and started rubbing it over my dripping hair. "Tomorrow, I'll have to clean ya' up again," she informed me.

Jesus, I'll have to go through this again, I thought. I began to cough again, this time even harder. I clutched my stomach to hold it in. With each heave I thought my guts would burst right out of my belly. Each cough propelled me forward. My muscles were working as hard as they could to keep everything inside of me, but the power of the cough overtook me and I started to pee myself. Standing in the tub, right there in front of her, I couldn't stop it.

"Come on," she said, I was still coughing and peeing as she lifted me from the tub. "Oh Jesus, are ya' peeing yur'self boy?"

"Yes, Ma'am, I'm sorry." She just shook her head as if disgusted with me, rolled her eyes, and wrapped me up in the drying rag.

I was humiliated and couldn't look at her. What must she think of me? I could feel my entire body turning red; my palms were sweating and I was shaking. "It's okay," she said. It's not yur' fault. Better ya' did this here than in all the nice bedclothes I've got for ya'. Her words helped put me at ease somewhat.

Bridie grabbed a brown, glass bottle from her cart and pulled out a large, metal spoon from her pocket. "This will settle you and that tummy of yur's down. Take it in now like a good boy." I opened my mouth and the large spoon deposited a thick, sweet liquid that immediately heated my lips, my throat, my chest, and my stomach. Although the taste was strong, I could feel the liquid move through my entire body, warming and relaxing every part of me as it passed. My coughing stopped. I was feeling wobbly and wanted to fall to the floor, but knew if I did I would be in trouble. My eyes wanted to close, but I strained to keep them open. My head dropped to my chest, I could barely stay awake.

"Sit here now; it's okay to close yur' eyes."

Bridie sat me down on a dark wooden chair and knelt in front of me. She lifted my foot into her lap and one more time squeezed out yellow puss and blood. Even my foot felt warm from the medicine she had given me. I felt no pain this time as she poked and squeezed, then wiped some yellow liquid over my heal and toes. She pulled a roll of white bandaging from the cart, wrapped my foot, pulled a heavy woolen sock over it and set my foot on the floor. Lifting herself up from her kneeling position, Bridie brushed off the front of her uniform and placed her hands on her wide hips. "Well, I think we've taken care of that. Now lets get on with fixing up the rest of ya'."

By now I was slouched down in the chair, with only one eye open.

"Alright then, arms up," she called out. I sat up, opened both my eyes, and tried to straighten myself up. I raised my arms and allowed Bridie to slip my body into clean bedclothes. The neck on the bed shirt hooked on my nose and I could feel the stiffness of the starch that had been pressed into the cloth. The smell of clean garments was something I had missed, and I remembered the fresh outdoor smell of clean shirts and trousers coming in off the line. These clothes didn't smell quite like that, but it was close. I didn't like the stiffness of this shirt as it scraped against my tender, over-scrubbed flesh, but it was still better than the dirty rags I had lived in for the past few weeks.

Jim and I were both dressed in clean clothes and woolen caps were placed on our heads.

"Well, I'm guessing ya' won't be able to make it up the stairs in the state you're in," Bridie thought out loud. Before I could respond, she had picked me up like a sack of potatoes and thrown me over her shoulder.

"Chris, can ya' come over and take this one?" Bridie called out to an orderly dressed in white, who was stacking up linens. The man came over and lifted Jim into his arms, but cradled him and didn't toss him over his shoulder like Bridie had done to me.

We were taken up two flights of well-polished wooden stairs. I kept my eyes closed most of the time and don't remember seeing too much other than her back-side. We arrived in some sort of meeting room and were again placed in chairs with handles and rubber wheels. The curiosity of the place had woken me up. The room was dark with no windows and only one bulb burning to light the entire place. Dark-paneled wood and tall ceilings reminded me of a church without pews and windows. No one else was in the room; it was almost empty, except for a few stands of books, a couple of long tables and a few empty wheel chairs. The sound from the rotating wheels of our chairs, the footsteps of Bridie and Chris, and the creaks from floorboards, echoed and bounced off the walls as we moved through the room.

Stopping in front of a small round table situated just outside an open doorway that led to some sort of an office, I could see three or four other nurses working. Sounds of a radio coming from the room peaked my interest, and I wondered if we would be able to listen while we were here. The women working in there sounded happy and pleasant. The tone of their voices made me think they were a friendly group of ladies and that I would not be afraid of them.

"You two stay here while I sort out where we're going to put yas'." Bridie said and then rushed off into the office. Stay put? Where the hell would we go? I strained my neck to look into the office to see what else was going on and to see if I could hear them talking about us. All I could hear was voices but could not make out any of the words. I tried to move my chair along the floor to see if I could get a better look or could hear something.

"Ya' see anything in there?" a voice asked.

I was caught off guard when a much younger lady came up behind us. She was bent down and looking over my shoulder. I pulled myself back and looked down towards the floor, and started to nervously rub my legs, I could feel the blood rush to my face and my body tense from the embarrassment of being caught looking into the office.

"Don't worry about it, you've got a right to be curious. I'd be taking a peak, too, if I didn't know what was behind there." My limbs relaxed and I looked up at her.

She was wearing the same sort of uniform as Bridie except she had red stripes on hers, and a red apron. She had long, beautiful, raven hair that was neatly pinned to the side of her olive coloured skin. Through her toothy grin, I saw the space between her teeth that reminded me of my family, we all had that gap. I must have stared at her for longer than what was considered polite as she said, "Do ya' like what ya' see little fella'?"

"Eileen, I mean Nurse, pardon me. I am, um, sorry for staring, but ya' look so much like..."

"Not to worry, you're not the first lad in here to stare at me. But my name's not Eileen. It's Donna, like the song. My Dad was an American; that's how I got the name ya' know." I had never heard the name, Donna, nor known what it had to do with being American, but I didn't ask. She sat a tray down on the little round table in front of us.

"He's not lying, Ma'am. Ya' really do look like our sister," Jim said in my defense.

"Ah, so ya' two are brothers than? Ya' can keep each other company in here."

On her tray Donna had two bowls of broth and two cups of tea. "Ya' better be drinking this stuff up quick-like, or Miss Bridie will surely be discharging me of my duties."

Normally, I would have drank something that smelt so good down in no time. Today, I barely had the strength to lift the cup. Jim didn't want to drink his either. Like me, he just wanted to sleep.

"Come on now. Be good boys and drink this up. You'll sleep better if ya' do," she said. Donna stood in front of us with her arms crossed like she was not going anywhere until we drank this stuff down. We both lifted the bowls to our lips and sipped back the broth. It was delicious, but I felt sick and had to drink it slow.

She was pretty and young, maybe only fourteen or fifteen, but looked like she could get very cross if you did not do what she asked you to. I wondered where Bessie and Eileen were, whether they had made out okay? I missed them both, and Sean and Billy. Would we ever all be together again?

After drinking down what we could, Bridie and the other nurse came back into the room. Donna dropped her arms and fumbled to gather our bowls and cups, then scurried off not saying another word and not making contact with either of the two older nurses, who appeared to be the ones in charge.

"Off we go," Bridie announced, "We've got two fine beds for yas'."

We were wheeled across the room towards a huge set of wooden doors. As Bridie opened the doors a gust of wind came rushing in to meet us. Now, where are they taking us? We were wheeled out to a large covered porch.

The porch was lined with lots of little iron cots. There had to be fifty or more of them, some cradling small sleeping bodies, others had nurses sitting next to them holding a child as he coughed or threw up. At one bed near the end of the deck, a priest dressed completely in black knelt, saying a 'pray'. Jim and I looked at each other and didn't say anything. We were taken to two beds across from each other near the opposite end of the deck where the priest was doing his job.

"We sleep out here, I asked?"

"Yes, it's good for yur' lungs." Although we were outside and I was scared, it was rather pleasant.

"Is there no room for us inside? What about that big empty room? Could we sleep in there?" I asked.

"I said, it's good for yur' lungs. You'll be sleeping out here for a while, until you get better," Bridie stated. This was odd. But, we would have our own beds, we seemed to have lots of blankets and it looked like they would feed us. Still, my stomach was a mess of knots as my head ran wild with thoughts of what would happen here and worried about how long we would be in this place.

"Am I here to die?" I ask Bridie as she pulled back the bedding on my cot.

"Ya' might be. Many boys do…depends how ya' behave and how yur' body heals itself." Bridie was so matter of fact. I guess she had done this a hundred, maybe a thousand times before.

"This is where you'll sleep until you're well. Climb in now. The doctor will see ya' in the morning." She held on to my arm and helped me get onto the bed and under the covers. "Here's a bottle; if ya' have to pee during the night, this is where you'll do it. Put the bottle between yur' legs and try not to spill it over on yur' bed sheets. When you're done, place the bottle at the end of yur' bed and we'll pick it up in the morning."

This was unbelievable. Why do they want me to pee in a bottle? I was too tired to try and figure it out. My chest was hurting and I started to cough up phlegm again. Bridie gave each of us one more spoonful of the thick, warming liquid and told us it would help settle us in. Again, I felt the warmth rush through my body as the fluid made its way into me.

"Get ta' sleep now and I'll see ya' tomorrow night. In the morning, Moira will be here; she will be yur' day nurse." Bridie headed down the deck leaving us there. I was still dazed from it all. As I drifted off to sleep, I looked down the row at all the other little beds. Who were these people? A choir of coughing hovered over the deck. I could hear the sounds of muffled coughing and voices beneath us as well. Must be another deck down below, I thought? I gazed at the white enamel bottle that stood at the edge of my bed. I never peed in a bottle before! I closed my eyes and started to fade away.

"Good night Jim," I said quietly to my brother, "Are ya' afraid?" There was no reply from my brother. He had already fallen off into a deep sleep.

I burrowed down into my covers. The air was good. I was still coughing, but hardly noticed as I was too tired. My breathing slowed and I disappeared into the dreamworld.

Always safe in the dreamworld.

Seven

WAKING UP AT PEADMONT

I had slept through the night without moving. In the morning, I woke to a collection of unfamiliar sounds—muted voices inside and outside of the building. The distant hum of motor cars and the continuous clopping of horse hooves pulling heavy wagons as they made their way by the sanatorium, filled my ears. These were the sounds of a city coming to life, odd but interesting; sounds I had never heard before. All around me I could hear young bodies coughing, crying, and vomiting. Like most days, I woke up coughing, sweating, and feeling the ach in my belly and chest. I could smell coal burning but did not know from where.

"Oh no!" I reached down and grabbed my privates to see if I had peed. Thank God, I hadn't. I released my grip and laid out on my back, relieved that I had not let go during the night. I let out a heavy sigh, then took in the taste of the clean air that was all around us. I had forgotten that we were outside. Not knowing what to do, I just lay there waiting for instructions.

"Boy," a raspy voice called out. "Boy, where are ya' from?" The raspy voice was coming from the next bed.

I rolled over pulled my knees to my chest and wrapped my arms around them in a timid fetal position. "Polrone, um' Mooncoin," I replied.

"Never heard of it," announced the boy. "I'm from Dublin, not far from here. Me sister Gwen is here, too, down below. I almost died ya' know, 'bout five months ago. I saw God, but he didn't want me, told me he had too many damned Irish orphans up there, didn't know what to do with us all, so sent me back to look after my sister.

"God said 'damned'?" I asked.

"Sure as hell he did, he ain't perfect ya' know. Sometimes he 'as a bad day just like any of em' What's yur' name?"

"Walter, Wattie. My brother, Jim, is sleeping over there." I turned and pointed towards Jim's bed. He was still in the same position he had been in when he had fallen asleep.

"He looks dead yur' brother does, not coughing, not breathing. Yup, he's dead. Musta' died in the night. Maybe they even poisoned him cause they thought he was too far-gone. I seen 'em do 'dat many a time."

A wave of panic moved through my body. No, not Jim, I thought. Oh God, had he died too?

"I'm not dead ya' stupid 'ediot. Now shut up, so I can get some more sleep," announced my brother from his bed.

"I'm glad you're not dead Jimmy. Do ya' still feel sick?"

"Ey', I'm mostly tired Wattie. Let me go back to sleep."

I let out a huge sigh and fell back on to my cot. The raspy-voiced kid lay kicking and giggling in his bed, coughing in between each snicker.

"God did not say 'damn'. Ya' made that up," I challenged the kid.

"Oh, ya' stupid little shit. You'll learn after being here a while, that ya' do what ya' can to get a laugh. You'll be doing it, too, you'll see. We could all be dead any day, so ya' may as well have a laugh about it. My name's Mickey O'Connell, before ya' ask. Call me Mick. A kid died in that there bed you're in just minutes before ya' got here. I don't think they even had a chance to clean the sheets."

"I see you've met Mr. O'Connell," announced a mature male voice. "Don't ya' believe a word he says there Mr. (pausing) Walter O'Keeffe," the man said as he looked at the chart that had been hung at the end of my cot.

"Mickey here has the best gift of the gab I've ever seen in a young Irishman; he should be writing storybooks, that's for sure…a storyteller like I've never seen, aren't ya' Mickey?"

"It's not all made up Doc. Most of my stories are true," Mickey stated defensively.

"Ah, ha"…the man turned towards me. "Walter, I'm Doctor Shea. The boys call me Doc. How are ya' feeling today?" Doctor Shea was a small man with light brown hair that was parted perfectly down the middle of his scalp and neatly waxed flatly to his head. He had a long moustache that curled up at the sides of his mouth and tiny blue eyes that peered over the spectacles that hung halfway down the bridge of his nose.

"I'm feeling fine," I replied. Really I wasn't, but I didn't know what to say.

"Well then, what are ya' doing here? This is a hospital for sick children. Get dressed, and be off with ya'," the doctor announced.

I was stunned." Okay, but, um…" I kicked off my blanket.

Doctor Shea took a seat at the edge of my cot and covered me back up.

"I'm teasing ya'," he said in a much softer and gentler tone. "You're very sick Walter and you are going to be here for a while. We will take care of you, but you also have to take care of yur'self. You have to get lots of rest, stay clean, take the medicines we give ya', and do the exercise we ask ya' to do. Can ya' do that?"

"Yes Doctor."

Doctor Shea proceeded to examine me, feeling here and there, making me breathe this way and that way, and then he moved over to examine Jim.

A nurse pushing a very large cart came on to the deck with what looked like several trays. It was. She was dressed in the same white uniform as Bridie had been. However, this nurse was tiny and much younger. After placing a tray beside a number of the beds, she made her way to our end of the deck.

"Good morning, ya' must be Walter. My name is Moira, and I will be yur' day nurse." I fell in love with her instantly. She had lovely, twinkling, brown eyes, long brown ringlets and a beautiful, friendly smile that was framed in with two big dimples. Just looking at her made me feel light-headed, warm, and safe.

Moira placed a tray of food beside me. "Now we're only starting ya' on the fluids for now. You'll get to the solid food in a few days. Isn't that right, Doc?" She smelt heavenly, like she had just stepped out of a bathing tub full of roses. "I'll be back to check on ya' a little bit later."

She moved on to tend to Jim. I could not take my eyes off of her. I gazed at how her uniform framed in her tiny body and got a bit of a shiver as I watched her bend over my brother's bed, exposing a small line of the slip she wore beneath her clothing.

"The nurses here will take good care of ya'," announced Doc. "Walter, are ya' listening to me?" I quickly drew my eyes back to Dr. Shea and went red-faced again thinking about how I had seen Moira's slip.

"Listen to what they say and behave up here. No going down to the deck below. No going anywhere, in fact," ordered Doc. "Do you have any questions?" I had a hundred questions, but could not think of one as my blood was still pumping to my face while my heart beat against my chest, thinking about our beautiful day nurse.

"Alright than. If ya' think of anything, I'll be around tomorrow." Doc made a few scribbles on the chart, asked me if I was a Catholic, and then hung the chart back on the end of the bed. He gave me two tablets and told me to get some rest. I watched Moira as she went from bed to bed serving the various boys on our deck. I am not sure how long I gazed at her because I fell back into a deep, peaceful sleep.

For the next week, Jim and I never left our beds. I spent these days slipping in and out of consciousness, forcing myself to stay awake when I knew Moira would be coming 'round. If I had to pee, I used the bottle; if I had to poop, there was a pan for that. One day rolled into the next. I really never knew how long we had been there. Now and then I would wake and find soup, juice, and tea by my bed, and be upset that I had missed a visit with my beautiful Moira. I would eat what was left for me and doze back off to sleep.

I had not been awake too long when a thunderous noise zoomed past my head and shook the entire deck. I dropped my tea into my lap messing my bedclothes. I held my eyes tight and grabbed the iron head board on my cot and held on for dear life. Another thunderous roar sped by. This time, I ducked into my pillow and covered my head with my arms. Again, the huge overhead sound came thundering through the deck shaking the pans, carts, and table trays. It was like the walls of the city were falling in.

"Jim!" I called out to my brother, he was also holding on to his cot.

"I'm here, Wattie. What the hell is that?" He yelled back.

"Look, look," shouted Mick. "It's the Air Force planes. They're low today."

Realizing that my deck mate was a bit of a storyteller I did not believe him, but had no idea what had made such a thunderous noise. I raised my head and looked up and I saw Moira heading towards Jim and me.

"'Tis," said Moira as she moved towards me. She wrapped her arm around my shoulder and pulled me in towards her covering my ear with her soft silky hand. "It's okay, don't be frightened. Most of the kids love to watch 'em. They're practising for the war ya' know. Jim, are ya' alright over there?" she called out.

"Yes Ma'am, I'm okay now," he replied.

"War," I asked. "There's a war?"

"Yes, ya' didn't know? Don't worry, though, it's not here. They're just practising. It's a fine sight to watch." She gave me a kiss on the top of my head and rose to go back to her cart.

Relieved that the place was not falling down, I lay back in my bed and watched overhead as row upon row of planes flew by. "Wonderful," I thought. I wonder who's at war?

Moira set a tray down next to me. "Here's another cup of tea, and I'll get ya' a new bed sheet. She set down her tray and pulled a clean sheet from below her cart and cleaned me up. I was so captivated by the aircraft in the sky, I had hardly been fazed by her cleaning me and the bed sheets up.

"Enjoy the show and eat up now. You've got to get well." She left us to enjoy this explosion of activity and excitement in the sky above us. Every few days, we would get a wonderful display of airplane aerobatics and formations. It was magnificent.

Weeks turned into months and I started to feel that I was getting stronger. I was now allowed to stray from my bed and go to the dayroom where we were allowed to rummage through a collection of picture books. I couldn't read at all, but the images were wonderful. The nurses and Doc never made us take any school lessons which I liked, but I was missing my school chums. Mostly I missed Josie, Billy, and Sean.

I was now well enough to go to the public toilet and to the shower once per week with the other boys.

"Wattie, come here," demanded Mick one day. I moved over to where Mick and a few other boys were standing in the washroom. "Put yur' finger right here."

I looked at the small unusual hole in the wall of the dayroom that he was pointing to. Having no idea what it was I took Mick's orders and I stuck my baby finger into the hole. Immediately, my entire body began to quiver. I shook so hard I could barely pull my hand away from the hole. Around me the group of boys were laughing intensely.

Finally, I was able to pull my finger out and fell to the floor.

"What is it?" I asked.

"It's electricity ya' dumb 'ediot. It's what makes the lights go on," one of the boys announced. How odd, I thought. Well, I wouldn't be doing that again.

"Clear out of here now you boys—back to bed with all of ya'," Bridie announced in a demanding and forceful tone. They all scurried back to their beds, but Bridie turned to me. "Have ya' not learnt that ya' cannot be listening to that boy?" She reached down and offered her hand and helped me up.

"Yes, Ma'am," I replied still tingling from the buzz of the electrical socket. I then staggered back to my bed.

Sleeping outside all these months had been wonderful...the sound of the city coming to life, the Air Force planes overhead, people down below, and birds swooping in looking for leftover pieces of bread. The sounds of outdoors, and the smell of rain as it dripped off the decks that protected all these young lives, were refreshing.

It was fall again, and I welcomed the evening wind each night as it gently danced through the deck where we slept, carrying in brown leaves that had been shed from the trees below. The night air cradled and caressed our healing bodies. It was marvelous. I must be getting better. I could breath, I was no longer coughing, and my belly did not hurt all too often.

I liked it here and I wanted to stay. Maybe they can bring Sean and Billy. This was a good place to be...finally, a safe place to be.

Eight

THE CONVICTION–OCTOBER 1940

Both Jim and I had regained our strength. During our months at the hospital we had not received any word on our family, nor did either of us really know how long we had been in.

"Walter and Jim O'Keeffe," called out an unfamiliar voice.

"Here," I called out and raised my hand.

A woman carrying two packages came towards our beds. I recognized the woman as the one who came around to send boys home. Oh no, what will happen now? I thought. My stomach began to tighten and the palms of my hands began to sweat.

"Doctor has said you two are well enough to head home. Here is a package of clothing for each of ya'. New trousers, under-shorts, socks, boots and a jumper. Get dressed now and I'll be back to get ya' ready for the bus." The woman headed out without allowing us time for questions or response.

Jim and I stood face-to-face holding the packages of clothing we had just been given. We stared at each other. I could see from the width of his eyes and his slightly parted lips that Jim was as shocked as I was about being sent out of this place that had become our home. We dressed without saying a word. I joined my brother on his cot and sat tightly beside him, waiting for the woman to return. The fear that had caused my stomach to tighten was now causing me terrible pain in my head. The pit of my gut ached and I felt like my bowels would fall out.

"Jim, do ya' think they're sending us home?

"I don't know. Wait and see."

"I'm scared to go home. What if she's still there, Jimmy? What'll we do?"

"Maybe she's dead Wattie. She's always sick and telling us she doesn't have much longer to live? Maybe she's died, and Eileen and Bessie are home and everything's all right."

The woman returned and motioned us to go with her. I jumped off my brother's cot and stayed close to him as we followed her out. She guided us through the large activity room down the two flights of stairs and back down that long, green, hallway. We were led outside where a bus was waiting. I could see other children, both boys and girls, peering through the foggy windows of the green bus. The driver opened the door.

"Can I say goodbye to Moira and Bridie, please?" I asked the woman. "They were very good to us, and I would like to say thank you."

"No," she said. "We have no time for that. She straightened her tight, woolen skirt and took one step on to the bus to address the driver. "These two can be dropped at Mooncoin," she announced. She stepped down and turned to us.

"Come along now; we haven't got all day. Get on up." She pushed me on to the bus and pushed Jim right into the back of me. That was it. No goodbyes to anyone. Just get on the bus and go. The driver pinned something on to our shirts, shut the door, and started up the engine. As we made our way down the isle the bus jerked, and we both fell to the bus floor. Nobody laughed—they did nothing. Everyone on the bus had long, frightened faces, including us. We found two seats together near the back and slid in.

I wiped the moisture from the window with the sleeve of my jumper and peered back at the hospital as we drove off. Now what? Were we going home? Would she be there? Would things be different? How long had we been gone? I always had so many questions, but no one to answer them. I guess we'll see soon enough, I thought.

It seemed as if we had been on the bus all day. The seats had some kind of spring in them, so every time we hit a hole in the road or ran over a rock we'd bounce out of our seats. The bouncing and the fumes made both of us, and a few others, sick. One poor kid puked up. The driver didn't look back. The kid just sat there covered in it.

The bus stopped in numerous towns to let a boy off here and a girl there. By the time we got to Mooncoin, it was nearing the dinner hour and our stomachs were making all sorts of noises. The driver pulled up in front of the Mooncoin sweetshop and opened the door. "Walter and Jim O'Keeffe."

We knew we had to get off, so slid out of our seats and made our way down the isle. The sun was disappearing beneath the Suir and a few drizzles of rain were starting to come down. Only one small red-headed girl was left on the bus. She had been there when we got on. My eyes met hers as we passed her seat. Her face was covered with freckles and she was biting down on her bottom lip nervously. She clutched the bar of the seat in front of her and I could tell she was scared. She reminded me of Sean. She was about his age and she had the same round face. I started to wonder how he had made out while we were gone. Maybe there was more food for him 'cause Jim and I had not been there. The driver pulled the tags off our shirts and opened the doors. We got off and were left standing in front of the sweetshop.

Nothing had changed in Mooncoin. Everything looked just as it had when we left about a year ago. Both of us were apprehensive about heading back to our house in Polrone. What would she be like? Had she changed at all? Did she even know we were coming back? Was she still alive? With no one to greet us or tell us what to do, we headed down the road to our home. The rain was coming down harder now and it began to thunder. By the time we reached our house we were soakin', tired, and famished.

As we approached our home, Ely was coming up from the ditch carrying a couple of pots. She looked old and worn down out. She did not appear pleased to see us and disappeared into the house. Within moments, Mary was at the front door. Damn, she was still alive. She had Sean by the back of his neck and was dragging his small body across the ground. My jaw fell open and my eyes bulged when I saw how frail, thin, and pale my younger brother looked. I ran forward to greet him. As I approached, Mary tossed Sean at me pushing us both to the wet, muddy, ground.

"God Wattie, Jim, I'm so glad you're back." Sean hugged my neck like he was drowning and I was the only thing that could save him.

"You will not be moving back into this house. Ya' take this piece of shit brother of yur's and ya' find somewhere else to live."

Nothing had changed.

"Where will we go?"

"I don't care. You've got other family. Go find 'em. I'm too sick to care for you lot," she screamed.

"Where's Billy? I asked in a concerned voice.

"Sent 'im away to fend for 'imself."

"He's been gone a long time now, Wattie," Sean whispered into my ear. "She gave 'im a royal beating; there was blood all over. Then she kicked 'im out."

"The authorities say if I'm ill I don't have to care for you bunch," she announced. "Now get out of here!"

Was this some sort of joke? Where were we supposed to go?

"Where should we go?" I asked her.

"Don't much care. All I know is I'm ill and you're not my responsibility anymore, so be off with yas'." She walked back into our house and shut the door, leaving the three of us dripping wet and in a state of disbelief.

It was now dark. Jim, Sean, and I huddled on the wet, dirt road outside of our home. I looked out towards to Phelans. Maybe we should go there. There were no lamps lit.

"Well what are we going to do? Maybe we should move into one of the out buildings?" Jim suggested.

I looked at Sean, he was skinny, dirty, with no shoes, and bruised all over.

"No, we have to get far away from here. We need to be away from her or she'll kill us." I took off the boots they had given me at the sanatorium and placed them on Sean's feet. Jim pulled off his jumper and wrapped it around our brother.

"Maybe Uncle Jim can take us in? We'll head back to Mooncoin to his house," I said. With nowhere else to turn, we headed back up the road to Mooncoin. Sean was exhausted and weak, so Jim and I took turns carrying him on our backs as he was unable to walk all that way on his own. We were all hungry, wet, and tired.

When we arrived at our Uncle Jim's, it was well past the supper hour. I banged on the door and called out for what seemed like a long time before someone came to answer. My Uncle opened the large wooden door looking a little dazed and rubbing his eyes.

"My Jesus, what are ya' doing here? Who brung ya'?" He stepped outside and looked around as if he was expecting someone to be coming in behind us. When he realized we were on our own he hurried us in. "Mary Mother of God, ya' look like a pack of wet dogs." He rushed about, grabbed a blanket, and wrapped it around Sean. He then found drying rags for Jim and me. "What happened? What's brought ya' here? Are you two well now?" he asked referring to Jim and I.

"Can we stay here with ya', Uncle?" I asked.

"Why? You've got yur' home in Polrone?"

"Mary kicked us out and she sent Billy away and she's been beating up on Sean. She told us we can't come back. Can we please stay here with ya'?" I asked again.

"Ah Jesus, Wattie. We've got no room for ya'." he said, anxiously rubbing his hands across his forehead trying to figure out what he should do. "Aunty is sick ya' know and could never tend to you boys. Ah Jesus. I'll go call up to the authorities and see what we can do."

Uncle Jim cut us each a slice of bread and covered it thick with butter and then he headed out. I thought about the last time I had been in this house. Father had been sitting right over there by the fire laughing and turning out tune after tune. Our Dad could pick up any instrument and play it—fiddle, flute, coronet...he never had a lesson in his life; it just came to him natural. He had taught both Jim and I how to play his coronet and said we were naturals at it just like him.

By the time Uncle Jim had returned with the Gardai we were all asleep, me with my head on the wooden table in the kitchen, Sean and Jim on the floor next to the hearth.

"Wattie, Sean, Jimmy. Wake up now, the authorities have to talk to you boys."

I rose from my slumber and looked up to see two uniformed men standing before me. Sean woke next; Jim lay there sleeping.

After Uncle Jim had given the authorities some information about our house, our parents, and Aunt Mary, they started to ask us questions. I explained how we had just come from the hospital and told them how Aunt Mary had thrown us out. I also told them how Eileen, Bessie, and Billy had all been sent away somewhere. I was so tired I really don't know what else I said.

The authorities advised us that they could take us back to our house and talk to Mary and make sure she looked after us, or, they could arrange for us to go to a lovely boys' school near Cork.

"What should we do, Wattie?" Sean asked.

"Jim wake up." I pushed him with my foot and he pulled his face up off of the floor. God, how were we to make a decision like this especially in the confused state we were in? All I wanted was to be home with my mother, father, and my brothers and sisters. I missed Prowler, and Josie, and the schoolhouse. I missed the graveyard and Mrs. Crowley's garden. I just wanted to go home. But I couldn't. It wasn't fair that an old bitch like Aunt Mary could steal our house from under us and send us all away to separate places. This was madness it was, like a bad dream.

Jim was now sitting up looking dazed. Sean was sitting on the floor leaning up against the wooden table leg, half asleep, still wrapped in Jim's wet sweater, and Uncle Jim's blanket.

"They want us to go back home Jim and they'll set Aunt Mary straight, or we can go to a boys' school where we would live with a bunch of other kids. What should we do?"

"I don't know, Wattie. You decide."

"I can't decide by myself Jim. You're the oldest, you decide."

"I don't know what to do Wattie," announced Jim.

"Wattie, please! We can't go back to Aunt Mary," cried Sean from his sleepy state. "She kicked me so bad she broke my bones right here." He lifted his shirt and pointed to his ribs. His skin was yellow from where his wounds were still healing.

"Ely taped me up 'cause she didn't want the authorities to find out. She sent me to the shed Wattie to heal up and to sleep by myself. She sent me out to that shed so many times, and it was always cold. She would be whacking me for nothing. Wattie, we can't go back there. Please!" he pleaded.

"But it's our home, I blurted out. Our mother and father wanted us to stay there."

"You're right boy," announced one of the Gardai. "We could force her to take ya' back in. But she's not well ya' know, and can't care for yas'."

I thought about the Peadmont and thought maybe the school would be like that.

"Jim, what do ya' think?" I asked again.

"I don't know, Wattie. You decide, I said!"

"The hospital wasn't a bad place 'cept we didn't get to go out 'cept to sleep. Would the school be like that?" I asked.

"I'm sure it is something like that," said one of the men, "except I'm sure ya' sleep inside. Lots of boys go there so it can't be all that bad.

"Maybe we could go live with our Grandmother Knox?" I suggested.

"She's too old, Wattie. She could never take care of yas' and she got no means," replied our uncle.

"Sean, the hospital was good and we were sick so maybe the school will be even better," I said. We had food everyday. They kept it, and us, nice and clean, and there were washrooms and storybooks, and the kinds of lights that ya' can flick on with yur' finger. I'm sure the school will be just as good." Sean got excited thinking about the three of us going to a place like that.

"Yes. Wattie, it sounds grand. Let's go there."

I turned to the Gardai and announced, "Okay, we'll go to the school."

"Good decision. Now get yur'selves together and let's 'get going. It's getting late, and we still have to get yas' over to Waterford." We said goodbye to our Uncle Jim and were hustled out by the officers. The three of us were packed into the back seat of the Gardai motor car.

"We'll be taking ya' to Waterford for processing," announced one of the men as we drove off.

"It's okay, Sean." I said, "Processing is not too bad, but try not to pee in the water." He looked confused.

After driving for quite a while, we pulled up in front of a red, brick building in Waterford. The building was well-lit with perfectly round, white bulbs. Each one about the size of my head—the biggest lights I had ever seen.

"We're here, boys. This is the Gardai station where we will keep ya' until we get ya' sorted out. By the way, my name's McCabe, Constable McCabe. If ya' need anything let me know."

We slid out of the auto and followed Mr. McCabe and the other man up the wide, stone steps to the building. Inside, there were all sorts of activities. Men were falling down drunk. Ladies dressed like I'd never seen were making arguments with the authorities. All the officers were dressed in neat, dark blue uniforms. We followed Mr. McCabe through a small, wooden gate and into a large office area with lots of wooden desks and other furnishings. We were shown to three wooden chairs and told to stay put while McCabe did our paperwork.

This was not at all like being processed at the hospital. This was very different and strange. McCabe moved in behind a big wooden desk and pulled out a bunch of papers from a drawer. One by one he asked us our birthdays, asked us if we could read, write, do math, and a bunch of other questions. He measured how tall each of us was and wrote down everything on a piece of paper. He got up and asked us to stay where we were until he returned. As we waited, Sean fell asleep with his head up against my arm. I could feel the tingling in my hand and wrist as my arm feel asleep. Not wanting to wake my brother, I endured the uncomfortable sensation. I was drawn to the activities going on around us…the people coming and going, the lights, the noise. It was all very odd.

"Okay boys," McCabe called out as he re-entered the room. Sean was startled awake and sat up. Thank God. I could feel the blood rush back down my arm and into my hand. "We can't get a car to take ya' over 'til the 22nd, so we will keep ya' here for a few nights, then take ya' up to Greenmount. The judge will see yas' tomorrow." The judge? Why are we seeing a judge?

"What is the date today?" I asked.

"October 19th," McCabe answered, "Come on, now. Let's get yas' settled in." He led us to a room that was full of furniture and sacks. We had no idea what was in them sacks, but there were lots of them.

"Here, you boys will sleep on these, tonight," announced McCabe. He gave each of us a blanket and helped us squish down the sacks so they flattened out for sleeping.

"What's in this here sack? Sean asked.

"Just paper, boy, lots of paper. In a few days, you'll be in yur' own beds at Greenmount."

Another man entered the room with a tray. He was an older fella' with not a hair on his head. He was a portly man and his uniform looked like all the buttons might burst open at any moment, but he had a kind face. On the tray was hot tea and bread with jam. "Any hungry boys in here?" the friendly looking fellow called out. All three of us jolted to attention and raised our arms. "Here ya' go. Eat this up and get some sleep. Name's Tanner and I'll be brining you young uns' yur' meals for the next few days." Tanner sat the tray down on a desk and the three of us pounced on it. It was great. Sweet blackberry jam with sugary tea and cream—nothing could have been better.

After finishing up every last crumb, we climbed on to the sacks and tried to settle in. I lay close to Sean. Jim took a spot at the other side of the room. I was terrified. My head was a mess of confusion. Had I made the right choice? Maybe I should have told the Gardai to talk to Aunt Mary and let us go home. I didn't know. I huddled in closer to my brother and drifted off to sleep.

The next morning I woke to the sound of the door opening. It was McCabe. "Okay, boys. Lets go finish off yur' paperwork. How did ya' sleep?"

Still barely awake and rubbing my face, I said, "Fine, thank you."

Jim was already awake and sitting up against the wall at the end of the room. He had not spoken to me since we had arrived here.

McCabe led us out of the room and down the hall to another waiting area. He asked us to take a seat on a wooden bench until they were ready. I didn't know what was going on. Sean and I sat next to each other while Jim took a seat across the hall next to a window. He just stared out and said nothing. McCabe disappeared behind a large, wooden door. After a few minutes, he came out and motioned us to come in.

When we entered the room we were shown to a bench in front of a large desk. The room looked like a classroom but bigger with one of them big, white lights in the center of the tall ceiling.

"O'Keeffe, Jim, O'Keeffe, Walter, O'Keeffe, Sean," announced the large man behind the desk. "Yes," we all replied. "Having found that you have a guardian who does not exercise proper guardianship, and yur' parents are dead, you are charged with wandering and will be detained to Greenmount Industrial School in Cork, until each of you turns sixteen years of age or, until it is deemed you can care for yur'selves. Thank you."

"Okay, we're done," announced McCabe. Done what? What had just happened? We were shuffled off and led back to the sack room.

McCabe got us some pencils and paper and told us we could spend the days while we waited to go to Greenmount, practicing our numbers and letters and mathematics. I used the paper to draw pictures of the River Suir, Josie and I, Mother and Father. Sean didn't know any letters or numbers so he drew pictures of birds, the kind that lived at our home in Polrone. Jim sat and stared out into space. Later in the day, Tanner came by with a bit of stew for us and let us go wandering about the station.

What an odd place it was. We watched as people came and went, some fighting when they were brought in. Some were rough looking, some were crying...all sorts of people came through this place. But no children like us. We were the only ones. I heard one of the officers say we were the youngest lock-ups they ever had. I didn't know what he meant. They brought us tea and bread, and we spent another two nights on the sacks until finally, it was time to go. Tanner had also brought in some clothes for Sean that he said had been his nephew's. They did not fit quite right, but they were clean and not torn apart like the rags Sean had been in.

It was early morning of October 22, 1940. We were sitting in the front waiting area, hoping Tanner would be coming by with something to eat when a younger, nice looking man came in. "Okay, where are these O'Keeffe boys?" He looked towards us. "Ay, you must be 'em. There's supposed to be three of ya'," he said, as he looked down on to his chart.

"Me brother Jim is over there by the window," I pointed.

He turned and spotted Jim. "Alright," he called out to Jim, "lets be off." Sean and I jumped from our chairs. I took Sean's hand and we headed to the door.

"Come on, Jim," I said as we were hurried out of the place.

"I don't want to, Wattie. I'm scared," he admitted. These were the first words he had uttered to me since we had been here.

"It's okay. We'll be okay. Come on, now." I took my younger and older brothers' hands and the three of us headed out towards the waiting car. We piled into the back seat of the vehicle and the door was shut behind us.

"Ya' boys hungry?"

"Oh yes, sir, we are." I called out.

A slim arm clad in a brown woolen sweater came over the back seat and passed us a brown package as we drove off. "Here, help yur'selves."

In the package were six slices of lemon cake. We each took a slice and I passed the package back up to him.

"No, eat 'em all. Ya' must be starving." I took the package back and we each inhaled another slice. Damn, that was good cake with lemon jelly inside. I had never had anything like it. Maybe it's not going to be that bad, I thought. We're all together eating cake; maybe everything will turn out all right.

In the car, it struck me that I had not even seen Josie when we went back to home. Would I ever see her again? God, I hoped so. During the trip, Sean recalled the past year and told us of the horrors that Mary had inflicted on him and Billy. Listening to him made me realize that I had made the right choice to go to the school for boys.

Sean described the day Billy was sent away covered in blood after Mary had given him a hell of a beating for eating raw spuds. Mary had told Sean that Jim and I were dead and were never coming back. She had also told him he was the last in his family, and that she could do whatever she wanted to him, and no one could save him. Like all of us, he was scared to death of her.

I was glad that I had the courage to make the decision to leave Mooncoin.

I was glad that I had saved Sean from a life of brutality. It felt good to be excited about life. If the school is anything like the hospital, at least we will be well-fed, clean, and together.

Yup, I did the right thing. So I had thought.

Guards can deges taking this boy
to School till 2nd October 1940 2794 *No. 212*

(34567) R.989.W.L.47952.3000.2/39.W.P.W.Ltd.20 *Moshe Justice*

ÉIRE.

AN CHÚIRT BHREITHIÚNAIS DÚITHCHE
(DISTRICT COURT OF JUSTICE).

CHILDREN ACT, 1908, 8 Edw. 7, Ch. 67.

John Ryan of 18
Baileys New Street Waterford
Inspector for the National Society
for the prevention of Cruelty to
Children

Order of Detention in a Certified Industrial School.

Complainant; District Court area of Waterford

Walter O'Keeffe

Defendant. District No. 23

WHEREAS *Walter O'Keeffe* who appears to the Court to be a child under the age of 14 years having been born so far as has been ascertained on the *18th* day of *November* 19*30* and who resides at *Pollroue mooncoin* in the County of *Kilkenny* has been found on the *7th* day of *October* 1940, at *Mooncoin* in said District (¹)Court Area, and in County Kilkenny, wandering

and having a guardian who does not exercise proper Guardianship

(¹) Insert one of the recitals in Schedule D of the Lord Chancellor's Rules appropriate to the case, including recital relating to the Council.

and whereas the Council of the said *County* has been given an opportunity of being heard.

And whereas the Court is satisfied that it is expedient to deal with the said Child by sending said Child to a Certified Industrial School.

And whereas the religious persuasion of the said child appears to the Court to be *Roman Catholic.*

It is Hereby Ordered that the said child shall be sent to the Certified Industrial School at *Greenmount Cork C.C.* (²) being a school conducted in accordance with the doctrines of the Roman Catholic Church, the Managers whereof are willing to receive said Child, to be there detained from and after this day, until but not including the (³) *18th* day of *November* 19*46*

And it is further ordered that

residing at

the said Child shall pay to the Inspector of Reformatory and Industrial Schools in Ireland a weekly sum of shillings (⁵)

(²) Insert "not" before "being" in the case of a child who is not a Roman Catholic.

(³) Date up to but not including, which detention is to continue.

(⁴) Insert "parent of" or "the person legally liable to maintain."

(⁵) Insert "during the whole of the time for which the said child is liable to be detained in the School," or until further order.

First payment on the day of 19

Given under my hand the *19th* day of *October* One thousand nine hundred and *Forty*

Justice of said District Court.

73

Nine

GREENMOUNT–OCTOBER 22, 1940

After a long drive, the car pulled up to a cold monstrosity of a building. We were in Cork, another place I had never been. Sean was stunned as he looked out the window and into the city. It was truly an awesome sight for young eyes that had never seen the likes of a city.

"Here we are boys, St. Joseph's Industrial School for Boys. Folks just call it Greenmount." It was huge, this place, bigger than the hospital in Dublin. I felt my guts tighten. Oh God, what will this be like? I imagined the boys inside the school playing soccer, eating marvelous food, taking interesting classes, and having a great time living here. No doubt the other kids would be happy to see three new boys arrive. I took in a deep breath then slowly released it, ready to start the rest of my life here at Greenmount.

The tension in my stomach did not let up. My back and neck were sweating, my hands were shaking, and I could feel the muscles across my shoulders tense up. Sean was silent. His wide eyes, hunched shoulders and the fact that he held both thumbs in his mouth was a good indication he was also feeling uneasy. His entire body was stiff; I could see it in his face and his legs. He was stiff with fear as he looked out the window towards this enormous, dirty, gray building that would now be our home. Sean had never left Polrone. I was terrified and my head began to hurt. I hoped that I had made the right decision for us. Sean trusted me to look out for him, Jesus, I didn't want to let him down.

Jim sat motionless, his head leaning up against the window. He looked as if he had already given up on life. He was not excited to be here, he was not afraid. He was nothing.

The brick school was located in the middle of the city and was massive and intimidating. Tall hedges and hawthorn bushes surrounded the place making it appear unfriendly. The Gardai got out of the car and opened the door closest to Sean. As the door opened we saw two lines of boys being led into the building. They were all dressed the same, walking with their heads down, in two side-by-side lines. A man in a long black robe walked in front of them, another man in a robe walked at the end of each line, and a fourth, robed man walking beside them. None of the boys looked happy. This was the first time I worried about our—my—decision to come here.

"Come on now, Sean. We've got to go in." I had to shake him to loosen him up and get him to move outside the vehicle. He slid off his seat slowly and allowed his feet to hit the ground. Sean turned and looked to me as I was trying to push out behind him. That look on his face, his eyes were wide and strained and his face was deathly white. God-damn, the kid was scared shit-less. The three of us, now out of the vehicle, stood and stared up at this cold, haunting building where we would now live. We didn't speak. I don't think any of us knew what to say. I held on to Sean's hand as we watched the two rows of boys being herded into the school.

"Come on now." The officer said. He proceeded to walk in front of us as we approached the building.

"This place is run by the Presentation Brothers; they're Christian Brothers," announced the officer. "So they should treat ya' well."

The Christian Brothers? I had heard stories of boys being sent away to live with the Christian Brothers. A boy from the Polrone school had been taken away when his father died. The boy's mother had taken up with another chap so the Gardai took the boy away from her. It made no sense. When the mother finally got him back, he was burnt all over his body and had turned real strange. No, this couldn't be one of those places, could it?

Once inside the building the scent of floor polish hit my nose. I gazed about at all the wood in the place. It shone and reflected like glass. Banisters, window trims, tall pillars, and wooden beams, all unbelievably shimmering and slick. We were taken through a large room and then into an office. The office was dimly lit and furnished with fancy chairs covered with red velvet seats. Maybe this is going to be a great place to live after all? It looked clean. Nice furniture. Maybe I was worrying about nothing.

The officer told us to sit on the fancy chairs until he came back. He disappeared down a small hallway with his chart and papers, leaving us still nervous, but sort of excited. I didn't know what I was feeling. Sean had relaxed a little and was gazing around the place. Jim kept his head down and didn't look at anything. We couldn't see any other part of the school from where we sat, but if this room was any indication, it looked good.

When the officer came back a Christian Brother was following him. "Boys, I'm going to leave ya' now with Brother Thomas. He'll take care of ya'. All the best now." Then the officer left.

The Brother was fierce looking. He was a tall, fat beast, with thinning orange hair and dressed in a long, black robe that hugged the layers of fat beneath it. It was impossible to see the colour of his eyes as they were hidden behind two tiny slits across the plump eye sockets that bulged out against his flabby, round cheeks.

"I don't like being called Brother Thomas, so you'll call me Blackie," he announced. Sean giggled when he said it. The Brother stepped up in front of Sean and looked at him. "Ya' think that's funny do ya'? Well, let's hope that's the last laugh ya' ever have while you're living here. Sean fell silent and placed his hand over mine.

"Ya' see this?" Blackie gestured to a huge, black, leather belt around his belly. "*This* gets lots of use around here. *This*," again pointing to the belt, "will make the difference between yur' little souls making it to heaven or being sent to hell. I am here to serve God and make sure yur' damaged souls are purified and stay pure. If I have to use this, and I know I will," he said staring straight into Sean's face again, "...it will be because I am trying to secure ya' a place with God. I always have it handy."

Now I was shaking. My hands were wet, and I thought I was going to piss myself. I slouched down in my chair as if I could hide from the being standing before me. This was nothing like Peadmont. I was numb. I didn't know where to look or what to say. Even Jim had now moved in closer to Sean and I.

Another Christian Brother came in, looked us over, then left the room without saying a word. He returned a few minutes later and handed each of us a bundle. The bundle included a pair of used, black boots, blue socks with black stripes that had been darned, faded gray short pants, a used blue shirt, and a tattered brown jacket. The garments Jim and I were wearing from Peadmont were better than what he had handed us, but I was afraid to ask if we would be allowed to keep the clothing we had on.

"Follow me," Blackie ordered. We slid off our chairs, took our bundles, and followed him across the room. We were led through the well-decorated office into a musty smelling room that was cold, untidy, and littered with boxes of rags or old clothing…some sort of supply room, I think, and quite a contrast to the fancy office we had just been in.

"Strip down."

What? We were stunned. What did he mean, strip down? "I said, strip down. Remove yur' clothing," he barked again.

"Right here?" I asked.

Blackie and the other Christian Brother looked at each other and then back at us. Blackie moved forward, right in front of me, bent down to look me directly in the face. "Yes right here," he replied, spitting in my face as the words came out of his mouth. "And, that will be the last time ya' question me. If it happens again, I will beat the living daylights out of ya'. Do you understand?"

I didn't understand, but I said yes anyway. Sean and Jim were frozen in terror.

"Strip down!" he yelled out at all of us.

Quickly we fumbled with buttons and laces to remove our clothing, until we stood naked before him. I started to put on my new uniform but was grabbed by the arm. "You will dress when I tell ya' that you can dress," Blackie announced. God, he was hurting my arm but I didn't dare challenge him or say anything. Finally, he released me. Jesus, my entire arm had gone numb from the pressure he had applied.

"Do ya' boys play with yur'selves?" Blackie asked. Again, we were horrified and could not say a word, any of us. Nobody had ever asked me or my brothers that kind of question. "I asked yas' if you play with yur'selves, yur' willys, do ya' play with 'em?"

Not sure where this was all going, I said, "No, Brother, we don't."

"Yur' a fuckin' liar; all boys play with 'emselves. Well, ya' won't be here cause if ya' do, I'll beat the bejeezuz out of ya'." Again, I had no words. I couldn't believe a Brother, a man so close to God, had used that sort of language.

"Pick up yur' clothes and come with me." Still naked we bundled up the items we had been issued and followed him out, leaving what was left of our lives before this place in three tiny mounds on the floor of the supply room.

We were walked naked through a dismal hallway trying to cover our behinds and privates. We were taken to a large shower room where two more Brothers stood. It smelt awful, like urine and mold and something else.

"Place yur' things here," he pointed to a small wooden bench, "and go stand in the shower." We were each given a smelly bar of something that stung my skin as soon as it was placed in my hand. We were then told to stand under the water-spout. Oh crap, I could tell that it was going to be cold.

"Ow!" I yelled out. The water was freezing.

"Come on, scrub yur'selves down, one of the Brothers ordered. "You have to wash the devil out of ya'." If I did have the devil in me, he would surely be dead after this frigid shower. I moved the bar of "stuff" over my body. It stung, and it didn't lather or anything. I didn't know what it was supposed to do.

"Scrub those willy's of yur's," the Brother beside Blackie called out, chuckling as he said his words. "Scrub those little peckers hard now," the two of them were now laughing.

It was all so uncomfortable. I felt uneasy and wondered why they were staring and laughing at us. After scrubbing ourselves down, the freezing water was shut off. The three of us stood there, cold, trembling, and dripping wet with these two fat Christian pigs looking us over. We stood huddled together shivering, confused, and not sure what would happen next. Sean's legs were turning purple and blue. The two fatties just chuckled to themselves getting some sort of pleasure out of our misery.

Finally, and to our relief, we were told we could put on our uniforms. We were not given anything to dry off with so it was a bit of a struggle to get dressed.

We fumbled about as we slipped wet arms and legs into sleeves and pant legs. Sean was having trouble with his shorts as they were getting stuck on his wet body. He sat on the wet shower floor to try and pull them over his foot. Without warning a huge hand came down and slapped him across the head and hauled him up by the hair from his sitting position.

"If you ever seat yur'self without being told, I'll whip you straight to hell," one of the Brothers yelled. Again, we were taken aback. What had he done wrong?

"You will sit when we tell ya' to sit," announced Blackie. "So for now, ya' can just stand there in that corner." He pointed his large crooked finger to the corner of the room. Sean stumbled to pull up his shorts. "Don't ya' dare,"

78

announced Blackie, "You stand as you are."

Sean staggered with his shorts half up, still dripping wet, to the corner where he had been ordered, his lips now turning blue from the cold. My heart was breaking for him. Here was this little boy, barely seven years old, my brother, scared, new to this place, wet, cold, turning blue and being sent to the corner for what? He had been so full of hope, we all had been. We hoped that this place would be good and fun. Now here we were. Was this how it would be from now on? Oh God.

Jim and I were taken out of the room and led down a large hall to a huge staircase. My stomach was sick, this time because I didn't know what was going to happen to Sean. "Can I stay with 'im, cause he's likely scared?" I timidly asked. "I don't mind staying with 'im."

"This will be yur' last warning," I was told. "I told ya', I'll beat ya' into the afterlife if you ever speak to me without being spoken to." Here we were in this a place where Ireland's most vulnerable and deprived children were sent to be cared for, and all we had seen so far was anger, brutality, and constant threats of beatings. And, we had only been here an hour or so.

I was led to a dormitory where about a hundred small beds lay head to head. A huge crucifix was mounted in the center of the back wall to remind us inmates that God was always watching. Large windows, too tall for a smaller child to look out of, surrounded the room. The tall, brown, wooden ceiling was held up with large white pillars making the room cold and unfriendly. The squeaky, wooden floors bounced with each step we took. Each tiny iron bed had a small mattress and one blanket. The beds were packed tightly together head to head. This was not at all like the hospital.

I was shown to a bed and told to wait. Wait for what I wondered? Jim was led out and taken to another dormitory I found out later. I sat there uncertain as to what was going to happen, worried that we had chosen to come here rather than stay in Polrone, wondering if we could change our minds, and go back to our house. Damn, I was so scared, and scared for Sean wondering if he was still standing in the cold with his shorts down around his knees. I was freezing. My hair was wet and cold, dripping down my back. My teeth began to rattle, and my body shook. If I was this cold, surely it must be worse for Sean standing in the cold shower room.

There were no other boys in the room, just me. I was too frightened to go over to the window to look out in case Blackie came back and whacked me for moving from my spot. Where is Sean? God, I hope they don't hurt him. I was always asking God for stuff, but he never seemed to hear me.

After sitting for what seemed to be hours, I heard the sounds of a distant rumble coming closer. The sound continued to grow. What is that? The sound grew louder, then all of a sudden it was at the entrance to the dorm. In came two rows of boys. All thin, pale, all looking miserable and all eyes held tight to the floor. Each one took their place beside a bed. Some of them looked over at me then moved along quickly.

I watched as each of them took a spot and stood next to what I assumed was their cot. I followed the crowd and got off my bed and stood like the others. When the last two boys had entered the room one of the Brothers entered behind them. He said nothing, looked around as if he was disgusted at the sight of all of us, and left. After he had exited, the boys all relaxed and fell on to their beds. Then a whisper of muffled chatting flowed over the room. Some of the boys started to rummage about under their beds pulling out odd looking night shorts. I didn't have any night pants. What was I supposed to do? Should I undress? Should I ask someone what I should do? I fidgeted nervously with the blanket on my cot, and waited. Damn, I hate this.

Again, I heard footsteps coming up the stairs towards the dorm. The boys scurried like rats and again took their places beside their beds. Another Brother entered the room. How many of these guys are there? This one had Sean with him.

I could see that my brother was scared and had been crying. He had his shorts on but was carrying his shirt and had goose pimples all over his tiny shivering blue body. He was walking like he was in pain, sort of bent over. What had the bastards done to him? I wanted to run up and take him and hold him, but was afraid of what might happen. Sean was led across the room to another bed. I could see his eyes scour the room to see if I was there. He didn't see me, and I knew he was afraid. He was handed night shorts and told to change.

"Walter O'Keeffe," my name was called out. I put up my hand.

"Here!" I announced at the top of my lungs so Sean knew I was there. The Brother walked over to me, said nothing, handed me a pair of night shorts that looked like a baby nappy, and left.

"Lights out five minute," he announced and exited the room.

I scrambled to change keeping my eyes on Sean the entire time. He was looking to me. I knew he was terrified, and I knew he wanted me to go over to him. I was so afraid. What the hell, I darted over to where my brother was and threw my arms around him. He fell into my chest and began to cry uncontrollably. "Wattie, let's go back to Aunt Mary. This place is bad. Can ya' please ask if we can go home?"

"What did they do to ya'?" He pulled back and pointed to the tops of his legs. Huge welts were coming up across both legs; it looked like he had been walloped a dozen times.

Those bastards. "Those fat Christian bastards," I yelled out and started running towards the door. Two sets of arms grabbed me and pulled me back. A hand covered my mouth. I wanted to scream and tried to bite the hand covering my lips. I kicked and struggled, but they wouldn't let me go.

"Calm down, it's not worth it," one of the voices hanging on to me called out. "I said calm down now. This is what they want ya' to do. They'll take both you and yur' brother there and beat the shit out of the two of yas'. If ya' want to help yur'self and yur' brother calm down." I stopped struggling and the two sets of arms let go. "That's the last time we'll help ya' out. Now go take care of yur' brother."

The two boys scrambled back to their beds and I went back to Sean. I didn't know what to tell him. I knew we would not be able to go home. This was home; there was nowhere else to go. I fought back the tears as I held on to my little brother. Jesus, Joseph, and Mary, what next?

"Don't cry," a voice whispered to us. "If they see ya' cry, they'll whack ya'. Try and hold it in; that pisses 'em off. You, the bigger one, go back to yur' bed or you'll get a whipping," the mousy voice warned. Sean wiped his face and fumbled around to dress himself into his night wear. I gave him one last hug.

"I'll look out for you here, Sean. I will, I promise."

"I believe ya', Wattie," he said. Then I scrambled back over to my iron cot.

All the other boys were laying flat on their backs with their hands outside the covers. "Ya' have to have yur' hands showing. Ya' have to sleep like this," the boy in the bed next to me announced. "If ya' don't, they beat ya' fur playing with yur'self. Ya' need to keep yur' hands out like this."

I looked over to where Sean's bed was and saw that he was being given the same instructions by another boy. I crawled into my bed and lay myself out like all the others. It was deathly cold and I was hungry. We had not had a bite to eat since we had eaten the cake in the car. I just lay there. I couldn't sleep. I couldn't think straight. There were a hundred thoughts rushing through my mind. As well, I had to pee. Where do I pee? No one had shown us to a toilet or pot. Oh no, where will I go pee? The room fell quiet and the lights went out. I heard the echoes of coughing and fidgeting as my room-mates, about a hundred of them, tried to get comfortable. Somewhere during all the madness in my brain I drifted off, but only for a short while.

When I woke in the middle of the night, I realized that I had peed the bed. Now what? I thought I should get up and flip over the mattress on my cot? That's it, that's what I'll do. As I sat up, I heard an odd sound. It was like the entire floor was being scratched. There was something, or many things, scurrying about under my bed and across the floor. As I tuned into the noise, I realized the sound was also coming from overhead.

"It's rats," the voice next to me announced. "They'll nibble on yur' toes if you leave 'em out. They lick yur' hands if you hang 'em over the edge of the bed."

"You're kiddin'," I said.

"I'm not. You'll get used to it." Then the voice fell silent.

All night I heard them scurry about. I was too frightened to get up and flip my mattress. I covered my entire body with my one blanket, afraid that at any moment a rat might pounce on me and start to nibble on my face. I worried about Sean on his side of the room. What if they were nibbling on him? Oh, what a terrible place I had brought us to. I lay in my soaking bed not sure about anything. Oh, how I missed my father and our home, and my mother. I missed the river and Josie. I missed it all. Dream now, I told myself, dream now and go to them. They'll keep you safe.

Ten

THE PILLAR OF TERROR

A large arm reached down and seized me by my scalp. The huge limb stole me from my cot and tossed my frail body on to the cold wooden floorboards of the dormitory. Confused, cold, and dazed with terror, I stumbled to my feet pushing the hair from my eyes and tried to steady myself on my two skinny legs.

"Turn around and place yur' arms on the pillar," roared the voice.

Stunned in absolute horror, and still in shock from being awoken in such a harsh and brutal manner, I looked up and saw the tussled, orange hair of Blackie with his black strap tied around his waist. He stood over me holding a long, thick cane tightly in his chubby, red fist.

"You do not own yur' body. It belongs to God. You dare come to the house of God and soil his flesh?"

What is he talking about? I didn't know what was happening or what this giant of a beast was going to do to me or why, but I sensed it would be painful and terrifying.

"You like to piss yur'self do ya' O'Keeffe? You're revolting!" With that Blackie took his large hand and pushed it into the back of my head thrusting my face into one of the large white pillars that held up the room. My nose was held tight against the pillar, I couldn't breath, and it hurt.

"Remove his shorts!" he shouted and signaled two boys, who stood in a sleepy state across from where my bed was positioned, to assist him. The two boys hurried forward and began to take down my underpants. "What the hell?" In an act of spontaneous resistance I lowered my arms in an attempt to stop them. The robed monster pulled my head back allowing me to inhale

83

once before he slammed my face back into the pillar. I could feel that my nose was now bleeding. I had inhaled the blood into my throat and was choking. I couldn't breath and was starting to panic. Again, he pulled back my head, I inhaled, he bent down looked straight into my face and spit his words into my mouth.

"You will not resist the wrath of God. You will accept yur' punishment for soiling yur'self. You will receive God's fury each night until you cease this disgusting addiction."

Addiction? What addiction, I asked myself. Stunned by fear, I stood there my entire body shaking as these two boys lowered my pants. I didn't dare resist. I was too afraid. Even when Aunt Mary beat the hell out of us we expected it? But this? What the hell was this?

"Now, part his legs and hold 'em so he cannot move." My entire body was now vibrating, my head was spinning; my god, I was so scared.

Standing before these strangers I was mortified as I felt the small cold hands of my two roommates grab my ankles to hold me in place. As tightly as they held me they couldn't control the shaking in my legs. Tremors of fear ran through my limbs and I shook uncontrollably. And cold, God I was cold. I felt the agonizing bite of the wooden cane as it cut across my naked flesh. Oh God, the pain was awful. Again, the cane came down upon my swollen bum cutting through a boil that had been there for days. The sting of the exposed wound was horrendous. Dear Jesus, what had I done to deserve this?

I looked down at the boys holding my legs. Neither of them were looking at me. Both of them had their heads turned down towards the floor. They too, were shaking. This wasn't their fault. One more time the cane came down, again cutting into my skin. It was more than I could bare. I'm going to puke up for sure. My stomach was coming up into my throat. I swallowed so that I would not spit up on the floor. My bowels were ready to release themselves right there. I was dizzy with confusion.

"Each time you wet yur' bed, know that I will be back," Blackie announced in a dominating tone, "Each time!" He released his hand and I fell to my knees. Blackie removed the leather whip from around his waist and with one flip of his wrist the belt came burning across my back, my bum and my legs. I fell forward on to my stomach and did not move hoping he would think I was dead. The two terrified assistants scurried back to their beds leaving me, demoralized and face down on the floor with my bloodied bum exposed to them all. I heard Blackie turn and leave, his heavy feet creating a weighty echo as he left the room.

The dorm fell silent; not a breath could be heard.

After I was sure that Blackie had left I slowly rose and sat on the floor. I just sat for what seemed to be a long time. I must have been in shock. With my head hung down, humiliated and confused, my eyes searched the floor for my shorts. Finding them hanging off my left foot I fumbled awkwardly to get them back on.

"Boy," a hand a little bigger than mine reached down to me. I looked up and saw a boy about the same age as me holding out his hand to help me up. I took his arm and struggled to my feet.

"Here wipe yur'self up." The fair-haired boy handed me a wet rag. I took the rag and shoved it into the back of my shorts in an attempt to wipe up the blood and the pus that had been released from the boil on my bottom.

"They normally beat the bed-wetters at night. This being yur' first day and all, he wanted to make a point. They come around in the night or early in the morning ta' see who's pissed their beds and make sure nobody's been touching 'emselves. Sick pigs they are, they're the ones playing with 'emselves, all the time. They even make some of the lads watch 'em as they do it."

What is this kid talking about? My God, I was baffled.

"Then, they make an announcement in the morning calling out the names of boys who are going to get a wallopin' before lights out. That way, they can have you in a mess of fear all day worrying about it. They're a bunch of fat assholes; there's nothing Christian about 'em fat Christian pigs." I was speechless. "Name's Charlie, Charlie McFarland. What's yur' name?"

"Wattie, Walter O'Keeffe."

"Well, Wattie. You'll sit with me today. I'll teach ya' a few things about this place, mostly how to stay alive."

"You mean each time I pee the bed that's gonna happen to me?" I asked in a shocked and terrified voice.

"'Fraid so. Don't worry, you're not the only one. We can teach ya' some tricks to hide it, but mostly they catch ya'. Sounds daft but you'll get use to it. Come on now. Get dressed. You'll line up with me today."

What had just happened to me? My God, this is a horrible place. I could never have imagined such pain and brutality. My head was spinning. I saw Sean seated on the edge of his bed, looking shocked at what had just happened. The rest of the boys were pretty oblivious to it. As the others moved freely around the room getting ready for whatever was next, I made my way over to Sean.

"Wattie, are ya' alright? Why did he do that?"

"I pissed the bed." My bum was so sore I couldn't even sit at the edge of Sean's cot.

"You two brothers?" a boy asked as he sat and tied his laces.

"Yes," I replied.

"How old are ya'?" I had to think about it.

"I think I'm nine, and Sean is seven, maybe eight I'm not sure."

"What ya' here fur?" he asked. "You orphans, criminals, come from bad seed, what?"

"Our parents died, and our aunt wouldn't take care of us no more," I replied.

"She was a real bitch," Sean added, his use of words shocked me again.

"My mother was a whore, so they took me away from her. She still comes around. I'm eleven, name's Frankie. I'll look after 'im over on this side," Frankie announced referring to Sean. "You two better get dressed. They'll be up soon."

"Thanks," I said and shuffled off in pain to dress myself.

Another huge Brother entered the room just as I had finished dressing myself. They were all big fat blokes. We were lined up in two rows. Sean was next to Frankie, and I was next to Charlie. We were marched out of the room and taken down two flights of stairs. I hoped they were taking us to get fed, but I was too afraid to ask. All the boys walked with their heads down, none of them wanting to stick out. I followed along and did the same, keeping my head and eyes down.

Each one of these boys had a sad face, a gray face. Skinny and bruised, all of them dressed in clothing that didn't fit right and was in need of repair. My clothes didn't fit right either. My shorts were much too big and I had to hang on to them so they didn't fall down.

"Good thing to keep yur' head down O'Keeffe," whispered Charlie. "Ya' don't want to make eye contact with any of them. Ya' just never know what they'll do to ya'."

We were taken down cold halls past rooms filled with desks. Everything was sparse, un-attractive, and dark. What a difference from the front office we had been brought into.

I was still in shock from what had happened. Wasn't there anybody I could tell? Every time I pee myself, was that going to happen? I began to sweat. What was I going to do? Maybe I could see a doctor to see if they could stop the bed-wetting. What if I really do go to hell for wetting the bed? No, this couldn't be right, could it? My mother never beat me like that for wetting the bed. Why was this such a bad thing? I didn't understand this place at all? My stomach growled and my mouth was dry. Maybe they'll feed us good like at Peadmont. Maybe the food will be good, and it won't be so bad living here after all.

But my hopes of food were crushed when we entered a large chapel where about another hundred boys were kneeling and reciting prayers. Another large, cold room. This place is full of them—rooms and boys. The chapel smelt musty, like the old church in Mooncoin. The smell reminded me of death. Each time we had been to a funeral, I recognized that sweet deathly smell. It must be that stuff they burnt at the altar.

All of the boys looked thin and scared. Not even one of them looked up from his place in front of the wooden benches where all the boys knelt. Brothers directed the boys to rows of benches. I followed the others as they knelt down to pray. How long would we stay here? What should I be reciting? I knew some 'pray's'. Were they the right ones? So many questions.

To be safe, I just closed my eyes, clasped my hands, and recited a few Hail Mary's…*"Hail Mary full of grace, the Lord is with thee, blessed art thou amongst women…, and blessed is the fruit of thy womb.,"*…and then the Lord's Prayer… *"Our father who art in heaven…hallowed be Thy name, Thy Kingdom come…on earth as it is in Heaven…give us this day artos epiousios (our daily bread)."* Should I be saying the prayers in Latin? Gaelic? Do I have the words right? *"Forgive us our trespasses…Forgive, Those who trespass against us,* Could I ever forgive or forget those who had treated us so harshly? *Lead us not into temptation, forgive us…* Jesus, I had it all mixed up.

Maybe I need to make up my own 'pray', I thought. Maybe God *is* listening; maybe this is the time that he will hear me. *"Dear Father, God of all life, Father of the mighty oceans, rivers and streams, Mother of the gentle earth, its deserts, mountains, green valleys, and trees. Please help me make it through this day. Thank you for the life you have given me. Thank you for the birds, the plants, and especially the bees that share this world. Thank you for the time I had with my parents. Dear Father please keep us safe. Please keep Eileen, Bessie, and Billy safe no matter where they are. Give me the strength, oh Lord, to survive this place and to keep my brothers safe from harm. God bless my mother and father, my brothers and sisters, Josie, and all living creatures on earth. Please let me survive this day and each day after until we are out of this place. Amen."*

I wondered if He heard me. I looked up and everyone else was still praying. So I started over again, and again. Finally, after an hour or so, a 'pray' bell rang and everyone rose and sat on the benches. No one spoke. One of the Brothers gave us a signal to stand. Again, each boy kept his head down as if he was hiding or afraid to stand out above the rest. I just stayed in my row and followed the crowd, scared to death of what might happen if I fell out of line. The boots they had given me were much too big and I had to concentrate really hard to keep them from slipping off my feet. I could feel that my bum was still bleeding and soaking into my shorts. God, what if I left a stain on the bench? Will they whack me again?

We were led from the chapel and taken to a large yard covered with grass and mud. It was raining, but most of the boys seemed to enjoy being led out here. The two rows of boys started to run around the yard, still in single file. I guess this was some sort of exercise. It was cold and I was starving. I just followed the lot of them, never fallin' out of line. I had to stay focused on my damn boots. I could have fit both my feet into one of them. After running two laps around the yard, we were led into another large room with more benches and tables. My stomach was grumbling as it waited for the food that I hoped was coming. I wiped my hand along the back of my shorts to see if anything was soaking through. No, I'm okay for now, I thought.

Before we could sit, we were led in another 'pray'. I pretty much faked it and continued to keep my head down. Finally, we were told we could line up. I followed the line in anticipation of getting something substantial in my belly. A row of boys came from behind a wall. It looked like they were carrying containers of food. The line moved forward and boys began to receive their meals. I couldn't remember ever being hungrier than I was at that moment. I could barely stand it and was pushing right up against Charlie, who was in front of me. As we got closer, I could see the boys who were handing out the food. What are we getting? What are we getting?

I reminded myself of Prowler when we brought him a food bucket. He'd jump around anticipating what he was about to eat. Right now, I was just like that, a hungry, wet dog who'd eat just about anything. Now I had my tray and could see the boys handing out something. Jim was with the boys handing out the stuff. When I came by him, he didn't look at me. He dropped a slice of bread on my plate, and I continued to be pushed along the line by the boys behind me. I looked back at my older brother and wondered why he had not even acknowledged me? Another boy placed a cup of black coffee on my tray without making a sound. So what else will be coming along with this...eggs maybe, fine sausage? Oh, I was hungry. But, that was it. That was the end of the line. There was nothing else. Maybe it comes later, I thought. I could smell it, bacon and warm bread. Where was it?

"Charlie, is that it or do they bring the other stuff out later?" I asked.

"What other stuff?" he questioned.

"I can smell meat and bread baking. Where is it?"

"Those bastards eat like kings. I've seen it," he said. "I've seen 'em roast an entire pig, probably one of their own," he giggled, "while we eat the slop that comes out of here. They also have one of the best bakeries around, but you'd never know it by the shit they make us eat." I sat next to Charlie, my eyes still looking back to see if the real food would be coming out.

"That's it O'Keeffe. Nothing else is coming," Charlie advised. I stared down at my tray. What a disappointment. I picked up the bread and looked down the table for butter or jam or something to put on it. There was nothing.

This was the strangest bread I had ever seen. When I pulled it apart it didn't separate. Long strands, like a rubber band, held the bread together like sticky glue. It was like a spider web that could not be broken. And it stank. It was sour. How could bread smell sour?

"It's rotten," said Charlie, but it won't kill ya'. Eat it, 'cause you'll be hungry before the day ends."

"We really won't be gettin' something else with this?" I asked him.

"O'Keeffe, you're a funny one. Now eat yur' stinky bread."

"Charlie, really, is this all we'll be getting?"

"Shut up, O'Keeffe. This'll be all ya' get 'til dinner tonight and don't be expecting no fancy feast than either, my friend."

Around me the other boys were gobbling up the awful stuff. One slice each and nothing to go on it. Some of them were putting the entire slice in their coffee cup and letting it soak up. They ate it by scooping it out of their cups with their hands. These boys, all of them, were ravenous. I shoved my bread in my coffee like the rest of them and ate it. Yes, this was awful stuff, but I was hungry and didn't care what it was. I just wanted to get something inside me. But my God, how will I survive 'til supper?

All of a sudden everyone stopped eating and put down their cups. Blackie had entered the room and was making his way to the front of the hall. He bellowed, "Finnegan Martin, Finnegan Thomas, Doyle Michael, O'Brien John, Reilly Patrick, Phelps Brendan."

As Blackie called out the names, different boys moved to the front of the room. As they did, Blackie removed his large leather whip from his belt. One by one he made the boys climb a short ladder and take down their trousers. Again, I was stunned at the horror of this place. Some of the boys were pretty casual about it all, like they had done this before.

Blackie mumbled a few words after each boy was up the ladder then gave them three hard whacks across the ass. What the hell was this, I wondered? Oh God, please don't call Sean's name. Please don't call my name.

"What did they do?" I whispered to Charlie.

"Could be anything. Could have looked at a Brother the wrong way, maybe failed a test, maybe they were sick and missed a class, might've spilt their coffee yesterday. Anything. I've been up there for just sneezing during mass," he added. "Was sick as a dog I was, burning up with fever. I tried to stop myself from sneezing, but when I did I crapped myself. Thank God they didn't know about that. Two seconds later I felt another sneeze coming on, and I had to let it out, right in the middle of 'prays'. Really pissed 'em off." So got my three whacks on the ass. Been up there a few times."

After the last boy had received his three whacks another list of names was called out: "O'Rourke John, Shannon Paddy, O'Sullivan John, Bartlett Kegan, Flaraty Walter, Raferty Fintan, Ahern Timothy, Pantazis Nik." This time, nobody came forward.

"Bed-wetters will not be tolerated," announced Blackie. "Tis a sin against God. You must have control. Those who urinate in their sleep are of bad seed and have been having indecent dreams. That's why they've wet the bed. Bed-wetters are disgusting. Each of you will receive yur' punishment before lights out tonight. Now, off to class." Then Blackie left the room.

So that was it, the morning drill. Get up, get paraded to mass, say pray's, run through the yard, eat rotten bread and coffee, watch boys get beaten for everything and nothing, and listen in terror to see if your name would be called out as a bed-wetter that would be punished before bedtime that night. What a place?

With Blackie now out of sight, the boys started to scuttle about and mingled. The level of their voices and activity rose. Kids moved freely. There was no lining up, that was a relief, but I had no idea what I was supposed to do next.

Then a voice called, "O'Keeffe Jim, O'Keeffe Walter, O'Keeffe Sean." Oh no, I thought. "Come forward."

The rest of the boys continued to rough each other up, chat, and move about. No one paid any attention to our names being called. Sean and I moved to the front of the room. Jim was already there. Still, he did not look at or speak to us.

"These are yur' classes. Each of us was handed a piece of paper with writing on it. I could not read a thing, nor could Sean. I was relieved that we had not been called forward for a beating. I don't think my butt could have handled another one that day.

"My name is Brother Eugene. Have you lads attended school before?" he asked.

"Yes sir," we all replied.

Brother Eugene was slim unlike the other Brothers. He had thick, black hair and was not as threatening as the other men we had come across in this place. Brother Eugene looked around as if he wanted to make sure there was no one that could hear what he was about to tell us. "Listen now lads. When you're replying to the Brothers you should be saying "Yes Brother," If you don't, some of 'em might get a wee bit nasty with ya'. You can call me what ever ya' like." This man was different than any of the others. But still I was not ready to trust him. "Now, can you all read what's on yur' class schedule?" Brother Eugene asked.

"Dem two can't read," announced Jim and pointed to Sean and me. I began to sweat and tremble. Were we going to get a whipping for not being able to read?

"That's alright. I'll read it for you and I'll show you where to go for yur' classes. Now, if you need anything here, come an' see me." The three of us just nodded this time.

Brother Eugene went through the timetable with each of us. When it was my turn he read out: Arithmetic, Reading, Writing, Band, Choir, Soccer and Shoemaking.

"I'll give ya' a walking tour of the school so you know where everything is and I'll tell yas' what's expected of you while you're here." The Brother guided us from the eating hall and out to the main entrance hall. I still kept my head down.

The floors of each room and hallway were unbelievably well polished. Brother Eugene took us to the various classrooms. Each one looked the same: a tall ceiling with one light and globe dangling down from the center, dark wooden walls, rows of desks, and a crucifix at the front of each class. A large wooden desk stood guard over all the others in each room, and a drawing board was attached to the wall, each one with chalk markings, that I could not read, scribbled about the board. The training room looked quite a bit different. This is where we would come for shoemaking. This space looked like a place that factory workers would go everyday. Greenmount was different than the schoolhouses we had gone to in Polrone and Mooncoin. Greenmount was cold, dark, and the air was thick with a damp, sour, musty smell.

Next, Brother Eugene showed us to the toilet. What a stench. The pissing room was done up with gray plaster or stone—it was hard to tell what it was. There was a trough running along the floor against the back wall.

"Now, when you lads have to do yur' number one, yur' pissing business, you just go and stand up in front of the trough. The pee will run down the wall and into the trench. If yas' have to do a number two, ya' go sit up on the bench there," he said, directing our attention to the long wooden bench with several holes cut out of it. The bench appeared to be well polished from all the bums that had sat on it over the years. Nothing was private; everything was out in the open.

My nostrils began to burn, and I could feel my eyes watering up and itching. The odor in the room was acidy. That's the only way to describe it. The stench burnt my nose, eyes, and skin. The humidity in the room settled on my lips, forcing me to taste the reek that hung in the air. Strips of well-aged newspaper were piled into a wooden box. We were told to use the paper to wipe our bums after we were done.

While we stood getting our instructions, a group of three boys, Sean's age, ran into the room. Never looking at us or Brother Eugene, all three of them faced the wall, peed, shook off their willys and ran back out...didn't wash their hands, just in and out. Now my throat was beginning to hurt. I had to get away from the stench. No wonder those boys flew in and out.

This place reeked.

"Now lads, from time to time you'll be assigned to come here to clean this room. Make sure ya' do a good job, or they'll send ya' back to do it over again." My head began to hurt and I felt sick in the stomach. I held my breath so I wouldn't have to breathe in the foul smell. It was hard to imagine how any boy could stay in here long enough to clean the place.

"Alright, follow me." Finally, the Brother led us out and I released the breath I had been holding. Christ, that was disgusting.

The toilets were nowhere near our sleeping room. How would I find my way to the bathroom in the middle of the night? I won't remember where everything is in this place. It's too big, much bigger than Peadmont. Little halls here and there, offices, doorways, staircases. Greenmount was a maze of confusion, just like my head. The building was enormous and each part of it was cold. As we were taken from one area to another, I saw boys hauling water, sweeping floors, and polishing stair rails. Everyone had a job that they 'took to' before classes started.

The Brother led us back out to the yard. This was our playing field. I hadn't taken much noticed when we had been out here just an hour ago. I had been too busy keeping my head down and keeping my boots on. Looking over the brown, untended field, it was clear that there was no way out of this place. Tall, gray, stone-walls protected the muddy field on three sides and a huge thick wall of hawthorn bushes protected the other side. It had been raining most of the morning and the yard was wet and muddy, like one large, mucky, puddle.

Brother Eugene quickly reviewed the day's routine one more time, and again described the duties that would be assigned to each of us. He told us where we would find mops, brooms, polish, and such. Several times, he asked if we had any questions, but none of us said a word. He went through it all very fast. I hoped that Charlie could show me around later 'cause I knew I wouldn't remember a thing.

Brother Eugene escorted each of us to our first class. Sean was left with one of the Brothers for his reading class. Through the glass window on the doorway to the class I watched as the teacher took Sean and pushed him along to the front of the classroom. Sean peered back over his shoulder and looked towards me. His wide eyes and turned down lips told me he was full of fear. So was I. Jim was taken to the training room for shoemaking and seemed rather calm about going in. The Brother took me to the arithmetic class. Oh Jesus, I don't know any numbers. Why did they have to start me with arithmetic?

"Mr. O'Keeffe, you will take the vacant desk at the end of the third row," the teacher called out. I walked between the two rows of desks keeping my head down and biting the hell out of my bottom lip. I found my place and slid in behind the one vacant, wooden seat at the back of the room. I was slouched down as far as I could get and not at all happy to be here.

The other boys looked close to my age, some maybe a little older. There would have been about forty of them in all. None of the boys spoke as I settled in. I hated that everyone was looking at me. To my relief, I saw that Charlie was seated one row over. He nodded at me as if to say it's okay, you'll be alright. The teacher headed down the row towards me and stopped at my desk. He slammed down a brown notebook and a pencil in front of me. I could tell he was annoyed that I had come in and interrupted his session.

"Okay O'Keeffe, let's see what ya' know." Oh no, please don't make me do this. I was terrified and could feel the sweat start to rush out of my skin, my shoulders stiffen up, and my chest begin to tighten. I don't know any of my numbers. I can count and add up a little, but that's about it. What am I going to do? I was scared beyond belief.

"O'Keeffe, come to the front of the class." He signaled with his hand commanding me to the front of the room. I straightened up and slid out from the desk and moved back down the aisle, again with all eyes in the room upon me. I stood with my back to all the other students and my head down, my eyes locked on the feet of the Brother standing before me.

At first the teacher just stood there, I could feel his eyes burning down on me. He turned and moved to the drawing board behind his desk and scratched out a bunch of numbers and signs that I did not understand. "Alright O'Keeffe, work this out. Show us what ya' can do." He then marched to the back of the room and left me, center stage, in front of them all.

I was panicked. I was sweating and nauseous. Without moving my head, I peered up and looked at the numbers he had written out. I swallowed. I couldn't understand any part of it. Should I tell him I cannot understand what he had written? I could feel my legs start to quiver and the tension across my shoulders grow tighter.

"What are ya', O'Keeffe? Stupid?" the teacher yelled out from the back of the room. Still, I said nothing my eyes frozen on the board. I could feel the pressure across my shoulder blades move into my neck and head, the pain of it forced me to hunch forward. The other boys in the class were silent. None of them made a sound.

Again, the Brother asked me to complete the question he had written out. Oh God Walter, make your mind work. Take control of it. Come on, figure it out. I nervously started to rub my forehead as if I was trying to figure it out. God, he'll belt me if I don't get this. Think, think, think.

"Is that it, O'Keeffe? You're stupid?" the Brother asked.

I said nothing.

"O'Keeffe, I asked you a question. Are ya' stupid?"

"No, Brother," I replied in a sheepish whisper."

"What did you say, O'Keeffe?"

"No,(clearing my throat) Brother." I haven't a hope in hell that I'm going to get out of this.

"Alright boys," he yelled from the back of the room. "What do we do to idiots who are too stupid to figure out even the simplest equation?"

The room was silent.

"I *said*, what do we do?" he yelled at all of them.

Behind me I heard a forced roar of laughter well up from the class. I was trembling, my legs were weak and could barely hold me. I peered over my right shoulder. Each boy was pointing at me laughing. I could tell that they knew if they didn't participate they could be the next one up here.

"I can't hear you boys. What do we do to idiots?

The level of laughter rose. Obscenities were thrown at me by the boys in the room. "Stupid asshole," one of them shouted out.

"Shit for brains idiot!" called out another.

"Stupid Paddy!"

I wanted the ground to open and swallow me up. I had never felt lower or more stupid than this. Those words! He was allowing them to say those words! Here in a Catholic place? If I had ever said words like this in the Mooncoin school or Polrone, I would surely have been sent to a corner or worse. This was madness.

"O'Keeffe, turn around and face yur' peers." Slowly, I turned not making eye contact with anyone. "Boys!" he shouted. "I said, what do we do to idiots?" he screamed like a crazy man at the top of his lungs.

Now the boys jumped to their feet laughing, "Fucker! Idiot! Stupid! Simple shit! Simple shit! O'Keeffe is a simple shit!"

The Brother continued to prompt the boys and encouraged them to laugh at me and to curse me. I looked over to Charlie. He stood with the others, but he did not laugh. I could see that he felt bad for me.

The Brother, whose name I still did not know, now leaned up against the wall at the back of the room with his large arms folded and picked the dirt, or food, out of his finger nails with his yellow teeth and then spat on to the floor. He seemed bored, yet slightly amused, by what was going on in his classroom.

Madness, pure madness.

The Brother straightened up and marched back to the front of the class. As he reached me, he raised his hand. The boys fell instantly silent and sat behind their desks. None of them laughed, not a smile or a smirk. Each one had played out their role, their part in this crazy scene to humiliate me, which they did. Each one knew he would have paid a big price if he had not taken part.

"Now O'Keeffe, that is not all we do to idiots such as yur'self." I looked up and saw him turn to reach for a long leather strap that hung on the wall next to his desk.

"Brother Gab," Charlie called out cutting off the Brother, who I now knew was Brother Gab, in mid-sentence.

"Damn it, McFarland. What is it?"

"Brother, I think I've shit myself," Charlie announced.

Oh, my God. Why would he say that? But thank God he did, because the focus was now off of me. The boys in the room roared with a different sort of laughter. It was real laughter.

"Silence," the Brother yelled out. "What the hell is the matter with you McFarland?"

"I said I shit myself, and need to wipe my ass."

Oh God, Charlie. What are you doing? You're going to get the beating of a lifetime for that.

Brother Gab's face was red with anger. He grabbed the long leather strap and walked down the isle to where Charlie stood.

Charlie was calm, did not look scared. He looked straight at the Brother, almost challenging him. Brother Gab grabbed Charlie by his upper arm and dragged him to the front of the room. He threw Charlie over the front of his desk.

"Remove his shorts," he called out to two boys who sat near the front of the room. They scrambled forward and did what they were told and then moved back. Charlie did not struggle. He was bent over the Brother's desk, his ass scarred from past beatings, fully exposed. Charlie never resisted at all, not even a little.

"Are you some sort of retard, McFarland?" asked the Brother.

"I guess I must be. I thought I crapped myself, must 'ave just been passing gas."

Brother Gab raised his arm and with the fury of a warrior bringing down his sword upon the enemy he belted him five, maybe six, times. Charlie never cried, never flinched. I thought he must be dead.

When the Brother was finished with him, Charlie rolled over and again stared the Brother straight in the face. He pulled up his shorts and said nothing. Charlie did not shed one tear. I have never seen a boy so tough in all of my life. Did he do this for me? Did he know that I was terrified and humiliated? Was it because he could not stand to watch what was being done to me, so he took this awful beating to stop the insanity? Had I found a real friend here?

Yes, I had.

Eleven

FITTING IN

The next several weeks were spent adjusting to this dreadful place, learning the routines, the prayers; learning where and when to be; learning how to survive and finally, who to trust, or not. Although he was the same age as me, Charlie was my guide. He always looked out for me. Every time I took a beating he consoled me and told me that these lard ass bastards didn't matter. They were the ones that were going to hell, he'd say, not those of us that had pissed the bed. He always made me laugh. Everything Charlie taught me about life in this place I passed on to Sean.

In our arithmetic class we had worked out a system where Charlie would pass me the answers to questions. If I was asked to solve a problem Charlie would try to give me the answer. Lots of times I couldn't read his lips and so would get a wallop from the Brother across the top on my hands and knuckles for not knowing.

Jim had disappeared into the crowd. Every now and then we would see him, or hear his name being called out for a bed-wetting beating. But mostly he kept his distance from us.

Within the first few weeks, I realized that there was an open market for just about anything. Kids would sell whatever they had, and use their pennies to buy comics and sweets if and when they ever got out of this terrible place. I had nothing to sell. That's what I thought anyway. One morning my coffee and bread were put in front of me. As hungry as I was, I could not bear to eat another piece of the sickly, gooey stuff.

"I'll give ya' a halfpenny for it, O'Keeffe," Tommy Fagan whispered to me. You've got to be kidden'. This kid must be stinking hungry if he wants to give me a halfpenny for a slice of rotten bread. So I sold it to him. And the day after that, I sold my bread to another kid for a penny. Can you imagine, a whole penny for a slice of disgusting, maggot-infested bread?

To fill my belly, I'd go out into the yard where I had found a rusty, leaking tap and stick my mouth under it. I'd pull up grass—roots, dirt, and all—eat it, and wash it down with water. I was not alone; most of the kids ate grass. The unbearable hunger in this place drove some boys to eat the prickly sticks from the thorny hedge in the yard, their tongues bleeding as they chewed the stuff up.

The worst part of it was we knew there was a lovely garden just on the other side of our yard, where the Brothers grew vegetables and fruit, then sold it off to the locals. We could also smell the luscious warm bread and buns that were baked in the school bakery. Again, these items were for the Brothers and, or, sold for profit. We, starving like we were, got the rotten stuff that could not be sold.

Two nights out of seven we would get a slice of tomato for supper along with a cup of broth that had nothing but water, a few spuds, and flavoring in it. I never liked tomatoes, so the first time I got one I gave it to Sean. When the other kids found out that I had given up my tomato, they all started offering me money for it. Taking advantage of the situation I started selling my tomato slices. By the time I had earned myself nine pennies I was starving. I had become light headed and was not pooping anymore, just had diarrhea all the time. So, it didn't take me long to learn to love a good slice of tomato. In fact, I started looking forward to tomato days.

I also stopped selling my bread and learnt to swallow it without smelling it, picking out the maggots, tasting, or examining it. I just needed anything in my gut to make me feel full. We were all hungry, and kids would do whatever they needed to do to get food into their bellies. When we weren't allowed outside kids would eat paper, others would pull the stuffing out of their mattresses and gnaw on that and some chewed on their leather laces—anything to feel full.

Some boys were forced to do awful things with the Brothers, like touch their privates or let the Brother watch while they touched themselves. Boys put up with it because they were afraid not to. Some of them might get a piece of candy or a cup of tea for participating in these ghastly deeds. Those of us who were bed-wetters, or had been sick with TB or other illness, never had to do these awful things. I suppose they thought we were sickly and they might catch whatever we had.

You always knew when a boy had been called off to "do" one of the Brothers. They would fetch them in the night while the rest of us lay frozen with fear in our beds, or even call them out of class. We'd hear or see the boy come back. Sometimes they were sobbing, sometimes they returned with blank looks on their faces and never made a sound. It was most often the boys who had no family or no one to protect them that the Brothers preyed on.

The days turned to weeks and before long, I had lost all track of time. It must have been close to Christmas because we were singing Christmas hymns in choir. It was getting colder and there was snow in the yard. I knew we had been here at least two months because we had been given two showers. Once a month we were lined up naked and marched into the cold shower room. It was always freezing in there. A Brother would go over each of us, including pulling on our willies, looking for lice, flees anything. Funny thing was we were full of boils, sores, bruises, and rotting teeth. They never seemed to care much about those ailments. They were more concerned that our body bugs might spread on to them. Each boy had his head and testicles washed down by one of the Brothers with this awful blue liquid they called Jay's Fluid.

They'd scrub our heads raw. It was not uncommon for boys to leave the room with their heads bleeding because a brother had burst a boil or scraped open a head wound while scrubbing in the Jay's. After our scrub down we were sent to stand under the cold shower. Some of the boys' lips, Sean's and mine included, turned blue and purple standing in there so long. As we came out of the shower we were handed a shirt and shorts. Nothing was our own and I never knew if what I has handed would be too big or too small or had buttons or working zippers. I also can't say I remember getting a clean pair of socks. Even after having a shower we'd roll the same filthy, frayed socks on to our feet. And boots...we were handed one used pair a year. If you grew out of them, too bad. Most of the time, boys ran around with nothing on their infected, filthy feet.

There wasn't much to look forward to in Greenmount, except going outside in the yard where we could see the sky, feel the grass, and breathe in fresh air. That was wonderful. Now that winter had settled in, the ground in the yard was thick with snow. We didn't care, we just wanted to be outside. We were never issued overcoats or vests, even to go out in the dead of winter.

Some kids, if they were lucky, might have had a sweater knit by an aunt or grandmother. Most of us had nothing to keep us warm, dry, and protected from the elements.

"Alright boys," announced Blackie following our morning beatings and coffee. "There will be no playing in the yard today." A heavy moan of disappointment hummed across the room.

"Oh, so some of you are disappointed are ya'?" he questioned. "Alright. If you really want to go play in the yard, you've got to come up to the front of the room and give me yur' boots. If yur' so desperate to play, you'll go out in yur' bare feet."

What an asshole. We kids suffered enough every day. Now, he wants to see us freeze our toes off running around in the snow. Blackie's challenge didn't stop Charlie, Franky, Sean, myself, and a bunch of others from rushing to take off our boots and bring them up to the front of the room, all desperate to feel the freedom of playing outside.

After handing over my boots I darted into the yard with the rest of them. It was bitter cold and my feet started to burn. I just kept running around hoping that the pain of the cold would eventually go away. At the entrance to the yard Blackie and a few of the other Brothers were laughing their asses off, getting huge pleasure watching us suffer.

But the fresh air, I loved it! The snow falling on my face felt clean and soft. Was it snowing back in Polrone? It was beautiful at home when it snowed. I loved to look out across the meadows, at the carpet of white that made everything appear clean, calm, and safe. Before we even had a chance to warm up, Blackie called us all back in. Crap, we were not even out there for 10 minutes.

"Alright, all you idiots who thought it was a good idea to run around in the snow barefooted, line up in the front of the dining hall."

The asshole. He was going to beat us for this? The torture that beast inflicted on us was inhumane. I hated him. One by one he made us climb the ladder and whacked us across the ass for being stupid enough to run around in the snow with bare feet. God, I loathed this demon.

We were victims of religion gone mad, each of us. Greenmount was insane, and we were not the crazy ones.

Twelve

HOME FOR CHRISTMAS–DECEMBER 1940

"I'm going home for Christmas," Charlie belted out as we readied ourselves to go to Mass.

"What do ya' mean, yur' going home?"

"Yup, just found out me Mum's coming to fetch me for Christmas."

Damn it, why is it that everyone I learn to trust and love leaves me. Now this boy, my best friend, was leaving me and I'd never see him again.

"Don't worry ya' dumb ass. I'll be back. I'd never leave ya' here on yur' own. You'd die in a day, you would."

What a relief, thank you God. "How long will ya' be gone?" I asked.

"Just fur the two days, then they'll bring me back. Maybe I'll bring ya' something."

"McFarland…Visitor!" a loud voice at the entrance to our dorm called out.

Charlie quickly finished tying his lace and jumped to his feet. Placing both of his hands on my shoulders he looked me square in the eyes. "I will be back, I promise." He scurried out of the room, turning to wave as he exited the dorm.

So many boys left Greenmount and we never saw them again. I don't know where they went. What if they put Charlie in another room when he comes back? What if he doesn't come back? I sat on the edge of my bed, my arms crossed, and hands held tightly under my pits looking down at the floor and wondered if I would ever see my best friend again.

As I stared downward my eyes caught the tiny eyes of a baby mouse squatting beside one of the legs of my bed. Just sitting there, looking up at me. I bent down and picked the tiny creature up. He never even tried to run off.

Maybe he was an orphan too. I had seen hundreds of mice before, this one was small, really tiny. He was mostly brown with little gray ears and tiny whiskers. He had a very short tail for a mouse. Maybe it had been cut off or something. It looked like the trigger on a toy revolver, I thought. It was the funniest tail I'd ever seen on a mouse.

"Poor little guy. What ya' doing up here? Where's yur' Mamma gone?" I gently stroked him on the top of his tiny head with one finger, trying to be very tender so that I didn't hurt him. "I'll take care of ya'," I said. The small mouse curled up in my hand and just lay there.

"All up," a voice roared. It was time for Mass. I tucked my new pet into my pocket very carefully and got in line with the others. I could hardly wait to show my little pal to Sean. He'll love him.

During Mass and breakfast I put my hand in my pocket to caress my new friend to let him know that I was still there. I took a few crumbs of my bread and put them in my pocket hoping my little buddy would eat up the morsels of food. Following breakfast, it was time to go out into the yard. On the way out, I wandered by a waste can and saw an empty Oxo soup box on top of the pile. This'll make a great little home for ya'. Jees', what am I going to call him? 'Trigger', that's what I'll call him, 'Trigger'. I had not been this happy in a long while. A pet, I had a pet! This was magnificent!

"O'Keeffe," a voice called out. It was Mr. O'Toole, the band teacher. So far, since we had been here, he had only taught us how to read a little bit of music, which I had a hard time with. Mostly, he did a lot of talking. He was nice enough, but still, I had no instrument so I didn't know why I was even in band. I loved music, and the thought of getting to play like my Dad was unimaginable. For now, I was forced to sit and look on while the other boys played.

"Yes, Mr. O'Toole."

"I've got a Coronet for you. Came in this morning. I'll hand it over to you next band class."

"Thank you sir!"

"Merry Christmas, O'Keeffe."

"Merry Christmas to you, too, sir. Thank you."

I was thrilled. This was incredible...a pet, and now a coronet to play in the band. My Dad played the coronet. He was marvelous. Nobody played like him and nobody 'sung' like him. He had shown both Jim and I how to play a couple of tunes. I wonder if I'll remember? This is great. I wasn't even hungry, just excited. Finally, I had something to look forward to—band.

During the two days of the Christmas season we didn't go to class. But, we prayed more than we ever did. The Brothers also herded us together and walked us through the streets. When they took us out they made sure we were well guarded. One of them in front of us, one behind, and a couple of them at the sides of us, so no one could run away.

Every now and then, you could hear a passerby saying, "Oh, those poor boys. Look at 'em. How lucky that the Brothers have taken 'em on." The odd person would hand money to the Brothers. "For the children," they'd say. We never got any of it. In fact, I'm pretty sure that's why we were paraded around, so the Brothers could get people to give them money for us. We never went anywhere; we were just marched around the streets so that the Brothers could show off their good work. With no hats or gloves, we were all freezing.

We were not allowed to talk to anyone, nor were we allowed to talk to each other. I didn't care why we were out there. I loved looking around the city, imagining all the families in their homes, looking at the shop-keepers and the people. It was nice to get away from the musty stench of Greenmount. I didn't like all the people staring at us like we were some sort of oddity. It was embarrassing, because we all looked bad. Every once in a while, I'd see nice lookin' well-dressed girls. They'd stare at us like we were a bunch of street beggars, and I guess in a way we were. But if we wanted outside the gates of hell, we had to put up with it.

Lots of the boys got visitors during this time of the year, and many, like Charlie, got taken out for a day or two. Not us. No one came. I guess we were too far away. I wondered if Josie even remembered who I was.

Christmas dinner was a little different than other days. We were given a chunk of meat and potatoes in our broth, lemonade and butter with our bread. Oh, the taste of the butter was grand, absolutely wonderful. Sweet, slippery, wonderful. I ate mine slowly and licked every part of my fingers to make sure I got it all.

We passed the time during the Christmas break hanging out in the snow-covered yard. We were given one soccer ball to share between 200 boys. A bunch of us cleared the snow with our bare hands to make an area to kick the ball around. Other than that, we hadn't any sort of toys to play with.

Some of the other kids passed the time collecting flies. These boys would walk about the halls with a pencil and paper and one shoe off. They used the shoe to whack the flies. Each time they whacked one they'd stick it in their pocket and give themselves a check mark. At the end of the day, boys would count up their flies to see who had caught the most. Anything to pass the time.

Santa Claus did come to the school. That was exciting. We were lined up and allowed to go and see him. Sean and I were together in the line, curious if we would be getting anything. As the line moved along, each boy was able to sit on his lap and was given an orange. Oh, my God! I had not had an orange for well over a couple of years.

When it was my turn, Santa Claus asked me if I had been good. I said yes. He asked me if I had any special prayers. I told him the only thing I wanted was to get out of this place. "One day boy," he said, and handed me an orange. Mine was rotten. Half of it had gone soft and turned brown. I didn't care. I ate the entire thing peel and all.

"Hey Wattie O'Keeffe, you great big arse, me Mum sent ya' something." Charlie had come back. I was so happy to see that fair head of hair come bouncing through the entrance to the dorm.

"Charlie, I've got news. Mr. O'Toole got me a Coronet, and I've got a pet. I've got to show 'im to ya'."

"That's great, Wattie, but look what I've got here for you and Sean." Charlie motioned Sean over to where we were. He pulled out a cotton napkin trimmed with lace. He slowly unwrapped it. Sean had his nose right in there anticipating what Charlie may have brought us. Once unwrapped, the napkin unveiled seven or eight pieces of fancy chocolate filled with gooey, sweet stuff, several biscuits, and a brown paper bag with hard, minty sweets in it. What a treat!

"They're all for you two, from me Mum."

"God, Charlie. Make sure ya' says thanks from us, will ya'?"

Charlie sat and watched as Sean and I pounced on, and ate up, the sweets. He didn't eat even one, but left them all for us.

I pulled Trigger out and presented him to my best friend.

"He's great, Wattie. Don't let the damn Brothers see 'im." We gave Trigger a few grains of sugar from the package and giggled as he licked the sweet stuff from his tiny paws. It was wonderful being reunited with my best buddy. He told us about his family and his grandmother and where they had been and what they had done.

"One day Wattie, I'm going to take you and Seany to my house. Me Mum's going to make us all up a big bunch of cake and bread and stew, and we're going to have a great party. And you can bring Trigger along, too. Yes sir, we will."

Sean and I continued to enjoy our treats as we listened to Charlie's adventure of his trip home. That was it, our first Christmas at Greenmount. No beatings, and treats from Charlie's Mum. So all in all, it wasn't too bad.

Thirteen

JANUARY 1941, FORCED TO KILL

It was finally band day. I had Trigger in my pocket and I was ready to wrap my hands around the Coronet Mr. O'Toole had brought in for me. The Brothers had changed the class schedule, so now Jim and I were in the same band class. Maybe things would be better between us, I hoped. I was the first one in the band room that day. Oh I hope I get it today.

The door to the cold band room opened up. It was Mr. O'Toole and Brother Eugene. Mr. O'Toole did not have a Coronet with him. Shit, he didn't bring it. I knew I should never get excited about these things. I sunk down into my chair.

"O'Keeffe, you ready to put those lips of yur's into action?" Mr. O'Toole moved behind his desk and from beneath it he pulled out a black case.

Oh, my God. That's it! That's it! I *am* getting it today. My hands were sweating.

By now some of the other boys had started coming in and were taking their instruments from the closet and putting them together.

"Yes, sir. I'm ready."

"Okay, here ya' go." Mr. O'Toole handed me the black case. This was the most beautiful thing I had ever seen in my life. I set the case on the floor, flipped the two brass latches, and lifted the cover. A red piece of velvet cloth covered the instrument. I pulled back the cloth and there it was…shiny, not quite new, but fantastic all the same.

I looked up and saw Mr. O'Toole and Brother Eugene looking down at me. Both of them were smiling. "Ya' think he likes it Brother?" Mr. O'Toole asked Brother Eugene.

"Aye, I think so. I think they'll be fine friends."

"Do ya' know how to put it together?" Mr. O'Toole asked me.

"Yes, sir."

I remembered my Dad letting me put his coronet together and letting me take it apart. The smell of the dried spit, the oil and the case reminded me of that time. Watching my Dad in the band had been outstanding.

I pulled the mouthpiece from its spot in the case and wiped it on my sweater, the way all the professional band players did, and gently wiggled it on to the end of the instrument. I placed my hands over the three instrument keys and placed the coronet to my lips. It tasted great. Isn't that odd? I loved the taste of it against my mouth. I took a deep breath and filled my lungs. I pinched my lips together and blasted a sound that I had never heard, not a good sound either.

"Well, you'll get better O'Keeffe. Go take a seat next to yur' brother up there."

That was embarrassing. I sounded like a donkey, nothing like the sounds that came out of my Dad's coronet. But I knew I'd improve, I just knew it.

"Nice playing," Jim said, as I sat next to him. Well, at least he was talking to me.

Over the next few days I practised until my lips were numb. I couldn't get enough of it. I would rush through my chores and spend every spare moment I had in the band room. Trigger seemed to like it. I'd take him out and let him sit on the top of my case. He never ran off, so I guess I wasn't all that bad. I visualized myself on stage in front of a crowd just like my Dad. The people were clapping and laughing and obviously impressed with my musical talent. That was it. I was going to be a musician and get out of this awful place. Finally, I knew what I wanted to do with my life.

It didn't take long for that donkey sound to work its way out of the instrument. Mr. O'Toole said I had a great set of lungs for playing. Imagine that, all that time in the hospital with sickly lungs, and here I was playing the coronet. Although I practised every day, I never practised reading music. I couldn't do it. I would listen to a piece and would just know how to play. Mr. O'Toole said I had a natural ear. Before long, he had me sitting in the first Coronet seat and playing solos.

I'd lay in bed at night dreaming about the day I had my own band. By now, I had Trigger sleeping right beside me in his little Oxo box, so I didn't squish him. "Aye, Trigger? One day, we will be up on that stage, you and me. I'll be the only coronet player in the world who has a mouse in his band. Won't that be grand, little buddy? Then one day, Josie Phelan will open the paper and see my picture. She'll see where my band is playing and she'll come watch us. She'll walk in, all beautiful like, and I'll play a special song just for her. Yup, its gonna' be just that way Trigger my friend." What a wonderful dream.

"Jees', I pissed again." I was woken up by the cold that ran up my back from laying on a wet mattress. The urine was all around me. I got up and flipped my mattress to try and hide it. I hadn't peed the bed for over a week. My bum had almost healed up. I must have peed a lot cause when I turned over the mattress it was wet on the down side as well. I rolled myself all over the bed trying to soak up the pee. That's what a lot of the boys did. I don't think it ever worked, but we tried everything. We'll see what happens in the morning. After Mass and coffee the next morning, I listened as the names were called: "Reagan Charles, O'Ryan Michael, O'Hara Timothy, Fitzgerald John, O'Keeffe Walter."

All day I'd worry about getting my beating. The bastards did this to make the entire ordeal worse. I couldn't think in class; I couldn't do anything, except worry about the beating and how painful it was going to be. That night, as we readied ourselves for bed, I saw Sean looking over feeling bad for me. Charlie felt bad, too. I could tell.

"Don't cry this time, Wattie. Try and hold it in. Ya' done good. Ya' went a whole week with out pissin' yur'self. Maybe after this, you'll go two, then three weeks, then it will stop all together."

I knew Charlie was trying to make me feel better, but it wasn't working. The only thing comforting me now was my little pal, Trigger. I sat petting his little head, waiting. I knew what was coming and I knew it would come again and again.

Blackie entered the room with the large wooden cane clutched in his hand. "O'Keeffe, up against the pillar."

I quickly tucked Trigger back in his box and hid him under my blanket, then rushed to take my place against the beating pillar, so that Blackie would not notice that I had something hidden in my bed.

"Wait a minute. What have ya' got there, O'Keeffe?" Blackie demanded.

"Nothing Brother," I replied, and turned to position myself up against the white post I had named 'The Pillar of Terror'.

"What ya' mean, nothing? I just saw you tuck something under yur' blanket. Come back here and pull back yur' covers so I can see."

Now I was scared, scared of what he might do to my wee friend. I slowly moved back towards my cot and pulled back the blankets that hid the soup box. I pulled the blanket back just enough so that the box was still hidden. I said nothing.

"Good God, boy." Blackie moved forward and threw back the blanket that protected my pet. "Have ya' been stealing food from the kitchen you disgusting thief?" he roared, as he raised his arm to whack me.

"No, Brother. There's no food in the box."

"Open it and let me see."

God, hide Trigger hide! I thought to myself. I opened the box to reveal my little buddy coiled up. He slowly stretched and looked up at me.

"What in God's name is this disgusting creature doing in here?" Now that was an odd statement, I thought, considering the entire place was ridden with rats and mice.

"I just found 'im, Brother. He was sick, so I put 'im in the box to let 'im get well. He's my pet."

"Yur' pet, is he? Well, *my pet*, you are not allowed to keep animals or pets, so he will have to be destroyed."

"But, Brother…"

Blackie's large arm rose and his fist came down upon my head, making me collapse to the floor. "Don't you ever question me? Pets are not allowed, and so this one must be destroyed."

Run, Trigger, run! I called out in my head. The day that Aunt Mary threw Prowler into the Suir came rushing back to me. The sick feeling in my stomach, the aching in my bowels. How can these grown-ups be so uncaring to other living creatures.

"Can't I just let 'im go, Brother, and he can run back to his family?" I asked. Again, Blackie's large hand came down upon me striking me on the back of my neck and pushing me forward making me fall on my face.

"You take that little beast and come with me." Blackie had me scoop up Trigger and the box, and took us down the stairs to the toilet.

"Throw 'im into the trough and let 'im drown," Blackie ordered.

"I can't. I can't kill this little thing," I cried.

"Well then, it will be you drowning in here tonight." Blackie grabbed me by the back of my neck and pushed my face into the wooden bench where we sat to do our business. It smelt terrible. He held my mouth so close to the edge of the hole that I could taste urine on my lips. "Do you want to die here tonight or shall the little mouse die?" he asked.

I figured if I elected to die myself, he would kill Trigger anyway, so what was I to do?

"If you do not take that mouse out right now, I will have yur' brother Sean put on the beating list every day for the next sixty days. Why was he doing this? Why? Would God approve of this madness? Is God upset that I have protected one of his creatures?

"I will ask ya' one more time. Will it be you or that mouse that dies here tonight?" Blackie blasted.

With tears in my eyes and a heavy heart, I replied, "The mouse."

Blackie pulled me back up by the neck. "Do it," he yelled.

I loved this little mouse. He had been my companion, and now I had to end his life. Oh, dear God. Please do not make him suffer. Please take him quickly. Please send him to Mother and Father and Prowler. I was crying uncontrollably now. I opened the box. I could not look at my little pal. I knelt beside the toilet bench.

"Thank you for being such a good friend," I said quietly. Then, I turned the box upside down and dumped him into the water below. I heard a small plop as he hit the water and was washed away.

This man was so unkind. I hated him more than any other person on the face of this earth. "Come on, we still have business to tend to." Even after this, the bastard was going to make sure I got my beating for wetting the bed. What a cruel, cruel pig.

Blackie dragged me back upstairs by my hair and tossed me on to the floor of the dorm. "Let this be a lesson to any of you who thinks he can bring animals into this house. There will be no pets allowed." With that he lifted me up and pushed me towards The Pillar of Terror. I knew what to do. I lowered my pants, raised my arms, and let him do what he loved to do...beat the living daylights out of me.

When I woke the following morning, again I had wet the bed. I hardly cared. No pain could be greater than what had been inflicted upon me the night before.

"Wattie, ya' stink man. Are ya' going to flip yur' mattress?" Charlie asked.

"No, can't be bothered," I replied, "Let 'im beat me. Let 'im kill me, I don't care."

"You do so care," Charlie shouted. Charlie rose up and came over to my cot and flipped my mattress.

"Don't let 'im get ya'. That's what he wants. Let 'im see that you're stronger than he is. Ya' have to fight back. Ya' have to." Charlie rubbed my blanket against the wall. He rubbed and rubbed to try and get the wetness out.

"One day, Wattie, you're going to be a great coronet player in a great band. Ya' will, Wattie."

I felt sorry for my friend. He was right. I could not let Blackie get the best of me. I could not let him see that I had been defeated.

"You're right, Charlie. I'll get out of here one day, and come back and smash that flabby bastard in the face, and knock out every one of his yellow, rotting teeth. Then, he'll never be able to eat another thing in his life."

"That's the way," Charlie replied.

Charlie helped me put my bed together and we got ready to march down to Mass. He was a great friend, Charlie McFarland was, a great friend.

Fourteen

LIFE ROLLED BY...

The weeks and months rolled by and I did my best to stay out of Blackie's way. I was still wetting the bed and getting beatings for it most days. My ass had become hard as leather and I hardly bled any more. My bum was thick with scars and calluses from the wounds that had to heal over and over again.

Many boys came and left the school. Mostly, we didn't know what happened to them. Lots of times boys were sent to the infirmary and never came back. If we ever asked what happened to Tommy or Jimmy, we were told their mothers came and got them. Most often, we knew these boys had no mothers. So where did they go? The infirmary was also used to confine boys who had contagious illness's like measles, pneumonia, or other disease's that might pass on to the Brothers. Funny thing was we were all starving, malnourished, and had cuts, bruises, and boils covering our bodies, and nobody cared. However, if we caught something that we might pass on to the Brothers, or that stopped us from working, they were quick to send us down to the infirmary.

This one time, I had a boil on my hand that had grown to be the size of an apple. We all had lots of boils, but this one was really horrible and painful. I could not hold the waxing cloth properly and was having trouble waxing the stairs 'cause the boil was so huge. The Brother supervising my efforts was mad as I was going too slow so he kicked me in the ass to speed me up. When I showed him the boil on my hand, he told me to go down to the infirmary to get it lanced.

The night before, a small boy, Tommy O'Connor, had been sent to the infirmary after getting the beating of his life for taking food from the kitchen garbage. Tommy was not in the infirmary when I got down there. I'm not sure but, I think they killed him.

I hated getting my boils lanced. The pain was horrific. The nurse called up four attendants, older boys, to hold me down. She then had another one squeeze and press until my skin erupted and the yellowish stuff oozed out. I felt my skin crack and heard the sound of it bursting open. She let the kids take turns squeezing the boil until the yellow and white puss turned to blood. I screamed and cried during the entire disgusting ordeal.

Lots of boys ended up with dreadful infections caused by their open boils. The worst were the boys who got them on the neck. The poor bastards walked around all hunched up. Thank God, I never had to work in the infirmary squeezing boils. Some boys loved it. Most, thought it was revolting.

I learnt to keep my head down, not wanting to draw attention to myself. I did my chores cleaning, polishing, laundry, wood hauling, tidying the yard, sweeping the chapel, but most often I worked in the kitchen setting rat traps. Chores killed the boredom, anyway.

I only went where I was supposed to go and stayed away from places I was not allowed. I'd say, "Yes Brother," "No Brother," "Thank you Brothers," "Praise you Brother," and learnt how to stay out the way of most of them.

Kids ran in gangs for protection. Ya' never wanted to stand out on yur' own. We all looked the same—tattered, woolen sweaters, dirty faces, uneven hair cuts, rotten and broken teeth, runny noses, bruises, scared and sad. We all looked miserable.

I never got used to the name calling…names like 'little maggots', 'bunch of dirty knickers', 'shit pots', 'dumb ass', 'stupid', and 'idiot'. They loved calling me an idiot, always asking me if I was dumb. "Are ya' dumb, O'Keeffe? Did yur' Daddy bang ya' around too much and knock the sense out of ya'?" They were always saying things like that. I hated it.

Going to class was a waste of time as I never learnt a thing. I was always too nervous worrying about getting an answer wrong and getting a beating for being stupid. Some mornings I'd wake up in such fear, I just wanted to march up to Blackie and say, give me a good whippin' and get it over with so I don't have to worry all day about it. We did learn swearing. God damn, we got good at that.

Another thing I got good at was catching bees. I had always been fascinated with them. One day, I was watching this huge bumble bee sitting on a dandelion. He was busy drinking up the nectar and rubbing pollen over his legs. He was a fascinating little creature, and I wanted to take a closer look at him.

The box I had kept Trigger in was in my pocket as I thought I might catch another mouse. Currently the box was full of flies. I pulled it from my pocket, dumped the flies, and carefully placed it over the dandelion, bee and all. Carefully I closed the lid of the box and broke off the stem of the flower, incredibly, I caught him. Curious to see if I could tie him on to a piece of thread and watch him buzz around, I pulled a thread from my jacket and made a small loop at one end, and damn it, I got it around his leg. I let him go and watched him fly around on the end of my string. I kept him for a whole day.

That night, in our dorm room, all the kids laughed as I let the bee out and had him buzzing around. I freed him in the morning and caught another one the following day. Kids couldn't believe it, and I became a bit of a circus act. I was odd that way. With animals, I could calm them down, tame them, or they'd just come to me, like Trigger had.

The only other thing that kept me interested in life was going to band. I loved it. I'd escape into the music and get lost in another world. I thought music would somehow shape the rest of my life. I hoped it would anyways.

When I wanted to flee from this place, I'd close my eyes and go deep, inside myself. I even learnt how to do this with my eyes opened. I'd see myself rising out of my body and flying away from this crazy place. Right out the window, I'd go. I'd fly over the walls in the yard, high over the city. I'd fly over green fields and stone-wall and beautiful gardens. I could see the River Suir from up high like this. It was beautiful, with the wooden boats painted in all sorts of colours—boats stacked full of rope, oars, nets, and fish.

I could see the ancient graveyard in Polrone, the Ivy and the headstones, this place gave me great strength. I felt safe there. Then I'd fly back to my home. I could see myself coming down out of the sky and landing upright on my two feet. The wind was blowing gently and I could smell the ocean salt and the scent of gutted fish on the air. I loved it. My Mom was waiting for me, waving as I moved towards her. The yard looked lovely, green and well tended. Father's livestock was well-fed and cared for. My brothers and sisters were playing by the river, Prowler was running about, the sun was shining down upon all of us. In the distance, I could hear my father singing soft, beautiful, Irish tunes.

Then I'd see Josie walking over. God, she was an angel. If not for her and the memories of my family and the hope that I would one day get out of here and return to the people and home I loved, I would have surely died in Greenmont, what a horrible, horrible place.

> *"Oh, the thoughts that come and go,*
> *like drifting shadows on fallen snow.*
> *Sometimes my thoughts are way out in space,*
> *and I'm speeding far away from the human race.*
> *Never wanting to look back,*
> *I'm excited beyond comprehension,*
> *Traveling at the speed of light to another dimension."*
> *— Walter O'Keeffe*

Fifteen

MARCH 1943 – NEW RESPONSIBILITIES

My chin rested in the palm of my hand as I sat peering out through the rain that drizzled down the classroom window, and tried to imagine what the rest of the world might be up to. I think it was March or maybe April. Sure, we had been here a couple of years now.

Where was Billy, and where had Eileen and Bessie been sent? I imagined Josie lying in the meadow beside the Suir in her pale blue dress, staring up into the sky enjoying the kiss of raindrops as they trickle down the sides of her cheeks, and wondered if she ever thought about me. My stomach growled, as it always did, as I remembered the splendid cakes and stews my Mum would prepare in our home in Polrone. I was miles away from Greenmount when my thoughts were interrupted.

Billy Fagan, a small boy whose face was covered in scabs, entered our class and handed the Brother a crumpled note and ran off, not even closing the door behind him.

"O'Keeffe, Brother Tom (Blackie) wants to see ya' in the kitchen."

Ah' Jesus, what have I done? I closed my hardcover math book, tucked my pencil in my jacket pocket, and headed off to the main dining hall.

This prison was familiar to me now. The narrow, dim hallways, the long stair cases, dark wood everywhere, white pillars, sacred figurines, the residue of incense that burnt during Mass, and the musty smell of leaky windows and dirty boys mixed up with the smell of floor polish. I knew it well, and I knew what to expect...most of the time.

I made my way to the small, dimly-lit office behind the kitchen. 'The Suffering Room' is what we called it. Blackie spent much of his time here beating, flogging, and ridiculing one boy after another. I walked in slowly keeping my head down so that I did not look at him. Even with my head down, I could see his hefty body behind the desk that was littered with stacks of papers and a plate of half eaten food that included chicken, potatoes, carrots, and a huge loaf of bread, all for himself, the bastard. I despised him.

"O'Keeffe, Tom Flarety has left the school. I'm puttin' you in charge of the kitchen." As he blurted out his words and rose from his chair, he sent crumbs falling from his chest on to the floor.

My head popped up, and my eyes strained as they nearly burst from their sockets. I held his gaze for only a fraction of a second, then quickly looked back down to his desk-top, afraid to make any lengthy eye contact with him.

"You've worked with 'im before. Ya' know what to do, don't ya'?" he asked as he opened a file cupboard and struggled to stuff a pile of disorganized papers into the draw.

"Well, yes Brother, I think so." I wasn't sure I could do it, but was too frightened to say I couldn't.

"Good, you'll start tomorrow, lighting the fires, getting the other boys organized, making the coffee, that sort of thing. That'll be yur' main work detail now." He turned from the file cupboard and moved towards me. He grabbed my chin and pulled it upwards so that he was looking right into my soul. "Lots of boys would kill for this job, so ya' better do it right. Remember now, you start tomorrow."

"Yes Brother, tomorrow," I replied as his hand scrunched my cheeks together. "Thank you Brother." He dropped his hand from my face and turned to move back behind his cluttered desk. I kept my head down and headed out of the room.

"O'Keeffe," he called me back.

Fuck, now what? Is he gonna' beat me for something?

"O'Toole needs you for some extra time in the band." Blackie announced as he ripped a slab of meat from the chicken and stuffed it into his mouth.

"I've told 'im he can have yur' ugly mug for some additional practise. Says the school can make some money from the band, O'Keeffe, so I expect ya' to be there when he needs you. You understand?" The food was spraying from his lips as he uttered his instructions. What a pig!

"Yes Brother."

"That's all, off with ya'." Blackie waved me off with his large arm and continued to fill his face. I left the room with my eyes held tightly to the floor, still afraid to look at him.

Jesus fuckin' Christ, I couldn't believe it. I'm being put in charge of the kitchen! My body felt stiff and my heart was racing. I stood outside his door with my eyes glued to the floor. What if I mess this up? I was sweating yet cold at the same time. My body started to tremble. I wanted to run from this spot but I could not move. I could feel my guts gurgling around and I felt like I was going to crap myself, I was scared stiff.

I had never run the kitchen by myself. I had worked with Tom for the past year. He was older than me and had shown me most things, like how to light the stove, how to set the rat traps, how much coffee went into the pots, how thick to slice the bread, that sort of thing. Here I was twelve years old, being given this kind of responsibility.

"O'Keeffe, what the Christ are you doing boy?" Blackie yelled out from his office. "Get back to class you idiot." The dread of him coming after me thawed my fear, and my legs took off. I sped down the hall right to the toilet where I sat my ass down and my gut exploded. Holy shit! How am I going to manage this?

When I crawled into bed that night I couldn't sleep. Incomplete thoughts were racing through my head. My brain was cluttered with uncertainty and worry. I'd turn one way and then flip myself over. I'd sit on the edge of my cot for a bit and then lay down. What if I don't get up on time? What if I can't light the fire? What if I can't do it by myself? Shit, I could be in a mess of trouble if I blow this. All night I tossed and turned. Ah, I wish the angels would come and take me now. I thought, better to die now, rather than mess this up and die at the hands of these pukes.

I lay in my bed agonizing and sweating over my new responsibilities. I was exhausted and I hadn't done a thing yet. I walked through the steps of my new duties in my mind. Alright, I've gotta' go to the boiler room to get things heated up, gotta' get the pots and haul the water, light the stoves, have to make sure…damn, just go to sleep. I wish I could quiet my brain, if only for a few minutes. In the middle of my agony, I felt a large hand touch me on the shoulder. What the hell? It startled me, and I sat up quickly.

"It's okay, boy." It was the night watchman, Fergy, come to fetch me. "It's time to go down and light the fires now," he said very quietly.

"Thank you Fergy," I replied.

"Let me know if ya' have any trouble and I'll come help ya', right then?"

"Yes sir, I'll be alright," I replied, even though I hadn't a clue how I would manage this great task.

It was dark as I tumbled out of my bed and began to dress. Only one oil lamp burnt at the entrance to our room, barely casting enough light to allow me to find my shorts and socks. Damn, it was freezing—that damp cold that cuts right to your bones and makes you shudder even on the inside. More than two years now we had been here, and I had never been given this much responsibility. God, I hope the angels are watching over me. I pulled my jumper over my head…please don't let me blow this…and pulled on my filthy, worn socks. Crap, what if I spill the coffee? I slid into my shorts. What if I can't get the furnace going? I tied on my leather boots. What if the water pump is not working? Who would I go to, Fergy?…and quietly headed out of the room while the rest of my mates slept.

I carefully made my way through the dark corridors and down the many flights of stairs of this gloomy, dismal hell. The halls were silent and lit only by the reflection of the moon and the oil lanterns that burnt at the end of each hallway. The tiny scratching of mouse and rat paws could be heard scurrying about. Above me, I heard the creaking of a door as it was slowly opened. I looked up and saw the figure of a boy, clad only in his bed shorts, run from the room of one of the Brothers. The click of the door, closing behind him as he left the Brothers chambers, echoed down the stairs. I saw the small frame of the body raise his hands to wipe his tear-drenched face, as he hurried to get back to his bed. Long shadows were cast throughout the building making things appear larger than they really were. Large intimidating crosses hung everywhere in Greenmount, always reminding us that God was watching, reminding us that God was to be feared.

As I headed down the well-polished staircase, polished by the thousands of little hands who had lived here over the years, my eyes caught the eyes of the Jesus that hung in the main foyer. This Jesus was the most ornate of all. I had never had much of a chance to look at him before as we always kept our heads down, and were nervously rushing from one place to another, one chore to another. I stopped at the bottom of the stairs and looked up to stare at him.

His eyes were open, looking right at me. He was sad, I could tell. He didn't like what he saw in this place. Did he suffer like we suffer here? Is that what life is about? Is he crying because he knows about the suffering in this place?

Does God want us to suffer? Why would he? I don't want the things I love to feel pain? I don't want the people I love to die? Is the purpose of my miserable life to suffer? Will I die in this place? Does God really want us to fear him?...so many questions.

Why is everything here done in the name of the Father? "In the name of the Father, we will cleanse yur' pathetic souls," we would hear as we were walloped for peeing the bed. "In the name of the Father, we will make sure you know each and every phrase of 'The Good Book'," we heard as one of us was flogged for not knowing a math question. "In the name of the Father, we will break you, humiliate, and degrade you, spit upon, and starve you.' All in the name of the Father? This is not a house of God. This is the house of the devil himself. But do I dare tell anyone? Never!

I did believe in God, but a kind and gentle God. A God that created beauty and love. I believed in my father, the father watching over me, the one who with my mother gave me life. The father who would watch down upon me and my brothers and sisters, and make sure we were reunited one day, free from this awful place. This is what I believed. Through the darkness of this place I would survive, in the name of my father, I would.

I took a deep breath, and hurried towards the long narrow hall that led to the boiler room. This hall was colder than the rest of the place. The walls were plastered with brick and paved with cobblestones. Kids said the bodies of hundreds of boys were buried down here behind these walls and under these stones. If there were boys buried here, they were better off resting where they were, rather than battling the day-to-day life in Greenmount. I ran my hand along the bumpy brickwork so I could find my way along this haunting corridor. I could smell the scent that had escaped from the coal room next to the boiler, indicating that I was almost there.

Finally, I came to the large wooden door and pulled it open. The scent of the coal pile that lay just inside the room was released. Coal was a good smell, mmm....the smell of my father. I knew exactly where the coal shovel was; I had done this chore many times in the light of day. It was different now in the early morning hours, with just one small light at the end of the hall casting a beam that barely allowed me to see where to place my spade.

This room was both peaceful and disturbing. Boys had been sent down here many times as punishment for a horde of deeds deemed to be despicable by the Presentation Brothers. Others, ran away during the day and came here to escape the torment, the beatings, the humiliation of not knowing a question, and the daily drudgery of life in this awful place. A million tears must have fallen on the floor of this room.

I did what I had to, and after I was sure I had a good fire going, I dusted myself off and placed the spade back in its spot. I left the room and started back down the hallway. A cold shiver ran up my legs into my spine and took over my entire body. It was a sinister, vibrating chill. I picked up my pace and began to run down the cold, dark passageway. Maybe there are bodies down here, I thought. I ran even faster now, and didn't stop or even take a breath until I had made my way to the kitchen.

As I entered the kitchen, I could hear the rats scatter. I heard the loud slap as one of them was caught in a trap. I'd have to take care of it later. Right now, I was too worried about getting things going. A long, brown, canvass apron hung on a brass hook next to the large, black stove where all the meals were prepared. I had to jump to snatch the apron from its spot. I slipped the stained and tattered garment over my head and pulled it up high around my waist so it did not drag on the floor. I wrapped the ends twice around my skinny body and tied them in a big knot right at the center of my stomach. This piece of clothing, this 'uniform', was filthy. It had hung here for months, years maybe and had never been washed. How many boys had worn this old piece of cloth, I wondered? How many boys had hauled themselves out of bed over the years to get up and make the coffee? Hundreds, maybe? Now it was my turn. I felt a bit of pride having been given such a big responsibility. Maybe they think I'm no good for nothing else so they put me in here? Nah, I deserve this chance. I'm gonna' be good at this. But I was scared shitless.

I pulled out a large wooden apple crate and slid it up to the stove to use as a step. A rat scurried across my foot as I moved the crate up to the stove. There were mice and rats everywhere in Greenmount. One at a time, I lifted two large, well-worn, copper pots down from the stove and slid them across the floor over to the water pump. I had to use both arms to pull the pump and fill each container halfway with water. I carefully dragged them back across the floor and lifted each one back on to the stove.

I used a smaller container to top up each pot with more water. Pretty smart, I thought. If I had overfilled them they would surely have spilt. This system is gonna' work great until I get a little taller. Once I had the stove going, I pulled out the huge loaves of uncut bread and got the trays ready for the boys that would be coming down. Most of the loaves had nibbles on them from the rodents that lived in the kitchen. I flicked away all the brown and black mouse droppings and began slicing up the bread.

I had never been in this place by myself. I had worked in the kitchen a lot and knew how things were done but never on my own. I was surprised at how efficient and resourceful I was. The other kitchen helpers would be arriving soon. Should I sneak a slice of bread for myself? Nobody would see me, would they? Maybe there was a Brother waiting in the shadows to see if I would steal anything. Maybe this was all a trick to catch me doing something bad? No, not today. I better wait and see how this all works out. As hungry as I was, I knew that this could work into a good opportunity, so I wasn't about to blow it this quickly. I carried on stacking the cups, cutting up the bread, and readying the room for the over two hundred hungry mouths that would be coming in from Mass. That was the one good thing about being in the kitchen—no morning Mass, and no line to march in.

The sun was well up now as the other boys started gathering in the food line, pushing up against one another, eager to get a measly piece of bread and a cup of coffee. On the other side of our kitchen, we could smell meat cooking and fresh bread baking, being prepared for the Brothers. Oh, yes! God fed those Brothers well, while we starved over on this side of the house.

The Brothers kept several animals, including chickens, turkeys, and cows to provide God's servants with fresh eggs, meat, and milk—the kinds of food we never saw in our kitchen. I thought maybe if I did a good job on this side, one day I'd get to work over there. I had heard stories of the boys who worked in the Brothers' kitchen. They were the lucky ones. They got to eat the scraps tossed into the trash buckets that were being sent out to the animals. If a boy was quick enough he could nibble on some fairly tasty rubbish on his way to feed the animals and be back before the Brothers ever caught him. The boys who had been caught eating from the trash bin, were punished more severely than anyone. Broken bones, dislocated limbs, or their short-lived lives, was the cost of stealing table scraps. Maybe I don't want to work over on that side; maybe the temptation would be too great?

"Hey O'Keeffe, give me an extra big slice would ya'? 'Fact, give me two," called out Nacho Mongolas. We didn't know where this kid was from but he was the toughest kid in the school. He was huge, mean, and made the Brothers look like angels the way he treated the other boys. Kids hated him, and we all feared him.

Was this some sort of test that the Brothers are putting me through? Maybe they told Nacho to ask me for extra bread to see what I would do? If I don't give him another slice, he'll beat the shit out of me. If I do and the Brothers catch me, they'll beat the shit out of me. God! Here I was again worrying about everything.

"Ya' know I can't Nacho, the Brothers will kill me."

"Well, I'll kill ya' and yur' pretty little brother, if ya' don't," he threatened.

Shit, what do I do, what do I do? "I'll give ya' my bread Nacho, after we're done in here." I thought that was a fair compromise.

"Listen, fuck. I want an extra slice right now." He leaned over the counter and grabbed me by the neck.

"Let 'im go," Brother Eugene announced. Just in time, I thought. "Nacho you cannot continue to threaten the other boys like this. Nothing will be gained."

Nacho released me and looked me straight in the eye. "You're fucked mister. You and yur' little maggot brother will be dead in a week." He took his tray and hurried off with his gang of followers trailing behind him.

Christ, now what's gonna' happen? Shit, he'll be after me for days. I'll have to figure this out, but not now. I wanted to do a good job. I continued to hand out the bread. The other helpers had arrived and were passing out coffee and collecting trays. Except for my interaction with Nacho, all in all, my first day went pretty well. I was tired but at least I had pulled it off.

Over the next few days I did my best to avoid Nacho. I was going to extra band practises like Blackie had asked and spent most of my time in the kitchen preparing the meals and keeping the fires going. Other than band, I hardly ever had to go to class anymore. The Brothers preferred to keep me busy doing other chores. Everyday, I got the same damn chill when I left that boiler room in the basement. Maybe little spirits were in there trying to call out to me. Maybe there were kids down there wanting their spirits set free. It was an eerie place, that's for sure.

I still worried every night that I wouldn't get up on time and would miss starting the fires. When I did sleep, I dreamt that I had forgotten to get up and Blackie was beating the daylights out of me. One morning, I woke up suddenly and found myself sitting at the bottom of the stairs in only my bed shorts.

"It's okay boy," Fergy said. "You're sleepwalking. Go back to bed, and I'll make sure ya' get up on time." Fergy was good to me and always made sure I was up. Over time, my body adjusted, and I would wake up when I was supposed to go down.

I was also getting real good on my coronet. I still couldn't read the music but I didn't have to. I could play by ear. I was now playing first seat, which meant I was the best in the band, and was getting most of the solos. Oh, if my Dad could see me, I know he'd love it. When we were good enough, Mr. O'Toole was going to line us up some concerts so that the school could make a few pounds.

Sean had also adjusted to Greenmont, and I looked out for him always. Sean, Frankie, Charlie, a few others, and me, had our own gang and tried to stay away from the likes of Nacho and some of the other toughies. Anytime one of us was called up for a beating the rest of our gang would go and stand near, to lend support. Sometimes all ya' could do was put your arm around a lad's shoulders and let him know he had friends. Without friends, a boy would not stand a chance of survival. Your pals were your family. Your pals were the only reason you were alive in this place, and we looked out for each other the best we could.

Sixteen

THE BAND PLAYS ON–SEPTEMBER 1943

M r. O'Toole was beaming when he came into the Band Room one morning. "Alright, boys. I think you're ready. They're going to start letting us out to play concerts. We're ready to start making some music and some money for the school."

The other boys and I were excited and nervous, but we were used to being nervous.

"Next weekend, we're going to play at the Boy Scout Jamboree outside of Cork. We better play our hearts out, or they'll never let us out of here again. The Brothers will all be there to see how we do."

For the next four days, we practised for hours upon hours. Right after breakfast, we would start and kept goin' right up 'til supper. I knew every note. I could play the pieces with my eyes closed, and I loved it.

On the day we were playing in the Jamboree, the entire school was buzzing. Kids who had never left this place for more than a block were over the wall with excitement.

We boarded the bus and headed out. From the bus window, I looked out at the streets and the people. It was marvelous. I loved being out of that place. It was fantastic—the people, the carts, the shops. I wanted to soak it all in, all of it. My jaw rested on the cold metal frame of the window. The breath of every child on the bus created a misty, wet fog that clung to the glass. I kept wiping it with my elbow so that I didn't miss a thing happening on the streets that were alive outside as our bus drove by. This was much better than being paraded around the streets, and having every one stare at us. I felt important being on the bus. This was good.

When we arrived at the Jamboree the Brothers made sure we stayed in a tight line and never strayed from their sight.

"Shit, I'm worried Wattie," announced Paddy Fagan. "I've never been around this many people."

"It'll be brilliant Paddy. Just do what we've done at practise. You'll be fine."

All the boys were scared and walking slowly with their heads and eyes down, huddled together like they did in the school. They were petrified. So was I, but I was also proud and eager to play.

We got to the area where we were going to perform. It was a large, outdoor auditorium partially covered by an enormous tent. We were told to set up on the large stage that looked out over a crowd of two hundred people at least. People were sitting inside and outside of the tent. Boys huddled together nervously as they put their instruments together and stayed close to one another while we set up the chairs. All of us gazed out over the crowd to see who was coming in to watch us. Sean was on the drums and tambourine. I could see that he was also anxious, but not as bad as some guys. I went over to him.

"Sean, listen. Daddy used to do this all the time. Do ya' remember how we loved to watch 'im, and it was wonderful?"

"I do, Wattie. I remember 'im in the band. I loved watching 'im."

"Well, today he's watching us. Don't be afraid. He will make sure we do just fine out here. This is what us O'Keeffes are good at, music and entertaining people. Are ya' alright?"

"Yes, Wattie, I'm alright. I'll be playin' fur Mummy and Daddy today. Let's give 'em the best show ever, just like Daddy used to do."

"Good lad. Good luck back here."

I took my place next to Jim and the other coronet players. Most boys were slouched down in their seats because they were so afraid. Most had never sat in front of an audience before.

"Come on, boys," announced O'Toole. "Ya' look like a pack 'a dyin' dogs. Pull it together now. Let's get goin'." Everyone was scared shitless. This was our first performance. We didn't know what to expect. I was excited—scared, but excited. In my mind, I was dedicating this performance to my parents.

"What if we screw this up and are given beatings for a week?" Paddy whispered to me. "Or they put us on food rations. Or what if we're really bad, and the crowd boos at us or throws stuff at us?"

"Shut up, Paddy. It ain't gonna' happen. We're going to be great."

"Wattie, I'm goin' to crap myself right here."

"Shut up, Paddy. Pull yur'self together before I punch ya' out."

I started to get tense when I looked at the rest of the boys. A couple of them were shaking like I had when I stuck my finger in that hole in the sanitarium wall. Some of them were frightened stiff, hardly moving, their eyes glued to the crowd that was set out in front of us. The drummer next to Sean bent over the back of the stage and puked his guts out but I don't think the crowd could see him.

"Boys, there's nothing to fear. I know you're scared. It will pass, and you will all be fine. Okay? Are yous' ready?" O'Toole asked. "Are yous' ready?"

Some of the fellows straightened up. Others were still frozen in fear. O'Toole tapped his stick on the edge of his music stand. He slicked his long bang off to the side of his face, took a deep breath and raised both of his arms.

"Ready boys?" he said again, this time louder. Our instruments came up in unison.

"Okay, we'll start with a simple C scale to warm ya' up."

His arm came down to count out the first note of the scale. Jesus, that first note was horrible, bloody awful, in fact. Hardly a sound crawled out from anyone. O'Toole's arms waved into position for our second note. Shit, it was not any better. The crowd, hearing us begin to warm up, started to settle down and take their seats.

O'Toole's arms came down and he nervously coughed into his clenched fist. With his head bent downward, into his chest, his eyes peering out at us over the top of his spectacles, he took in another deep breath. He looked tense but spoke in a calm tone.

"Boys, pull it together. Ya' know what to do. You've done it a thousand times. Now, be the men ya' are and play yur' damn hearts out." Again, he raised his arms.

"Ready boys, lets try the C scale again." His wand came down and a little more sound came out of us this time, but we were still a mess. The crowd was huge now, and the Brothers were in the very front row staring us down. Oh, my God!

O'Toole looked at me.

"O'Keeffe, this is one of those days in yur' life that will make all the difference. This is a day you will not soon forget. I want you to rise up and show the rest of these poor, scared lads how it's done. Give me a C scale Walter, one that will belt right through the roof of this place. Show the other boys how to do this. I know you're not scared. You're not afraid of anything. Walter, you're the best I've got. Don't let me and the other boys down."

Jesus, why was it up to me? I closed my eyes and said one of my private prayers, one of the ones I wrote myself. *"God of all life, please let the life force of your Universe flow through me and give me strength."* I took a deep breath and for a moment disappeared deep inside myself. O'Toole is right, I'm not afraid. I want to perform. I will take all the anger and the hatred that is locked up inside of me and belt it out through the end of my Coronet. I will send the sound flying right into that front row where each of those fat bastard Brothers are sitting. Yes, I can do this.

I rose from my seat and, with the courage of my parents' blood running through me, I took in a deep breath and belted out a perfect C scale. I stretched my neck making it crack, took another deep breath, and belted out a perfect G scale. Every note was a bullet aimed at that front row. I was okay. I could do this. I was warmed up and ready to go. I turned to the rest of the boys in the band.

"Alright, mates, we can do this. We're going to blast those fat Brothers right out of their seats. Fire every note ya' have right at 'em. Take all the anger, the fear, the pain, and the hatred ya' have for these assholes and toss it at 'em. Think of every note as a bullet that you are firing at those bastard fucks and shoot 'em down. Let's kill these pricks with our music. For every mean, disgusting thing they have done to ya', let's gun 'em down." The rest of the boys got excited, giggled, and were ready to go.

O'Toole heard everything I said. He nodded, and I could tell he thought my words would work.

"We're ready, Mr. O'Toole," I announced and took my seat.

"Okay boys, a C scale, just like Mr. O'Keeffe said." He raised his arms again, and this time we had it right. The sound was wonderful. Once we had warmed up with our scales we relaxed and were ready to perform.

Off we went, fantastic rhythms and harmonies flowed from our instruments. This was grand. March after march we played on. This was the best we had ever performed. Even the Brothers were tapping their feet and clapping their hands. Each tune was aimed right at 'em, invisible bullets shooting 'em down.

After playing for over an hour, we were exhausted, but it was good. Blackie arrived as we were readying ourselves for our last tune and positioned himself right in front of us. The band was tired and our fingers were sore.

"One more," Mr. O'Toole shouted out. "Blackie is here now, boys. He will decide if we come out and do this again. I need ya' to give me everything you've got." He raised his arms and we began to play a Souza March. We were offbeat and not together at all. The sight of Blackie had scared some of the boys.

Mr. O'Toole brought down his arms, tapped his music stand with his wand, and again stared at us. "Look at me, boys. Right now, this means everything. This last tune will change some of your lives. If we do this right, we will get more practise time, you'll have fewer chores to do. Come on, now." Again, he raised his arms, then he looked at me. "O'Keeffe, when my arms come down, let me hear you. Let everybody hear ya'. Let the God damn world hear ya'!" he implored.

His arms came down signaling the start of our last tune. With that direction, I sprung to my feet and my fingers took off. I belted out every breath of life in me. The other band members came to life. They also rose. The sound grew louder and better. O'Toole was sweating and waving his arms madly. Everyone was in sync now. The trombones, the trumpets, the baritones, French horns, drums—it was magnificent and a sight to behold; we went wild. The crowd rose to their feet. They were dancing, clapping, cheering, and full of the excitement. Our music was bringing all of these people to life. What a feeling!

When we came to the last five bars in the march, O'Toole motioned his hands to slow us down. He raised his arms higher, creased his brow into a hundred tiny wrinkles and directed us into a crescendo and a magnificent finale. We held that last note for at least ten seconds. When his hands motioned for us to stop, the crowd went silent. They were stunned. O'Toole, with his arms frozen in the air, looked out at us and revealed the biggest, yellow grin I had ever seen. His arms slowly came down to his sides, and he turned to the address the crowd.

Instead of bowing, like he usually did at the school, he turned and acknowledged the band with his left arm fully extended. And then, he started to clap. The rest of the crowd rose to their feet and clapped along with him. He looked over at me, still clapping, nodded his head and mouthed the words, "Thank you." This was the greatest moment in my life.

Seventeen

TAKING ON NACHO

During the ride home, we were all still full of life, singing out tunes, laughing, and jumping from one seat to another. The Brothers couldn't control us, nor did they try. This was our celebration. I had never seen this kind of excitement or happiness come from these boys, ever. When we pulled up in front of the school, the roar of laughter quickly fell silent. It was over. We were back. It was pouring down rain as we stepped off the bus. Pulling our jackets over our heads, each boy ran quickly into the main hall of the school. I was dripping wet, but feeling mighty proud.

"O'Keeffe, kitchen," Blackie called out. "Ya' haven't much time now, so get going."

That was it, back to reality. I pulled off my wet jacket and used it to brush off my dripping hair and wipe the water running down my legs. I hadn't much time to get the dinner started. When I arrived in the kitchen, the other helpers had already arrived.

"Wattie, how was it? What did ya' see?" All the other boys were eager to hear tales of the outside world.

"It was grand; I'll tell yas' about it later. Let's get this goin'."

I grabbed my apron and quickly began mixing up the dinner stew. I dumped a bag of flour into a special pot we used for our stew. I added salt, water, and a few spuds and had one of the other boys stir it up. The pot was almost as tall as the small, dirty boy trying to stir the contents inside. I unwrapped a package of some sort of ground meat. It was gray; I never knew what it was, but each Sunday, the same type of package was left out for me to add into the stew pot. One small package of meat—I think it was meat—to feed over two hundred hungry boys. I sighed and tossed it into the caldron.

The others were starting to line up now. I saw Sean in the line telling the other boys about our adventure. I could tell he was proud; I was happy for him. I was glad that he had been a part of something wonderful. My Dad would have been so proud of us. I hoped he was. As each boy came along the line, I scooped them out one full ladle of stew. I tried to make sure there was at least a little bit of meat in each scoop. I could see Nacho in the line just ahead of Sean. Crap, I just did not feel like dealing with him today, not after everything else had gone so well.

When it was Nacho's turn to be served, he grabbed the ladle from my hand to try and get himself some extra meat and an extra scoop. I grabbed the ladle back from him, and in the struggle I whacked him in the face with it and lost an entire ladle of food. Like a swarm of bees boys fell to the ground to lick what had been lost on the floorboards.

"Nacho, you asshole! Fuck off!" I shouted right into his face.

"This time, O'Keeffe you're dead. Tonight, you're dead." He marched off with his tray and his gang. I was terrified. Sean looked worried.

"Don't worry, Sean, he can't do nothin' to me. I can take care of that pig. After today, I can take care of anything."

"I'm proud of ya', Wattie. I'm proud that you're my brother."

"I'm proud of you, too, Seany. Ya' did good today; ya' really did great."

After everyone else was fed, the kitchen helpers and I were able to eat. I took my time eating and cleaning up. I feared that if I left this safe haven, the kitchen, Nacho would be out there waiting to kick the life out of me. I stayed and scrubbed the floors just to kill time. It was getting close to the end of the day, almost time for prayers and bed. What was I going to do? Was he going to kill me tonight? Was I going to spend every single day of my life in this shit-hole worrying about Nacho? Fuck no. I had found an inner strength today that I did not know I had. Let's see if it's still there.

I threw off my apron and left it on the floor. I grabbed my jacket, still wet, from its hanging place and marched out to the yard to find Nacho. There he was with his gang of merry-suck ups. As soon as he looked my way, I took my jacket and threw it to the ground. This was the signal that I was ready to take him on. Nacho was more than willing to meet my challenge and came running towards me. The other boys started gathering 'round as they knew a fight was about to unfold. You could hear the chanting start to build for both camps.

"Wa–ttie, Wa–ttie," roared one group of kids. Charlie came running to my side.

"Do ya' need some back-up, mate?"

"No, I'm going to do this on my own."

"Na–cho, Na–cho," roared the other group of boys. A few small boys sat on the fringe of the entire event not knowing which side to choose. Charlie, Sean, and Jim were part of the crowd that were gathering behind me. I could see that Jim wasn't chanting anything, but at least he was on my side. Sean and Charlie, on the other hand, were screaming at the top of their lungs. Nacho now stood in front of me. His jacket laying on top of mine.

"Ya' fuckin' piece of shit Irishman," Nacho screamed into my face. "I'm goin' to kill ya' and break every bone in yur' face and yur' body and leave ya' out here so the rats can feed on yur' rotting flesh."

Just like I had done earlier in the day at the concert, I disappeared deep into my inner self. Again, I asked my mother and my father to guide me, to be with me, to lend me their strength. The echoes of the boys screaming now became muffled background noise. I could only hear my own inner voice, saying I can do this, I can do this. I then heard my father's voice, "Walter, you come from a line of strong and mighty men. Nothing is difficult for the strong and courageous. You will not let anyone, ever, call you down or beat you down—*not ever!*"

With my father's voice still ringing in my ears, I raised my right arm, clenching my fist so hard I could feel my nails puncture the skin on my sweating palm. As my arm swung about, I belted out the loud barreling call of a warrior, "Ahhhhhhhh!"

My fist hit the front of Nacho's face. As it did, I heard a loud crack. I raised my left arm to stop the blow coming towards me from Nacho, it never reached me. His eyes rolled back into his head, blood sprayed from his nose and his arms moved up towards his face to catch the blood and teeth that were falling from his mouth. He was in shock. With his hands cupped in front of his nose, he looked at me confused. I knew what he was thinking…where the fuck did that come from?

I was shaking, my knees were rattling, and I could hardly stand. My right arm was still raised where it had intercepted with his face. My teeth were clenched in a warrior's pose. I was stunned. Like him, I was thinking, where the fuck did that come from? I had done it; I had taken on the brutal bully. I had again called on my inner power, a force that had been growing inside me just waiting to explode.

Nacho snatched his jacket from the ground. "Come on," he called out to his pack of pawns. They, too, were confused. A few of them nervously hesitated and then slowly moved over behind me. "Fuck you," Nacho screamed out and ran off the field.

I let out a huge sigh and finally dropped my arm. The roar of boys behind me was still muffled. I was in some sort of trance, having some sort of spiritual awakening. In that moment, I knew I would survive this place. A calm, warm, tingling sensation wrapped my entire being. Every pore of my body filled with a sense of understanding, a sense of knowing that there was a higher power looking out for me. I could feel my body wrapped in this beautiful gown of protection. I had never felt such an incredible feeling in all my life. I didn't move. I wanted to continue to feel this warmth, this connectedness to my higher power for a little while longer. It was amazing.

The sounds behind me grew louder; I still had not moved from my place. Boys started to shake me, pat me on the back. They were laughing. Sean was in front of me now, hugging me, calling out my name. Charlie was clapping and jumping up and down. My ears were buzzing as I was brought back to this place, with a new understanding that no matter what happened, I would survive.

Across the field, I could see Brother Paul, our shoemaking teacher, running towards the crowd of boys. We all scattered like mice and ran up to our dorm rooms.

"That was fuckin' brilliant," announced Charlie as he tossed his jacket on to his bed. "You, my friend, were fuckin' marvelous. When we get out of this place, I am going to manage yur' boxing career. We'll both be rich, rich, rich."

All the boys in our room were huddled around me yakking about how I had taken Nacho out. It was good.

"Come on, see if ya' can take me," Charlie jested, bouncing around in a boxer's pose. I jumped up and we started to spar, all in jest.

"O'Keeffe Walter," Brother Gabe shouted as he barged into our dorm.

The room fell silent and every boy in the place put their head down. He marched up to me, said nothing, and whacked me on my ear. Shit, my ear was ringing. These bastards loved walloping us on the ears. I was dizzy from the blow I had just received. I pulled my hand from my ear and saw that it was bleeding. The ringing was unbearable. He then grabbed me by the hair and started to drag me out of the room.

"Ya' like fighting do ya', and setting a bad example for the rest of the boys? O'Keeffe, that is not something we like around here. Blackie will set you straight."

The other boys followed as the Brother dragged me out of the room. When we got to the top of the stairs he shoved me forward just enough so that I lost my footing and fell, knocking my head against the wooden railing, the same side of the head that he had whacked me on. The force of the fall sent me rolling down the steps. I was able to grab hold of the railing to stop myself from tumbling all the way to the bottom at about the sixth step. I landed backwards on the stairs bracing myself with the railing and holding my ear. Christ, I was in pain.

The Brother took about three steps towards me. He stood, smiled at me, and then with the force one might use to kick a soccer ball all the way across the field, he kicked me in the shoulder sending me flying down the rest of the steps. When I hit the bottom my nose was bleeding, and the pain in my head was unbearable. He slowly marched down the stairs with a grin of extreme pleasure on his face. When he reached the bottom where I lay, he looked at me with that same smile and gave me a swift kick in the ribs. Oh fuck, that hurt. He reached down and grabbed me by my scalp and dragged me off to the dining hall, all the other boys following cautiously behind him. The pain was excruciating; I just wanted to pass out. Please, God, let me pass out or die.

When we reached the dining hall, there was Blackie seated at the front of the room tapping his cane on the side of one of the wooden tables. Nacho was knelt on the ground beside him looking demoralized, his nose still bleeding. Blackie rose.

"All of you little maggots, you scum of the earth, you are the lowest form of life in our great Ireland. We here in this place have given you a chance at life, something yur' despicable parents never gave ya'. You have no gratitude, any of ya', for how hard we all work to keep ya' alive. Without us, each of ya' would be dead, or close to it, living on the streets like the bunch of mangy rats that you are. You disgust me, every one of ya'." He then spat on the floor. "This is how you repay us for our charity, starting riots, taking us away from our dinner to break up schoolyard fights? O'Keeffe, I expect more from you. Mongolas, you lowlife, wimpy, piece of shit, you embarrass me."

Having humiliated and ridiculed us for a good while, he then had Nacho take down his trousers and step on to the ladder. I lost count at how many times his hand rose to beat Nacho, but I knew that I was next. When it was my turn I could barely pull myself up off the floor. The pain in my head, the ringing in my ear, and the excruciating pain coming from my side where Brother Gabe had kicked me, were horrendous. I'm sure I had cracked or broken ribs. Still, he wanted me to climb the ladder. With my arm holding my side tightly I tired to walk forward. I couldn't do it.

"O'Keeffe, get on the fuckin' ladder or I will surely kill ya' right here right now."

Death would have been a welcome relief from the pain I was in.

As I could not get up, I crawled across the floor towards the ladder, holding my broken body together. I crawled up the ladder using my one arm. The boys in the room were silent. Brothers Eugene and Fergy stood at the back of the room, obviously distressed by what was going on. Why didn't they stop this madness? I rested my head on one of the rungs in the ladder and braced my body with my feet to hold myself in place. I could not undo my own trousers, Blackie called another boy forward to do it. I was slouched over the ladder, likely had broken ribs and a concussion, and still, he felt I needed more.

His cane came down upon my ass. The pain in my side and in my head was so bad that the beating on the ass was nothing. I don't know how many times he struck me. Each time he did, he bellowed out some sort of ridiculous religious calling:

"God save his treacherous soul." Whack.

"May the will of God be served on this day." Whack.

"Forgive the ghastly deeds of this damaged soul." Whack, and so it went on.

When he was done, I released the muscles in my legs that were strained from keeping me braced on the ladder. I slid off and lay face down on the floor barely able to move. Charlie and Sean came to my side. They tried to lift me, but I was in too much pain.

"Maybe we better take 'im to the infirmary," someone suggested.

"Nonsense, he's not contagious. Take 'im up to his room," Blackie replied.

Charlie, Sean, Frankie, Paddy, and some of the other boys—even little Kenny, the newest and smallest boy in our dorm—lifted me up and carried me off to our room. Jesus, the pain was awful. As they carried me up the stairs I must have blacked out a few times 'cause I cannot remember them laying me on my cot. When I came to, Charlie had ripped up his blanket and was binding up my side to keep my ribs together. Somebody, probably Sean, had stuffed a piece of cloth up my nose, to stop the bleeding, I suppose. I couldn't speak, and just let them do what they were doing to try and put me back together. The only thought that came to mind now, was Christ, how will I get up in the morning and start the breakfast? Fuck. I must have passed out again from the pain because I don't remember falling asleep.

Like always, Fergy came 'round to wake me. This morning was different.

"Don't worry, boy. I'll get the fires goin' fur ya'. You've got to stay put or ya' won't heal up right. Take these." Fergy put two tablets in my mouth and told me to chew them up and swallow them. I did as he said and then passed out again. When I woke, I had been properly taped up. Fergy must have told somebody something. Thank God for that man.

I was given two days off from the kitchen to allow me to heal up. I pretty much slept the entire time. I wasn't sure if I was glad to be alive or not.

It wasn't but a few days later that the lady inspector came 'round. She was a medical doctor. When the inspectors came 'round everything was done up nice. I'm not sure what happened. Maybe somebody got word out. Maybe a housekeeper or Fergy told somebody what was going on in here. I'll never know. The inspector spoke to me and a few of the other boys. She never looked at my injuries. She never asked me what had happened. I was scared to tell her anything. But if she had asked, I would have told her. If she had asked to see my bandages, I would have shown her. She never asked.

The Brothers behaved for a few days after that. They always did after an inspector had been through. But Fergy disappeared; he had been fired. One of the Brothers said he had been caught stealing loaves of bread. I knew that wasn't true, but I didn't question it. I felt really bad about that. Fergy had been a good fellow and I think he felt bad about how things ran at Greenmount. He was the only adult in this place that we could have a bit of fun with.

I used to tie a string on to the light switch in our dorm room. When Fergy came around at night to put out the lights, we'd pull the switch and the lights would go back on. All the boys would giggle. He'd come back in and turn the lights off again, and again, we'd pull the thread and on they'd go. He would make a bit of a fuss, and the boys would laugh. He must have seen that string on there. He must have also known that we were a bunch of boys who didn't get much fun in our lives, so he played along. What a good old fella' he was. Never for one second did I believe that he had stolen anything from this place. Who would want to steal the maggot-infested shit we ate? I think the Brothers had him fired because he complained about this place. I think he told the authorities what was going on in here. Finally, somebody had the courage to tell our story, and he was let go.

Nacho never bothered Sean or me again. In fact, he was very different after that. I suppose the humiliation of a boy half his size taking him on did something to him. I don't know what happened to him. One day, his things were packed up and he was taken away; never said goodbye to anyone. He was just gone, which happened a lot at the school. Boys would just disappear, without a word. We never even asked where they went, for fear that we might end up in the same place.

I healed up and went back to my work detail. The routines of the day never changed; nothing ever changed.

Playing in the band gave me something to anchor a little hope to. I knew that I had great talent and one day hoped I would be able to use it. Our Dad would have loved that the three of us were playing in a band together. All three of us were good. Jim was different when we played music together, which I liked. Music was the thing that brought us together in this place. I think he liked it, too, but would never say.

I never got used to the beatings for wetting the bed, but they did become routine. They still hurt, but not as bad. My ass had built up such thick scar tissue that I think the nerve endings must have been damaged. I was older now, almost thirteen, and here I was still wetting the bed and being publicly flogged for it. No, nothing ever changed, just the faces of the boys who would come and go from this hell on earth.

Eighteen

THE STRIKE–DECEMBER 1943

As I grew older, I had various young 'uns that I was charged to look after and I always tried to treat them well. I taught them how to survive in Greenmount, like Charlie had taught me. I made up great stories and entertained them night after night with tales of banshees, leprechauns, and fairies. I also told them how much their mothers loved them and how my Mum had loved me. I told them that the Presentation Brothers were jealous because nobody loved them, not even God.

Kenny was one of my charges and he had become pretty attached to me. He had no family in this place and did not know why he was here. He had been taken from his father after his Mum passed away from tuberculosis. Kenny's Dad had come 'round once since Kenny was brought in over a year ago. He was a good lad, very quiet. I did my best to look out for him and tried to teach him how to keep his head down and how to stay out of trouble. He was smaller than most of the boys his age. He wore thick glasses and didn't walk quite right; he had rickets or something when he was a baby. We were all pale and thin, but he was really pale and thin. His whitish skin and fair hair made him look even more sickly. Because he was so frail and couldn't run properly, he didn't play in the yard with the other kids and so didn't have a lot of friends. He was smart though, knew his numbers and all his letters, and he loved stories.

One particular day, when we were all in the dining hall, I was doing duty in the kitchen while the rest of the boys were scooping out their bread from their coffee cups. I could see Kenny from where I was. He had his head down chewing on his bread. Not bothering anyone. A couple of boys from another group started roughing him up.

"Hey Kenny, ya' little faggot. Whose dick ya' suckin'? How about suckin' on this?" one boy taunted as he pulled out his dick and shook it at Kenny.

I jumped out from around the counter and started heading over to break it off. Kenny moved to elbow the kid just as Brother Gabe was moving in to break up the scuffle. As Kenny nudged his elbow towards the kid, he accidentally hit a coffee cup that was in another kid's hand and splashed it on to Brother Gabe. Shit, this is not going to be good, I thought, so I rushed over to try and defuse the situation. "Brother, it wasn't Kenny's fault," I tried to tell him.

"Shut the fuck up, O'Keeffe, and get back into the kitchen," roared Brother Gabe.

"But Brother..." He whacked me across the face.

I backed away but I could not leave this defenseless, almost blind kid to fend for himself. I remembered how little Kenny had tried to help the boys carry me up the stairs when I had been so badly beaten. I had to stand up for him. "Brother, really, it was not his fault." I pleaded. Again, he whacked me across the face and I fell to the floor.

Brother Gabe grabbed Kenny by the collar of his shirt and dragged him out of the room. I could see that Kenny was gagging and choking from the shirt being tugged against his throat. Gabe hauled him out to the muddy yard and called over two onlookers about Kenny's age and told them to strip him naked. The Brother then shoved Kenny to the ground and had him lay face down in the mud and the snow. Kenny must have been freezing. Brother Gabe pulled out his cane and started beating Kenny mercilessly.

The Brother was out of control beating and beating him. I couldn't stand to watch it nor could I walk away and leave the poor kid there. After he had hit him over a dozen times, he pulled him to his feet. Kenny's glasses were half hanging off his face and were muddied up. I was sure he couldn't see a thing. He was crying and must have been terribly confused. Using Kenny's socks, Brother Gabe tied Kenny's two hands together behind his back and left him standing there naked, freezing in the yard. Kenny started to cry, sobbing uncontrollably, heaving, and fell to his knees. Brother Gabe grabbed his hair and pulled him back to his feet. "You will stand here until this stain dries from my robe," he yelled.

I wanted to run out and kill the Brother. Never had I hated anyone so much as I hated this mean bastard. Kenny sobbed and sobbed; it was heart wrenching. All I could do was look on and let him know that I was nearby. I felt guilty that I could not do anything for him.

After a long while, Blackie came out and told me to bring him in. The poor little bastard was near death. I wrapped my apron around him and carried him in. I took him up to our room and covered him with the blankets from the other beds. He was shaking uncontrollably.

"This is bullshit. We're not going to take it anymore," Charlie said as he helped me bundle Kenny with blankets to warm him up.

"Walter," Charlie whispered. "Get the boys. We're going to have a meeting."

I ran around the room and quietly told all the others to gather 'round. Charlie assigned one boy to watch over the door in case any of the Brothers were coming. We all gathered around Kenny's cot.

"This is bullshit," Charlie said. "The shitty food, they way they beat us and talk down to us, the chores, the crap we put up with, it's not normal. This is not right." The boys were listening. "This has to stop, and we can stop it."

"How the fuck can we stop it?" someone called out from the back.

"We'll have a strike," answered Charlie. "None of us will go to class, none of us will lift a finger, suck a dick, nothing—until things change around here."

"Wattie, I'm not sure about this," Sean said. But I stood beside Charlie.

"Sean, all of yas', Charlie is right. We're going to die in this place. Is that what ya' want? I have been here for over three years and it only gets worse. The more they get away with, the more pain and suffering they bring down on us. We've got to stand up for ourselves 'cause nobody else in this God damn world is. If you fellas are waiting for a miracle to pull ya' out of here, you'll be waiting forever."

Some of the boys started to agree with Charlie and me, and then a few more. In minutes, the entire room was onside with the idea of a strike. But how were we going to make it work? We had to get word to the other boys in the school.

Charlie, Paddy, and I snuck out that night while the others kept a look out for us. We crept into the other rooms and told the boys what we wanted to do. They were all in. Even Jim thought it was a good idea. The plan was that in the morning after breakfast we would take over the dining hall and refuse to come out until they sent in the Gardai or an inspector. Then, we would tell our story. That night, no one could sleep. The place was humming as boys talked about the strike. It was exciting, yet frightful.

I got up the next morning like I always did and got the fire and kitchen going. Charlie was busy organizing the boys and coordinating the strike. He was our leader, 'The General'. As the boys started lining up for coffee, I could see that they were excited. Please, God, give us all strength today. Oh God, please keep us strong enough to go through with it; don't let anyone chicken out.

Breakfast had ended. Boys nervously scuttled about wondering what to do next. Oh shit, here we go. I saw Charlie stand and move to the front of the room. He stood on the very front table and called out to the pack.

"Lock it down boys." I jumped out from behind the kitchen and into the dining hall to assist.

Brother Eugene was sitting near the back of the room. He slowly rose and looked confused. The other Brothers in the room didn't know what the hell was going on.

"Strike! Strike! Strike! Strike!" Charlie started yelling out loudly.

Boys started yelling and screaming, banging their tin cups on the tables. "Strike! Strike! Strike! Strike!" they chanted with him.

The Brothers were stunned. None of them moved.

Charlie and Paddy and a few others started to wrestle the Brothers out of the room. It was crazy; we were crazy. The rest of the boys got involved getting the Brothers out. Me and a few others locked down the windows and doors. Some of the kids jumped into the kitchen looking for weapons to beat the Brothers out of the room. All we had were big stirring spoons and ladles, which was good enough. Boys were whacking the Brothers on the heads, the legs, anywhere to get them out. We were like a herd of wild animals on the charge, and it was great. The adrenaline was pumping through me and I didn't give a shit. I didn't care what the consequences would be; we were taking over this place. The boys, who weren't pushing the Brothers out of the room, were now on the tables jumping up and down waving their arms and utensils.

A few boys who didn't want to participate were dragged into the storage room. We didn't want even one boy left outside with the Brothers. It was loud; it was chaotic; it was mad but it was working. When we had all the Brothers out of the room and the doors and windows sealed off, Charlie got back on the table and started leading the chant again.

"Strike! Strike! Strike! Strike!" We were warriors.

I moved up front where I could see the Brothers outside the door through the beveled glass. They were all dancing around in a state of confusion and shock. God damn, it was funny to see them like that. All the boys were waving their arms in the air chanting, "Strike! Strike! Strike! Strike!"

Finally, Brothers Eugene, Gabe, and Edward were lined up in front of the door wanting in. Blackie and a few others were lined up behind them. The housekeeper and other staff (members) were also out there. Blackie pushed his way through Eugene and Gabe and stuck his ugly red face into the glass pane on the door.

Shit! Now I was scared, and stepped back from the door. We had taken it this far, we had to go all the way now. Boys were still chanting, waving, and banging cups.

"What in God's name is going on in there, McFarland?" Blackie screamed through the glass.

"I'll tell ya' what's going on in here," Charlie screamed back. The boys started to quiet down. "Starvation, humiliation, torture, abuse, neglect, that's what's going on here, and we want it to stop."

"Let me in so we can talk," Blackie suggested. Charlie turned to me, I nodded to him indicating that it was a good idea.

"Alright then, but just you," Charlie called out. "The rest of ya' stand back." Brothers Eugene, Gabe, and Edward listened to Charlie's command and stepped back from the door. A bunch of boys helped slide back the table blocking the door and gave Charlie just enough space to let Blackie's fat body squeeze through.

Once Blackie was in and standing face to face with Charlie, he screamed into Charlie's face, "What the fuck is wrong with you boy?"

"What the fuck's wrong with you and all 'em out there, and this fuckin' place?" Charlie screamed back at him. "This *place* is what's wrong with me!" Charlie yelled, releasing all of his pent up frustration, almost spitting into Blackie's face. I loved it.

Blackie went for his belt like he always did. This time, I put my hand over his to stop him. Blackie was stunned. Charlie grabbed Blackie's other arm as he tried to pull me off of him. Charlie then took the strap away from Blackie and held it high over his head presenting it to the boys like soldiers do when they capture the flag of an enemy. A thunderous roar came up from the boys and rose to fill the room. Again, they started to jump up and down on the tables and wave their weapons.

"What the hell do ya' think yur' doing?" he screamed at us.

"We're doing a strike, and until we can talk to the Gardai or an inspector, we're not coming out," Charlie yelled out. The boys cheered.

Paddy then stepped out in front and shouted through the crack in the door towards the other Brothers and the staff standing outside the dining hall. "Do the right thing. Go tell somebody we're here. Tell 'em what goes on in this place. Help us! You can help us!"

Blackie turned to me. "O'Keeffe, you get these boys to come out of here right now or I'll kill ya'," he threatened.

I moved right up into his face. "Death is better than living everyday in this hell, so yur' threats of death don't scare me." I moved in closer to him. "You can't do this anymore. You can't treat us this way. We want to talk to someone in authority, and if ya' don't bring us someone, we'll kill ya'. We've got nothing to lose."

"McFarland, O'Keeffe, the punishment I'll inflict on the two of ya' after this is over will give me great pleasure," was all he said.

"Get 'im out of here," Charlie screamed. A bunch of boys got together and shoved Blackie back out of the room.

"And ya' don't fuckin' come back unless ya' have the authorities with ya'," Charlie screamed at him.

"Tell people about this place!" Paddy called out again as the door opened to release our hostage. "Tell 'em to come and see what goes on here."

"Strike! Strike! Strike! Strike!" the chant continued.

I turned to Charlie. "Now what?" I asked.

"We wait," he answered. And we did.

That night, we all slept in the dining hall taking shifts to guard the windows and doors in case they tried to come in and drag us out. We had thought ahead and a few of the kitchen helpers and I had stashed coal and wood out the back so we could keep a fire going, even if they shut down the boiler. We made up lots of coffee and still had loaves of bread to keep us fed. Lots of the boys had stuffed their blankets down their trousers so we could keep warm while we were down here.

None of the staff or the Brothers came to the door during the night. Nor did they try to get in through the back or the windows. They were waiting us out. That was fine; we were prepared. Still, in the morning no one came. Occasionally, we saw them peer through the windows waiting for someone to crack. As the day wore on boys started to get restless, but we held on to them. We had to stay united. "Stay tough," we kept telling them. "There is nothing outside of this room for ya'."

Finally, late in the day Mr. O'Toole came to the door. I guess they thought he could talk some sense into us. He knocked gently and appeared quite calm.

"Let 'im in," Charlie decided. The table was slid back and O'Toole was allowed to squeeze through.

He walked towards me slowly. Now, he looked nervous. He didn't have to be. I would never let anyone hurt him, ever.

"Walter, what are ya' doing? What's it going to take to get you lads out of here?"

"Mr. O'Toole, they can't treat us like this, beating kids, starving us. You know it's bad. You've seen it. We want to tell some body."

"Walter, I know this is not the best place in the world, but it's better than nothing, and look, ya' can play in the band, yur' in charge of the kitchen. Why are ya' putting all of that at risk?"

"Because I want to live long enough to get out of here. I want all of these boys to survive this place and have normal lives and have families and get jobs. There is so much to see and do outside these walls and I want 'em to see it. I don't want another boy to die in this place. Please help us." My eyes flooded with tears.

Mr. O'Toole stared at me, then he nodded. "Okay," he said, "I'll see what I can do." Then he turned and walked back towards the door to squeeze back out.

Oh God, what had we done? What had Charlie, Paddy, and I got all these poor kids into? Shit.

Darkness set in for the second night. We still had enough coffee to last until the morning, and the fire in the kitchen kept burning. When the bread and coffee run out, then what? I didn't know. I looked out over the room.

It was dark, yet I could see a row of boys seated on the floor, their backs against the wall, rocking back and forth not saying a word, worried that they might never get out of this place, and if they did, worried about what would be waiting for them. Under each table, and in every corner of the room, was a pack of seven or eight boys huddled together, some trying to sleep, others counting up the flies they had caught since they had been in here.

I caught sight of Sean and moved over to where he lay on the floor. I stood over him and stared down at his gentle, small face. He had very soft features, and many of the boys teased him about being pretty. God, he would never survive in here without me. I knelt beside him. He was sound asleep, with his arms crossed and his hands tucked in under his armpits keeping his fingers warm. Like all the others, he was wearing his jacket, shorts, and his well-worn leather boots, one without a lace. His exposed legs were covered with bruises, scabs, and scars, and both woolen socks were pushed down around his bony ankles.

I reached down and pulled his socks up over his wrinkled, dirty knees to warm him. I placed my hand on his cheeks to see how cold he was and to push the sticky, dirty hair out of his eyes. As my hand touched him, he rolled into the cup of my palm as if my warmth was drawing him in. This is not what my parents had hoped for us. My mother's tears must surely have been filling the clouds in heaven as she looked down upon us.

I lay down beside my brother and passed my arm under his head to cradle him and keep him warm. He snuggled right into me. I loved him so much and wanted to keep him safe and get him out of here. All I could do right now was to hold on to him and let him feel the warmth of someone who loved him. I was exhausted; we all were.

We were like the men who had gone to war. We were soldiers fighting for our rights. Throughout the day, Charlie had reminded the boys of this and kept telling them that we had to stick together. I felt the back of another body nuzzle up behind me to stay warm. It was Jim.

"Here, put this over 'im," he said, as he tossed me a small blanket. "And don't wet yur'self," he added. I snickered because I knew what he was thinking. He was remembering how the three of us used to sleep together in our parents' house. I wrapped the blanket over both Sean and me.

"Do ya' think we'll survive this place, Jimmy?" I asked my older brother.

"I don't know, but I guess we've got to try," he answered. It was odd that Jim had come over to us. He hung with another pack of boys, and we rarely saw him. It was good to have the three of us together, battling this war. If my Mum and Dad were looking down, I think they would be a little happier now, I thought, as I closed my eyes and drifted off.

"Wake up, Wattie, wake up," Paddy said, shaking me awake. "There is a man and a woman at the door; they want in."

I rose, rubbed my eyes, and looked towards the guarded door. I saw a man and a woman standing outside the glass both looking down towards the floor. These were faces we had not seen before. I quickly pulled my arm out from under Sean's head. It hit the floor, and he woke rather suddenly and dazed. I rose to my feet and moved to stand next to Charlie and Paddy. My arm was numb and tingling, and I was not quite awake yet.

"Do we let 'em in?" Charlie asked.

"Do we know who they are?" I questioned.

"Nah," replied Paddy. "I think they must be the inspectors or something."

"Okay," Charlie commanded, "Let 'em in."

The man squeezed through first followed by the well-dressed woman, all fancied up in a brown woolen skirt and hat. I could see that she was worried about wrinkling up herself, since she kept pulling on the front of her skirt and holding on to her fancy hat so it wouldn't fall off. Once inside, they stood shoulder to shoulder and asked to see whoever was in charge. Charlie moved forward while Paddy and I stood behind him.

"So, what is the problem in here boys?" the man asked.

"Who are ya'?" questioned Charlie.

"We're school inspectors for the Department. We are here to see that you are being well cared for," the man replied.

"Well, we're not well cared for. We're beaten, we're all starving.' Look at us! We're a pathetic lot, don't ya' think?" asked Charlie.

The man looked out over the crowd of boys and then looked back at Charlie.

"I want you boys to know that we will do everything in our power to make sure the Brothers are treating you in ways that are fair and within the guidelines for the treatment of children that they are supposed to follow."

"What does that mean?" Paddy asked.

"It means if you come out of here in an orderly fashion, we will conduct a full inspection of the school, the kitchen, the conditions, and the treatment of boys here," said the woman. "If there are any wrongdoings we will report them and have the problems corrected," she said. "You can trust us."

Charlie turned to Paddy and me. "What should we do?"

"Ask the rest of the boys," Paddy suggested.

"Good idea," said Charlie. He stood up on the table and quieted the crowd. "These two here are inspectors. They say that if we come out in an orderly way they will have the whole place inspected and change all the crap that is going on in here. What do ya' boys think?" he asked.

Boys talked amongst themselves; they were confused and didn't know what to do. They wanted out but were all scared.

The man then stepped forward and climbed on to the table next to Charlie. "Listen boys, I know you're scared. I know things are not alright in this place. We are going to look into it, but for us to do that you have to come out and let us do out jobs. You can trust us."

Again, boys talked amongst themselves; they still did not know what to do. Neither did Charlie.

"Alright then," called out the man. "Lets have you line up in two rows here," he pointed to the front of the room, "and we will all march out together peacefully," he suggested.

"What if they beat us?" a voice called out from the back.

"I will not let that happen," he said. "You can trust me. If you come out peacefully, I will make sure no one ever hurts you again."

"What about the food? We're starvin' in here everyday; they don't feed us," another voice called out.

"I will look into that, too. I promise," said the man.

Boys were still nervous.

"Listen boys, you won!" said the man "You wanted the inspectors to come in to see if anything was going on, and here we are. You boys have won yur' war."

"He's right," said Paddy. "This is what we asked for."

"Can we really trust ya'?" Charlie asked.

"Yes, you can really trust me," the man replied.

Charlie stared into the man's eyes for a long time. "Alright then," Charlie said as he turned to the crowd, "We have won the war boys. These inspectors here are going to look over the place and make some changes. We have won our battle."

The boys cheered a little, not too loudly. I sensed a great deal of fear amongst them. I was scared, too, so I knew they all must be. Slowly, boys moved towards the front of the room and started to line up preparing for our exit.

What would happen next, I wondered. Would things change? Would they start feeding us and stop beaten us? God, I hoped so. I felt sick to my stomach. What had we done? Will things be worse, better? Shit, I was confused. We slid the tables away from the door. Paddy pulled the door open and ran back to fall in line. Now, what?

"Okay boys, lets go," the man said.

Slowly, the two lines of boys, with their heads hung down started to move out. Brothers Eugene and Gabe were outside of the door directing us. Blackie was nowhere in sight. Maybe they canned the fat bastard, I hoped.

"Straight up to yur' rooms now boys. Clean up for yur' supper." Both Brothers were smiling. They were very pleasant and soft-spoken. Maybe things will be different. Time will tell.

That same night, following our strike, all of us were nervous and scared. We had gone up to our rooms and just waited. The inspectors had wandered about, talked to a few kids, and looked about. We were finally called down to dinner later in the day. Holy Mother Mary of God were we stunned.

A great meal was prepared for the boys. We had a stew with lots of meat, potatoes, turnips, carrots, and a yummy broth. We had bread—good bread with butter—not the crappy stuff we usually had, and oh God, it was good. Milk was even put on the tables for our coffee. Some of the boys were drinking the cream straight from the container. I did not have to cook that night; none of the other boys had to help or clean up. The Brothers got together in the kitchen and did the cooking and clean up. Well, we really did win this. It was great.

Following our dinner, we were allowed out into the yard, and there were seven or eight soccer balls out there, which was fantastic. The man inspector even came out into the yard and kicked the ball around with us. When we were called up to go to bed, each of us had a nice clean bed shirt to wear. Brother Eugene came to me just before bed to advise that I did not have to rise to light the boilers, that it would be done for me and that breakfast would be prepared, so I could sleep in. This was more than we had hoped for. We really had won, or so we thought.

I got up in the morning with all the other boys and readied myself to start the day. Following Mass, we went to breakfast and again were surprised. We were each given a boiled egg—my God, an egg!—with bread and butter again, and cream with our coffee. The inspectors moved around the room and made small talk with boys, and I could see everyone was happy. All the boys in the place were at ease and feeling proud that we had taken on these bastards.

Following breakfast, I returned to our dorm to gather my things for class. I gazed out the window feeling good and thought about what we had done. As I stared out across the yard, I saw the two inspectors getting into their automobile. They both shook hands with Blackie and then they were off. Did we really win, I wondered?

Nineteen

BLACKIE'S WRATH

When the inspectors were in, I had been told that I could go back to class if I wanted, so this morning I did. As I sat in my writing class, I thought about Polrone, the meadowlarks, the swans floating down the River Suir; how I loved that place. I was drawing a picture of Josie and me on the riverbank. Off in the distance, I drew in the boats, the men fishing, and the houses. I'm a good artist, I thought to myself. Music, art and nature, that's me. That's what I love; that's who I am. Math and stuff, I don't like. I continued to doodle.

"O'Keeffe, McFarland, Blackie wants to see ya'," disturbed my thoughts. I had been so lost in my wonderful daydream that I had not noticed the boy who had come to the door to deliver the note.

"Shit, what does he want?" Charlie mumbled.

Both Charlie and I gathered our things and headed off. "Shit I'm scared, Charlie. What do ya' think he is going to do?" I asked my friend.

"Nothing. He wouldn't do a thing, cause if he does we will strike all over again. We have 'im by 'is fat sweaty balls."

As we entered Blackie's 'office', my stomach began to turn over. I felt sick. Paddy was standing in there with a few of the other boys. We stood for a few minutes before he said anything. Keeping his head down, Blackie rose and started to walk around the room. He moved his large arm behind the door and pulled out a brand new, larger, beating strap.

Oh Shit. He tied it on to his belt, still saying nothing. With his head down he stood right in front of Charlie as he tied it up. He then raised his chin and stood face to face with Charlie.

Whack! Blackie's large arm came up and slammed Charlie so hard across the head that he fell to the ground. He was limp, like a rag doll.

"Oh, my God." I went to kneel beside him to see if he was alive.

Wallop! Blackie struck me with such force that I lost consciousness for a second or two, and then found myself laid out on top of Charlie. The other boys were frozen with fear. Charlie was motionless. I started to shake. Should I lay here and pretend I'm dead or should I get up? I didn't have a choice as Blackie grabbed the back of my neck and pulled me to my feet. He then shoved me up against the wall smashing my shoulder against an iron hook that was attached to the wall. It jabbed right through my flesh. Even though I was in great pain, I did not dare move.

Charlie's feet started to twitch and he slowly started to pull himself up. As he did, Blackie kicked him in the side of his ribs and down he went again. Charlie was curled up with his knees to his stomach and his hand on his head. Shit, he would be better off if he was still passed out.

I could feel blood running down my back from where the hook had punctured my shoulder. Blackie walked past the line of boys giving each one a swift kick or blow to the gut. It was terrible. None of us had the nerve to defend ourselves.

"So ya' think you're in charge of this place do ya'?" Blackie questioned us in an evil tone. None of us said a word. "I asked ya' a question," he screamed out.

"No Brother, we don't," replied Paddy.

Blackie turned and smacked Paddy across the side of the face with the back of his hand. "That's right, you are not in charge. And because ya' think you have it so bad in this place, I have arranged for a few of ya' to be transferred out to another school, Upton School for Boys, a place that will make Greenmount look like heaven on earth. I have sent word ahead that you're all troublemakers and that you should be watched closely.

Oh my God, not Upton. Upton is a nightmare. The stories of that place were more horrific than anything that goes on in here. Nobody spoke. I wanted to ask about Sean, whether he would be coming, but did not want to bring any attention to myself.

"And Doyle," Blackie spat into Paddy's face, "ya' have a nice little sister up in Dublin in one of the schools. We have sent word that she is to be severely punished and told it is because of you. I could see the wetness fill up Paddy's eyes. He did not say a word. None of us did. "The rest of ya' ugly 'paddies'," he continued, "will resume yur' chores until we arrange yur' transfers." Blackie then opened the door and left.

Still, we were silent. We were stunned. Nothing had changed. In fact, things were about to get a whole lot worse.

Twenty

LOSS OF A FRIEND–NOVEMBER 1944

Paddy and the other boys were transferred out right away. They never got to say goodbye, nothing. Why they kept Charlie and me around was a great mystery. I think they wanted to torture us, leave us wondering if this was the day we would be sent out to Upton with the others. It was horrible living like this all these months, not knowing. Everyday I woke up in fear. Charlie and I were both on our best behavior, never questioned anyone, and never caused a problem. We did what we were supposed to for the next few months. Following the strike and the beating in his office, Blackie stayed away from us. Why? Was he afraid of another uprising? Why hadn't they split Charlie and I up? It was all so odd.

"McFarland," The door of our dorm flew open as we were getting ready for lights out and Brother Gabe marched in.

"McFarland, its time to go," announced the Brother.

"Where brother?" Charlie asked.

"You're leaving. Get yur' things."

We were all surprised, Charlie mostly.

"Brother, where am I going?" asked Charlie.

"Shut up, McFarland, and get yur' things," ordered Brother Gabe.

"Am I coming back? Am I going to Upton?" Charlie persisted.

"No! Now get yur' things before I beat the living daylights out of ya'."

Charlie scrambled about picking up the few personal effects he had. The tears pooled in my eyes. My best friend, my very best friend. Oh God, how would I survive this place without him? He had shown me how to survive and had kept a watch over me. He took care of me, took beatings for me. I had loved this boy like a brother for four years. Now, just like that, he was being taken away. We had stopped thinking about the transfer to Upton; nothing had been said or done for months. Now, just like that, when we weren't ready for it, he was being taken away. To where we were not sure.

We stood side-by-side. I could see that he also had tears in his eyes.

"You'll be okay Wattie, and I'll come and see ya'. Remember, me Mum's goin' to have you and Seany over, and we'll eat cake and…" he began to sob. I grabbed hold of my best friend and hugged him for dear life. Here he was, not knowing where he was off to and he was worried about me.

"Charlie, thank you for keeping me alive in this place. I'll come and find ya' when I'm out."

Charlie quickly grabbed his pencil and a piece of paper from the side of his cot and scribbled some numbers and letters on it. "Here is where me Mum lives. When ya' get out, come and find me," he said.

"Come on, ya' two faggots, let go of each other. McFarland, grab yur' things," interrupted Brother Gabe. He grabbed Charlie by the arm and pulled him away from me to hustle him out the door. "The rest of ya' lot stay here. Lights out in five minutes," Brother Gabe called out as they left.

That was it then. He was gone. I think I was in shock. Lots of the boys were. Charlie had been a real leader in Greenmont. Another person I loved, stripped from my life. I wandered over to his empty cot. His few possessions, the picture of his Mum, gone. Nobody would ever take his place. I pulled the blanket from his cot and wrapped it around my shoulders like an old woman's shawl and sat on the edge of his bed. Sean came over and sat next to me. I lifted my arm and wrapped the blanket around the two of us, remembering our good, good friend, Charlie McFarland.

I cried that entire night. I worried about what would happen to him and where he would end up. The next day, not a word was mentioned. I kept my head down, did my chores fearing that I might be next. How would I survive this place without him?

The following night, I looked out over the large, well-polished, wooden window sills of our dorm room and worried about Charlie, where he was, and how he was. I wondered how other people lived beyond this place and how I would live once I left. On this night, most of the other boys were also lined up along the window peering out, silently thinking about the lives they never had and the lives they might have, if they lived long enough to get out. Like me, I'm sure many of them worried and wondered about their families, the sisters and brothers who had been taken away, grandparents who had been left behind, many of them wondering why they were here at all. Tonight, everyone was silent—no whispering, no comic book swapping, no fly catching. We were still mourning the loss of a good friend and leader.

Over the following months, I continued to keep my head down and follow the rules, worried that at any moment I would be moved out, leaving Sean behind. I learnt how to tolerate this place, the intimidation, threats, and insults to our families. It was heart-wrenching to watch small boys being told their mothers were tramps and that they were here because their mothers had traded them in for a man to keep their bed warm. How can a child understand that?

Things had gone back to the way they were before our strike. The Brothers continued to tell us that if it weren't for them, we'd be on the streets starving, begging, and sleeping with the rats. I wondered what the difference was. We were starving, begging for our lives every day, and living with the rats in Greenmount.

The chores got harder and we had to work longer. Every week, every stick of wood in the damn place had to be polished. The stairs were the worst. The smallest kids were given this horrible task. A group of small boys would start at the top of the large staircase and would work their way down. Hunched over for hours, bracing themselves on bent knees, these young boys worked until they got to the bottom row of the staircase. They were not allowed to rise until they had finished. An older boy was always appointed by the Brothers to watch over them and whack their tiny fingers and bums with an ash cane if they stopped polishing for even a second or kick them down if they tried to stand to stretch their backs. I'm sure the reddish-brown stain in the wood got its colour from the blood of the thousands of little fingers that had been whacked while polishing over the years.

No, nothing changed in this place, nothing. Even the faces of new boys arriving had the same pale, thin, scared look. Poor little bastard, I thought, as each new one entered the place. The only thing any boy could look forward to in Greenmont was reaching the age of sixteen and being set free. Lots of boys didn't make it.

By now, I had my routine down good and had become numb to the place. Up early, run the kitchen, wet the bed, get a beating, do other chores including now having to control the rat population, or at least try to. There were more rats in Greenmount than there were boys. Rats were everywhere. Trying to catch them and rid the school of them was useless. Still, everyday I would set the traps in the kitchen. Each trap was about the size of a large man's boot. When I set a trap, I had to bait it. It killed me placing bread in those traps knowing the boys were starving. I'd set out about ten traps a day and by day's end they were always full, sometimes with a couple of rats sitting on top of the trap trying to get in.

They were bold little creatures, use to being 'round the likes of all of us. When a rat crawled into the trap, the door shut, locking the little beast in there. I was supposed to wallop them over the head to kill them, then throw them in the fire. Instead, I'd take them out to the yard where there were always stray dogs hanging around. I don't know where these damn dogs came from; they were just there. I'd take two or three traps out to the yard. When the kids saw me coming, they'd start gathering 'round because they knew there was about to be a slaughter.

I'd set down the traps, open them one at a time, and let the rats run free. The dogs and the boys, would go wild chasing them. Those poor bastard rats never got away. Either a dog caught them and chewed them to bits or the kids would catch them first and stomp them to death. Then the dogs would eat the remains. It was a game between the stray boys and stray dogs—see who could get the rat first and kill it. The boys loved it. I knew it was cruel, but it entertained the rest of the kids so I kept on doing it. Even a few of the Brothers would come out to watch. Greenmount was a sick, sick place.

Twenty one

FALSE HOPES

The only thing that gave me joy in this place was band. Damn, I was good, and kept getting better. I came to believe that this was why they kept me here. O'Toole needed me in the band. I think the school was paid pretty well when we went out to perform, and I played an important part in keeping the band together. Audiences loved me and I loved to entertain. Jim was no longer coming to band, and I had not seen him in weeks. I had also not seen him in the kitchen or in the yard. Although he didn't have much to do with us, I was worried that they had done something with him.

"Brother Eugene," I called out one day as he rushed past the band room before our practise started. "I haven't seen my brother, Jim, about for awhile. Is he sick?" I asked.

The Brother placed his hand on my shoulder. "No, Wattie. He's been let out to a farmer in Kinsale. I'm sorry, Wattie, but I have to run."

I stood there stunned. Jim had been let out? Nobody had told us. He hadn't said goodbye. He hadn't taken us with him? My God, he must really hate me for bringing us to this place. My stomach ached. I loved my brother. We had been through so much together. Even though he stayed away from Sean and me, I know that deep in his heart he had love for us. He was just hurtin' the same way we were. Will this be the way it always is, I asked myself, with people being stripped from our lives without any time to heal wounds, or to say goodbye, no reconciliation? I hated this. My Mum, my Dad, Prowler, Eileen, Bessie, Billy, Trigger, Charlie, and now, Jim. To love anything is the ultimate pain, I thought.

I stood in the middle of the hall as boys rushed by hurrying about to get where they were supposed to be. So, it's just Sean and me now. I have to keep him close; I cannot lose him, too. I love him and fear for him too much. I knew what they did to the boys with no families. Those poor kids were raped and assaulted repeatedly, with no one to stick up for them. I could never leave Sean here on his own. Over the next few weeks, I kept a close watch over my brother and made extra efforts to spend time with him.

He didn't seem to have the same reaction as I did to Jim's leaving. It was just one more loss he had to endure. I remembered the day that he snapped the neck of that little bird. Sean deals with loss differently than me. He was hurting; he just didn't show it, kind of like Jim.

"O'Keeffe, get over here," called out Mr. O'Toole.

The band had been outside practising marches when a tall distinguished looking fellow had arrived to speak with Mr. O'Toole so we were told to take a break. We could tell this man was from the city. He wore a fancy suit and had a very neat mustache that curled up at the sides, like Dr. Shea's at Peadmont. We often saw people coming in to speak with Mr. O'Toole. Mostly, they wanted to book the band for a parade or concert. While they were speaking, Sean and I had run over to a small patch of gooseberries and were picking them quickly in hopes of not being caught. When O'Toole called me over, I thought we were in big trouble.

"O'Keeffe, this is Mr. O'Rourke from the city. He has a big band that plays around the clubs and halls in Ireland. Mr. O'Rourke thinks you're pretty good and wants to know if you're interested in joining up."

I was taken aback and absolutely stunned. "Excuse me, sir?" I replied in a daft, confused, and completely idiotic manner.

Mr. O'Rourke took a long puff of the cigar he was holding. It was one of those really thick cigars, almost as thick as the mouthpiece on my coronet. He tilted his chin back and blew the smoke out the side of his mouth.

"I've heard ya' play when yur' band here, has been out on parade. You're as good as, if not better than, many of the lads I've got in my band. We travel 'round, go over to England now and then. You've got real talent. I think you'd do well with us, that is if yur' interested?" He spoke to me in a tone of voice that no one ever had. Almost like he thought I was someone important or that I was special. He was such a friendly looking fellow with a big belly, I liked him instantly.

"God yes, I'm interested," I said quickly. "Yes, please. I'm very interested.

Can I Mr. O'Toole? Can I go?"

"I don't see why not. You're fourteen now; it's a good opportunity for ya'. I'll talk to Blackie and we'll see what we can do." he answered.

"That'll be grand, then," said Mr. O'Rourke. "I'll call 'round tomorrow evening, and we can make the preparations. Mr. O'Keeffe, it has been very nice to meet you. You are very talented. You could make a lot of money and I hope we can work together." He then extended his arm and offered me his hand. I wiped my hand down the front of my shorts and shook his hand. "Good grip you have, O'Keeffe," he said smiling, as he placed his hat upon his head and turned to leave the field.

I've made it! I've survived this terrible place and we'll finally get to leave... and play in a band! My God, my father really is watching me from heaven, I thought. I'll be just like him. I'll take Sean with me, and we will travel with the band. This was marvelous, too good to be true.

Blackie was away somewhere at the time. Mr. O'Toole wasn't going to be able to talk to him until the following morning so I had to wait, but Mr. O'Toole said it wouldn't be a problem, and I trusted him more than anyone else in this place.

I could not contain the excitement I felt as I ran over to my brother.

"Sean, we're leaving here," I told him excitedly. "That man, he wants me to play in his band. I'm taking ya' with me, and we're leaving this place. He's going to pay me money. Can ya' believe it, money to play in his band? God, we'll find Billy, and Bessie, and Eileen, and Jim, and my God, Sean, I can't believe this!" I hugged my brother with all the strength I had.

Sean let out a huge scream. He was excited beyond description. The two of us danced around the field like silly imps. Making faces at the school, pulling down our trousers, and telling the Brothers to kiss our asses, not directly at them of courses, but in our minds that was what we were doing.

That night, we told everyone we were leaving. The other boys were jealous. For four years we had been here, endured the humiliations, the beatings, and the insults. We had watched others leave, and now it was our turn. Neither of us slept that night. We had each packed up our meager belongings into small bundles, ready to leave the next day.

As usual, I got up, lit the fires, and prepared the kitchen. All the helpers had heard that we were going so there was lots of chatter and laughter going on.

"Wattie, who do ya' think they'll put in charge?" one of the kids asked.

"Not sure, maybe Michael. I really don't know." Michael had been working with me for the last year. He was getting pretty good at running things.

"But don't worry, lads. I'm gonna' come back ta' see yas'," I told them.

In the four years that we had lived in the school, we had never had a visitor, never had a guest. Many of the other boys had family that would come and go and drop off packages. We never saw anyone. I knew some of these younger boys had no one, so I thought how great it would be to come back one day with lots of sweets and have a visit with them all. Yes, this was a great day. I nervously anticipated everything…leaving, playing in the band, being free. It was all unreal.

I saw Mr. O'Toole enter the room and I quickly moved through the crowd to catch up with him. He had his head down and looked rather concerned. I figured he was worried over how he would replace Sean and me in the band. We were both good, so he would have to find some fine replacements.

"Mr. O'Toole," I shouted across the hall.

He looked up at me and sighed. He took a deep breath and stood straight as I approached him.

"Did ya' speak with Blackie? Did ya' ask 'im? Did ya' tell 'im we're going?" I blurted excitedly.

O'Toole placed his hand on my shoulder and guided me out of the room. I could smell pipe smoke on his tweed jacket. It smelt sweet. I thought I might start smoking a pipe when I get out of here. He led me into the hall where it was quiet. His hand still on my shoulder, he stood directly in front of me and looked down at the floor.

"Jees', I'm so nervous," I said, "I've tied my finger right into the front of my apron. I guess I'll have to take the apron with me when we go." He still said nothing, his eyes held tightly to the floor. "Sean and I, we packed up our things," I continued chattering. "We can go anytime. Will the man be coming 'round to fetch us?" Still, he said nothing. I could feel my eyes becoming wet, a ache deep in the pit of my stomach started to rise. "I've told the other boys I'll be coming round to visit with sweets and…"

"Wattie," he cut me off.

"I could still maybe come 'round and play in the band once in a while," I said, my eyes now clouded. I knew, but I didn't want to know. I didn't want to hear it…

In a soft and loving tone, he said, "Blackie won't let ya' go, said he needs ya' here."

I began to shake, my damn finger still tied into my apron. Don't let me cry, God. Sweet Jesus, don't let me cry in front of Mr. O'Toole. But it was unstoppable. With only one free hand I tried to wipe my tears.

"It's okay, lad. I'd be crying, too." Mr. O'Toole pulled me into his chest and hugged me tight. I completely surrendered to his comforting arms and let the weight of my body fall into his chest. It was uncontrollable. I had not lost my emotions, or cried like this, since Charlie left. I remembered this ache; it was the aching that came from a broken soul...the ache I felt when we drove away from Sean and Billy as we drove off to the sanatorium...the ache I felt when that sack was hurled into the Suir with Prowler in it...the ache that filled my heart when I was forced to dump Trigger in the toilet...the same ache that was a constant reminder that I was born to suffer.

None of the other boys taunted Sean and me about not leaving; they all felt bad for us. Even Sean said it was okay, it wasn't my fault. I wasn't quite the same after that. I sort of lost a bit of me. That could have been the one chance in my life to do something great, to do something really big. And it was taken from me because they needed me as a workhorse. Well, if that's what you get for working hard in this place, fuck them.

I decided I would do whatever I had to, to get out of this stupid hell we lived in. I started selling slices of bread off the side of the kitchen. Each time we were off playing in a concert, I would slip away and purchase a comic book or two with my bread money and then rent them out to the other boys for a penny. I started to save up quite a little bit. My only focus now, was to get Sean and I out of this place even if we had to escape, because I knew now they were never going to let us out.

Another new year and my fifteenth birthday had come and gone. We never celebrated birthdays. I knew it was my birthday 'cause on your birthday they always came 'round and measured you up to see how tall you were. Maybe they were measuring us up for our coffins, I didn't know.

On this day, I was out in the yard and had made my way to a part of the wall where the apple trees hung over our field. In the late summer the apples were ripe with fruit, but we were forbidden to pick it. What torture to see these lush red apples hanging over the fence and not allow us to have them. At this time of the year, the trees were not bearing fruit, so there were not a lot of boys hanging around this part of the yard. From where I sat on the ground, I could see through the thorny, thick hedge that made up one side of our field. I could see straight through to the other side. I could get myself through there, I thought. I might get scratched and scraped and bleed a little, but that happens every day in here. I could run out of here, get the Gardai, and come back for Sean. I could really do this. I am going to do this, I decided.

I looked around and no one was paying much attention to me. The rest of the boys were playing soccer. I rose to my feet and started walking towards the hedge. If we got too close, the Brothers usually called out for us to move back. I heard nothing. I got closer; my heart was pounding. I'm really going to do this and I am going to escape. Now I was sweating and started to quicken my pace. I looked behind me and could see that a few boys were looking in my direction. I knew they were saying, "Go, Wattie, go." I started to run now. Jees', I'm actually going to make it to the hedge.

"O'Keeffe, come back from there," a loud voice called out. Now, I ran at full speed. I didn't look back.

"O'Keeffe!"

The whistle was blown and the Brothers' henchmen, those suck ups that did whatever the Brothers told them to, started chasing me. Boys, who I had known for years in this place, boys who wanted out of here as badly as I did, were now trying to catch me, hunt me, and pull me back.

I got to the hedge and started to burrow my way through. I was down on my knees and could feel the tear of my flesh as a thousand thorns cut into my exposed legs, hands, and face. I could feel the blood running down my skin. I didn't care. I was getting out of here. I pushed hard against the thick branches of the hedge, crawling, climbing, rolling, and contorting my body in every which way I could to make it through.

I had burrowed about halfway into the hedge when I felt someone grab my leg. I shook it free, but within seconds, I felt another hand—a large hand—grab my ankle. I tried to kick the hand from me, but it would not release its grip. Shit! I was being pulled back. Now, another hand grabbed my other ankle. I could feel many hands upon me pulling me out, pulling me back to hell.

I was covered in blood; it was streaming into my eyes, and I couldn't see who had a hold of me. They dragged me along the ground through the yard. Boys were screaming and yelling. It was complete chaos. Then, I was grabbed by my hair and pulled to my feet. Although I could not see whose hand it was, I had felt that strong grip on my head many times. It was Blackie.

I was dragged into the main hall where we gathered. The other boys were brought into the room. The noise was incredible. We had not had an escape or attempted escape for years. My trousers were stripped from me and I was dragged to the front of the room. Two large fingers poked into my eyes.

"Ow, that fuckin' hurts," I screamed out.

"I want you to see what's happening to you, you little shit. After everything I have done for ya', to pull this kind of stunt." Blackie scraped the blood from my eyes so that he could look right into my face. "I will teach ya' and every boy in this place a lesson for what ya' have done today." He then pushed my head into the back of the ladder that stood behind me. "Get on that fucking ladder, O'Keeffe," he spat at me.

Bare-assed, covered in blood, with the entire school surrounding me, I climbed the ladder.

Whack! The pain of the ash stick cut deep into my flesh. He kept hitting me and hitting me. I don't even know how times he struck me. I didn't cry. I didn't care and I was not sorry for what I had done. Even as I stood there being beaten, all I could think about was doing it again.

Blackie was a madman attacking my body. I did not try to resist. I did not try to get away. I took it. And that made him even more angry. "Are ya' sorry for what ya' have done?" he called out.

I did not reply.

"Are ya' sorry for what ya' have done?" he yelled out louder.

Still, I did not reply.

He continued to beat me, then screamed again, "Are ya' sorry for what ya' have done?"

"He is sorry! He is sorry!" Sean cried. He was at the front of the room crying uncontrollably. Oh, my God! This was so hard for him to watch.

"Yes, I am sorry for what I have done," I called out. I wasn't sorry and I would try it again, but I could not stand for my brother to see me this way.

Finally, Blackie stopped striking me and turned to the rest of the boys. "Kneel! he commanded.

Every boy in the place fell to his knees and turned his head down towards to the floor.

"We strike the beast because the beast is full of evil thoughts," screamed Blackie. "This boy is evil and he is the beast; you are all the beast. I will dispel all evil thoughts from each of you and purify yur' hearts and yur' souls. In the name of God, I will." Blackie ranted on and preached to the boys about how good he was to us.

I don't remember all of what he said. My eyes were fixed on my brother as he knelt beside me with his head down, shaking, as Blackie screamed to the crowd.

"I'm okay, Sean. I'll get us out of here," I whispered. "I promise I will get us out of here."

Blackie continued on with his rant. "Tonight, each of ya' will go to bed with no supper! Instead, you will kneel by yur' beds and pray for this soul." Blackie pulled back my head by my hair and exposed my bloody face to the crowd of boys. When he let go my chin hit the ladder causing me to bite through my lip. "Pray for his soul and ask God to forgive him, his evil thoughts, deeds, and trespasses," finished Blackie, finally.

I felt bad that the others were punished for what I had done. The Brothers regularly made us all pay for what a boy had done. It was their way of getting us pissed off at each other.

I was suspended from band practise and given the worst of the worst jobs for the next several months. Each job was made easier as my mind drifted off to think about my next escape attempt. After some pleading from Brother Eugene and Mr. O'Toole, I was allowed back into band. I was also put back in charge of the kitchen.

I had learnt how to escape this place by going into my deepest self, to that place that had given me the strength to defeat Nacho, that place where I was able to connect with my spirit and my parents. Each night I would disappear into my deepest self and travel back to Polrone, back to our family home. I would visit Josie and see how beautiful she had become. I'd pick apples in Mrs. Crowley's yard. All the people I loved were there. It was a marvelous adventure. If I wasn't able to escape the physicals walls of this place, I would allow my mind and my spirit to escape. I continued to say my own daily prayers, too, the ones I had created…

"God of all life, Father of the mighty oceans and lakes, rivers and streams,
Mother of the gentle earth, its deserts, mountains, green valleys, and trees,
Please help me make it through this day."

They gave me enormous strength because they were mine.

Twenty two

A SURPRISE VISIT–SUMMER 1945

It was summer and I had fallen back into the monotony of the place. I had expected that they would have transferred me out of here after my escape attempt, or split Sean and I up. That would have been the ultimate punishment. But for whatever reason, they didn't get rid of me. They always sent the boys who caused the most trouble away. But they kept me. They needed me here, in the band and in the kitchen. As long as they need me, I guess they'd keep me and keep me alive.

I was now doing milk runs into the city for the school, always under the watchful eyes of the Brothers of course, and was still saving money from comic book and bread sales, always planning the day I would leave here for good. I had trained Michael to light the fires, but was always back from my milk run in time to supervise him and keep things going in the kitchen.

We were finishing up from morning coffee and preparing to go to our classes when Sean and I were both called out. Shit, we had both been really good. Why were we being called out?

"Ya' have a visitor," Brother Eugene announced.

"What?" Sean and I looked at each other in complete shock.

"Who is it?" I asked.

"I'm not sure. It's a lady who says she was a friend of yur' family in Polrone."

Sean and I were thrilled. Who could be here? Who would come for us after all this time?

We were led into a well-decorated meeting room. We had never been in here before but had heard about it from the others boys. It was a lovely room, with velvet curtains, high back leather chairs, lots of well-polished wood trim, empty glass vases, and well-polished mirrors. Christ, maybe somebody died and they are coming to tell us? Maybe this is bad. There was an older woman standing in the corner of the room. At first, I didn't recognize her. Then I did. It was Mrs. Crowley; how wonderful! But why was she here?

Sean and I both moved quickly towards her. How wonderful to see a familiar and friendly face.

She wrapped her arms around the both of us. "Oh Wattie, Sean, 'tis so nice to see ya' two boys. You've both grown, but you're both so skinny."

How nice it felt to be in familiar arms, to be in kind, gentle arms. Yes it felt good. She smelt wonderful, like soap.

"I've come to bring Nelly up to the nunnery," Mrs. Crowley explained. "She's going to serve our Lord and teach in the Catholic school. We're so proud of her. So I thought I'd come up and see how ya' boys are doing."

Mrs. Crowley looked older than I remembered her. The thick, dark edges under her eyes aged her and made her look tired. Long strands of gray hair had slid out from the brown, woolen cap that was neatly pinned in place on her head. But still, she looked neatly put together and she was a joy to behold. She brought us up to date on the people of the town. Old Aunt Mary, that bitch, was still alive and living in our house with a few of my cousins. I asked about my grandmother, and she told us Grandmother Knox was still alive and often asked if anyone had heard from any of us.

"And yur' sister, Eileen, she came back to Mooncoin, ya' know, though she didn't stay long. I think she's gone to Dublin," Mrs. Crowley told us. Eileen was okay, I loved my sister; she was beautiful, and I was happy to hear that she was alive. She also informed us that one of the Walsh boys had brought home information that Bessie was now living in England, and that Billy had headed to Derbyshire, England. I didn't even know where that was. But at least they were alive. Bessie, Eileen, and Billy had all made it. Just hearing their names and knowing that they were alright made my entire body tingle. That warm, safe feeling that sometimes flowed over and through my body, now wrapped me in this moment. They were alive! Nothing else mattered right then, and for a few seconds, I felt completely relieved of all pain and worry. Bessie, Eileen, and Billy were alive.

"Oh Mother Mary, I almost forgot. I brought ya' boys something. She pulled out a brown paper bag from the black leather purse she had been clutching tightly in front of her belly and handed it to us. I opened it up. It was a bag full of sweets, lemon drops and peppermints. Oh damn, they looked good.

"Oh Jees', thank you, Ma'am. This is wonderful," I said as Sean and I dug in.

"Let's save some of 'em, Sean, for later when we're starving," I suggested.

"I'm starvin' now, Wattie," he answered.

"I know, but you'll get sick eating too much of it. Pace yur'self, boy." Sean continued to gobble them down; I didn't try to stop him. He deserved a binge like this.

"Have ya' seen much of Josie Phelan, Ma'am?" I asked.

"Oh yes, see her all the time. She's still living with her folks. They're saving up to send her away to nursing school in England."

My heart dropped into the pit of my stomach, and the lemon drop in my cheek fell to the back of my throat as my mouth dropped open, making me gag. "England?" I questioned, coughing up the sweet.

"Yes, not for a few years yet; she's still a bit young. Would ya' like me to tell her you were asking about her?"

"Yes, please! Tell her...tell her...that I'll be home one day and 'um.....I don't know what ya' should tell her, maybe that I'm okay and asking about her," I said.

"I'll do that for ya', Wattie. Ya' boys are so thin and gray. Do they treat ya' alright?" she asked.

I thought about how I should respond to that question. Would it make any difference if she knew what a hellhole this was? If I told her about what really went on in here, would she be able to do anything about it? Likely not, and it would surely get back to the Brothers that I had said something. Then Sean and I would get some sort of punishment.

"Yes, Ma'am, they treat us fine," I told her.

"I'm so sorry for ya' boys; I'm sorry for the whole lot of yas'. Yur' mother, God rest her soul, was a beautiful woman and yur' Da', what talent that man had...and the way they loved the lot of you."

I loved this, Mrs. Crowley telling us tales of my Mum and Dad. It was lovely listening to her. Sometimes, while in this place, I wondered if they had ever existed. It was nice to sit and remember them.

"Times up," a voice called out, before too long. It was time for Mrs. Crowley to go.

"Thank you for coming to see us and for bringing the sweets," I said. She wrapped her arms around both Sean and me. Oh, how I missed the love of my mother, the way she hugged me and loved me. This was nice. I loved the scent of Mrs. Crowley. I rested my head on her shoulder as she hugged Sean and me. I was taller than her now, not by much. I would have loved to keep her there for a while longer.

"Time," the voice called out again.

I pulled myself back from her and thanked her again for coming.

"Now Wattie, Sean, when ya' get out come and see me. I will find work for ya' and help ya' get started." She gave each of us a kiss on the cheek and then turned to leave. What a wonderful visit. What a wonderful hug. The only human contact we got in Greenmount was the inhumane kind. The loving embrace of caring arms was overwhelming and moved me to tears.

I had never really thought about where I would go or what I might do if we ever got out of this place. After Mrs. Crowley's visit and her invitation to come and see her when we got out, I had a bit of hope that maybe one day I would actually be able to go back to my home in Polrone. Maybe.

Twenty three

THE HURLING STICK

Hurling was a huge sport in Ireland and a popular sport when we lived in Polrone. The hurling teams from Mooncoin were home to some of the best hurlers in Ireland. When my Dad was alive we'd go watch the men play. He had a couple of hurling sticks and let us mess about with them. It was great fun. Eddie Doyle was one of the greatest hurling champions of all time, and he was from Mooncoin. We got to watch him play, back in about 1936, when he came out of retirement to help the Mooncoin Senior Team win the finals that year. What a great game!

As a boy I had always imagined the day I would have one of them fancy sticks, and a jersey. When I get back to Mooncoin, I thought, I'm gettin' on the team.

The school had started up a hurling team. Only the boys whose families could afford to buy them a stick were allowed to play. I loved to watch, and like some of the other boys, would occasionally find a tree stick and try to play along with them. Damn, I wanted one of those sticks.

I was doing pretty well saving up a penny here and a penny there for my 'Run Away Fund'. I decided that if I wanted one of them sticks, I would have to increase my saving efforts. To assist with my attempt to buy a stick, I went back to selling off my bread slices. This deed, selling bread and other food items, was not allowed in the school, and boys who did so were brutally punished, like we were for everything else. I knew I would have to be careful, but a new hurling stick would be worth the hunger and the risk.

In the Spring, we were taken into Cork and paraded around so the towns-folk could feel sorry for the pack of us and take pity on the charity work done by the Brothers on our behalf. What a laugh! If they only knew what terrible deeds were inflicted upon us by these assholes. The Brothers would also now let the boys who had money go into shops and buy comics and sweets. This year's trip was a few weeks away, and I decided it would be on this trip that I would buy my stick, so I really had to put forth a good effort to save up.

Within a few weeks, I was starving from selling off my food but had a couple of pounds stashed away. I was proud of how much I had saved from selling food and renting out comics.

"Alright lads, I'm buying a stick," I announced to a hoard of boys in my dormitory.

"What ya' mean yur' buying a stick, O'Keeffe, ya' dumb sod. Ya' ain't got two pennies to yur' bastard name," called out Joe Byrne.

"That so? Well, ya' daft paddy, I've got meself more than two pennies and I'm going to buy the best damn hurling stick in all of Ireland," I called back in a cocky sort of voice.

"How the hell are ya' going to do that, O'Keeffe? Ya' gonna' sell yur' little brother here on the streets of Cork to make a couple pounds? He's pretty. Some horny, old bastard will pay ya'." They all laughed and thought they were pretty smart.

"So I don't have two pennies, ya' say?" I announced again probably just a bit too cocky in my tone. "Well then, what's this?" I challenged them as I pulled out my savings and threw it down on the bed.

"Where'd ya' get that, O'Keeffe? Who'd ya' stick one into to get all that?" one of the boys asked.

"I didn't steal nothin'. I saved this up myself."

"Well, if ya' don't share it with us, we'll tell the Brothers you stole it," announced Joe.

I scooped up my savings and tucked it back into my pocket. Why had I opened my big mouth? "I'm not givin' ya' prickheads one penny of this."

"Oh, I think you are," announced Joe, 'cause if ya' don't, we'll all say you've stole' the money from us, or that you've been selling stuff from the kitchen to line yur' own pocket. Now, share it 'round, O'Keeffe, before we call Blackie up here."

"No fuckin' way," I protested.

"Yes fuckin' way," demanded Joe. "Tom, run and get Blackie. He'll love this."

"No, don't!" I shouted. "Okay, I'll share it around ya' fuckin' little bastards."

They all pounced on me an' stole every penny I had, didn't leave me anything. Why had I been so stupid? Why had I bragged about this? Damn, keep yur' mouth shut in the future, I told myself.

The trip to Cork was only a few days away and I had nothing, not even a penny to put towards a hurling stick. I had to figure something out. On the day we went to Cork I had no plan, and like many of the other boys, I had no money. I wanted to kill Joe and his gang for taking my savings; I couldn't let them get the best of me.

When our bus arrived in Cork, we all got off and lined up like always. One Brother in front, one behind, and a couple in between. We were led into a large shop where the Brothers would purchase supplies and other such stuff. They had us come along so the shop owners would feel sorry for us and give the Brothers a good price for whatever they were buying.

Inside the store, I saw them—new, never been used hurling sticks—calling out to me, Wattie, pick me up, feel the fine finish on me. Oh, how grand ya' would look with me in your hands, I heard them call. I had to have one. I had no worldly possessions. All I wanted was a damn hurling stick. Was that too much to ask? I didn't think so. I'm not sure how I did it, but I managed to take one of the new sticks from the shelf and put it down the back of my trousers and under my jacket. Except for Mrs. Crowley's cabbage, I had never stolen anything ever, in my entire life, and now, here I was a thief taking a hurling stick. Damn it, I didn't care. I wanted it so badly. Other boys used their money to buy this and that, lots of comic books, sweets, a few bought sticks, but most of the boys had nothing. It was cruel to bring boys in here.

I was sweating. Once I got back out on to the street, I calmed down and was eager to get back to Greenmount. Imagine being so eager to get back to that hell. That's how scared I was for what I had done. My stick and I made it back safe and sound. Damn, I was relieved. I put the stick under my mattress that night and could hardly wait to get out into the yard the next day. I was so proud of that stick. Joe and his gang were amazed that I had got it. In fact, I think they looked up to me for what I had done.

The next day in the yard, I was ready to go. Two teams of boys were lined up with their sticks, mine, one of the newest on the field. This will be grand, I thought. Oh yes, it was worth it. I was playing defense. My team won the toss and we were off. The ball was flying around the field being shot from boy to boy. Finally, it came towards me, and I ran to meet it. This was great. I'll make my mark here today, like most of the men in Mooncoin and Polrone, I'll be a hurling champion, even if it's only in this place. I pulled back my stick and with all my strength struck the ball hard.

CRACK!

I hit the ball alright, so hard it flew to the other end of the field, so hard that it cracked the entire length of my brand new stick. The stick fell into two pieces right then and there. After all I had gone through to get this stick, the saving and thieving and finally, getting here to the field—I only got to take one shot! Was God telling me something? I think so. I was devastated. So that was it; my hurling days were over.

Twenty four

NO GOOD-BYES

It was well past my fifteenth birthday. More and more I was obsessed with getting out of this shit-hole. When I get out, maybe I'd try and find that band fellow and see if he still wanted to take me on, and I'll bring Sean with me, I thought. Maybe Mrs. Crowley will give me a job. I just knew I needed to get out.

As I delivered milk beyond the walls of the school early in the morning, I enjoyed gazing at the smoke that billowed from chimneys and wondered about the families who lived in these houses. The hills off in the distance reminded me that there was more to life than this terrible place. I had a family out there and one day I'd find them.

I knew I didn't have more than a year left in this place. When I'm sixteen or seventeen, I figured, I'd leave, get a job and then come back for Sean. One more year maybe, if I can survive one more year in this sinister, horrible place, we will be fine.

This morning, I returned from my milk rounds like always and headed straight to the kitchen to oversee the preparation for the morning coffee. When I arrived things were in good order, so I walked back to unload the milk churns from my wagon. Like all days, I passed the gate to the yard that we were not allowed to enter. Behind the gate was a garden growing tomatoes, carrots, lettuce, berries, and an abundance of other tasty gifts from the earth. These delicious fruits and vegetables never found their way to the bellies of the starving boys in the school. This garden was for the Brothers only, and we were not allowed to enter it. Over the years, a few boys had managed to slip in to take a peak. They told the rest of us about the lovely apples and vegetables that were growing in there.

This day, I am not sure why, I decided that I was going in. It was early so no one would be out there. I didn't even hesitate. I unhooked the latch of the gate and walked right in. Once inside, I was amazed at what I saw. It was like my Dad's garden back in Polrone. I recognized almost every plant: tomatoes, carrots, apples, turnips, spuds, rhubarb, all sorts of things. The amount of food inside this yard was beyond belief. While we boys were starved, all this was so nearby.

Off into one corner of the garden, I saw a pile of rotting fruit and vegetables. It pissed me off. Christ, there was enough food in here to feed all of us, and those assholes are letting it all go bad. I pulled all sorts of things from the rotting pile taking whatever I could into my pockets and my mouth...tomatoes, carrots, whatever I could find. Funny thing was, I never thought about taking the fresh, ripe stuff. I came across a low growing creeping plant that I had never seen before. I snipped a piece off and chewed it up. It tasted marvelous, like an apple. I pulled a hold of the vine, ripped it from the ground, and stuffed it into my socks. I stuffed carrots into my cap, tomatoes under my jacket, and other bits in my underpants. I was not quite sure how I would get this back to my room, but I figured I'd worry about that later. My clothes and my gut were busting.

I hurried to the edge of the yard to make my exit. With no one around, I shot off down the path before anyone could catch sight of me. I darted through the halls and up the stairs towards my room. I could feel tomato juice running down my pant leg. On the way up the stairs to my room, I ran straight into Brother Eugene. Shit.

"O'Keeffe, what are ya' up too?"

"Just a bit of diarrhea, Brother," I said, as I darted off.

He never came after me, thank God.

Once inside my room, I unpacked my load and hid everything under my mattress. None of the other boys were there so I didn't have to fear being turned in by one of the fags who reported to the Brothers. I put myself together and headed back down to the kitchen to finish off supervising the breakfast preparations and clean up. I was safe. I had gotten' away with it, and what a feast Sean and I would have later that night.

The kitchen helpers were all done and had gone off to class. I was alone in the kitchen setting the traps when a boy came in to call me out. "Wattie,

Blackie wants to see ya',” and then the boy ran off.

Fuck, someone had seen me in the garden. I hadn't gotten away with it after all. God damn this place. God damn this fuckin' place. I threw down the rat trap I had been setting and kicked it hard and far across the kitchen. I was so pissed off. I untied my apron and flung it to the floor knowing I was heading out for a beating. How could I have been so stupid? God damn me. As I walked towards Blackie's office, I was actually pulling the hair off the top of my head, I was so frustrated and mad at myself.

I took a deep breath just before I entered Blackie's office, then walked in. Blackie was seated with, and chatting to, another fella' I had never seen before. When I entered the room they both stood up.

“O'Keeffe, this is Mr. Jim Reagan. You'll be going to work for 'im now. You'll be living with 'im. We expect you'll be on yur' best behavior.”

I was stunned. “How long will I be gone?” I asked.

“You're leaving here, O'Keeffe. Ya' won't be coming back. Mr. Reagan will be in charge of ya' now. You'll go collect yur' things and be leaving with Mr. Reagan here. Be quick now, Mr. Reagan is a busy man.”

“Ya' mean I'm done? I'm leaving here and I'm not coming back?” I questioned.

“That's right. Now go collect yur' things.”

“But what about Sean? Can he come along too?”

“No,” snapped Blackie, “now go collect yur' things.”

Oh, my God. Oh, my fucking God. I was going to pass out. This day that I had waited for all these years had arrived, so quickly, so unexpectedly, I wasn't ready. I started to sweat, it was hard to breath, my head felt funny, and I was getting dizzy.

“What's the matter with ya', boy? Mr. Reagan asked.”

“I'm not sure. I'm just a little surprised, I guess.”

“Go get yur' things now like the Brother asked ya', and we'll be off,” said Mr. Reagan.

I took a few deep breaths and calmed myself. I slowly headed back to my room to collect the few possessions I had. On my way up to the dorm I started to panic. I had to find Sean. I had to say goodbye to him. I had to let him know that I would be coming back for him. I turned back down the stairs and headed towards the classrooms so I could find him. When I reached the bottom of the stairs, Blackie and Mr. Reagan were there.

"What are ya' doing, O'Keeffe? Go get yur' things."

"I'd just like to say goodbye to my brother and let 'im know I'll be back for 'im."

"There's no time for that. Now go get yur' things at once."

I headed back up to our room, confused, and filled with a mix of emotions. I was overjoyed and terrified at the same time. What would happen to Sean in here on his own? Would I be able to come back to see him? Was I getting paid for work? What would I be doing? Where would I live? So many questions, so many emotions, I had to think quick.

As I got to my cot, I remembered the food I had stashed under my mattress. I quickly loaded up the items and took them over to Sean's bed. Shit, what if one of the Brothers finds this stuff and thinks Sean stole it? Crap. I ran back to my cot and just left the items out hoping that Sean, or whomever, would find them and eat them up before the Brothers did. I grabbed my measly possessions, a couple of comic books, a pencil and notepad, and my cap. That was it. After almost six years, that was all I had.

As I left the room, I took one look back and my eyes filled with tears, not because I was sad to leave this place. I was sad for all the things that had happened here. The boys who had been beaten and abused, the boys who were famished, the boys who disappeared. I was leaving this horrible place, but others would come behind me. Others would be sent here to endure years of fear and suffering like I, and hundreds of other boys, had. God so many tears had fallen on these floors, and no doubt more would fall in the years ahead. I was not sad to leave; I was terrified for those who had to stay. I turned and left the room.

Is this what Jim went through when he left? Was it this quick? Is this why he didn't say goodbye to us? It must have been. As I reached the bottom of the stairs, I could see Mr. Reagan was paying Blackie a sum of money.

"It'll go towards the boys," Blackie said.

Bullshit, I thought. Mr. Reagan's donation will end up right in yur' fat stomach you fuckin' pig. Blackie extended his hand, which shocked the hell out of me.

"Good luck, O'Keeffe. We've turned ya' into a man in this place. Now go out there and act like one. Mr. Reagan here will be paying ya' seven and six a week to be working for 'im, so ya' do a good job now."

Seven and six! Christ, that's a lot of money. My God, I'll be able to save up in no time and come back for Sean.

"Please, I would really like to say goodbye to Sean, Brother," I asked once more.

Blackie placed his arm on my shoulder and pushed me towards the door.

"There's no time. Mr. Reagan has to get back to Crosshaven. Now, off with ya'."

Crosshaven, I'm off to Crosshaven. I've never been there. Jesus, I was nervous. Blackie hustled us out the door. I stopped on the stairs for just a moment remembering the day Jim, Sean, and I had arrived at Greenmount. What would it have been like if we had stayed in Polrone? Would it have been worse than this? I'll never know. I turned and ran to catch up with Mr. Reagan. I walked slightly just behind him not sure where my life would go from here.

Kilkenny Co.

Register of Industrial Schools of Ireland

Register No. 2794   Height 4' 3"

Name Walter O'Keeffe ... Born 18th Nov 30 Figure Stout

Age 9½ yrs   Complexion Dark

Date of Admission 22nd Oct '40   Hair Dark

Where, when and by whom ordered to be detained

Wat. 19th Oct '40
Mr. McCabe   Eyes Brown

With what charged Wandering   Nose Regular

Under what Section of Act 58   Marks on person and other
                                           peculiarities None

Sentence of Detention 18th November '46   General Health Good

Previous Character Good

State if "illegitimate" No

Parentage   ### Educational State

Names of Parents, or...   Reads Yes

Step-parents Both parents dead   Writes Yes

Address   Calculates Yes

                                           Previous Instruction,
                                           and for how long
                                           Stand T

Occupation

                                           Mental Capacity Good

Character

Circumstances and other Particulars   Particulars as to
                                           Leaving the School,
                                           by Licence or
                                           Discharge Licensed
Religious Persuasion   8.6.46 to
                                           Mrs. O'Regan
                                           Fountainstown.
                                           Crosshaven, Farming
                                           Wages 7/6 per wk, with
                                           board & lodging

Date	Report on Conduct and Character in School
Dec '40	A very good child
Dec '41	Continues a good boy
Dec '42	A very good boy
Dec '43	" " " "

Twenty five

THE REAGAN FARM–AUGUST 1946

We drove in the Reagan automobile for quite some time before he spoke to me. "Well, I've paid a good price for ya' boy. I hope ya' were worth it. You'll be expected to help us run the two farms, care for the animals, and other such duties. Me Mum's getting on in age so she can't do a great deal anymore."

Beyond that, Mr. Reagan never said much else to me the entire trip, nor did I 'utter a word. I sat nervously rubbing my hands together between my knees, and shaking my legs up and down with my meager bag of possessions tucked under my arm. From what he told me, my chores didn't sound too bad, and, Blackie said I would get paid.

As we drove on, I gazed out over the quilts of green farmland lined with rock walls and dotted with sheep. It was beautiful. It felt good to be out of that school. What a wonderful site. I had missed the countryside. My Dad used to tell us stories about the little people, the leprechauns that lived hidden in the fields and hills of Ireland. We were captivated as he told us how they roamed freely from field to field hiding their gold under stone-walls and beneath tree trunks. Sean and I had spent hours searching for that damn gold and chasing the wee folk. How I loved those stories. I would often tell the same tales to the younger boys at Greenmount to give them hope and to give them something to take their minds off the hunger and misery of that place.

I worried about Sean now, and how he would react once he knew I was gone. I hope he had found the food on my bed and had eaten it all. Damn, he'll be wondering why I left him. Shit, why wouldn't Blackie let me say goodbye? That asshole tortured me from the moment I stepped through those doors right until the moment I left, and he's still torturing me now, even though I'm out from under his guard. I sat anxiously chewing at the sides of my fingers, ripping the skin from around my fingernails. I hadn't even noticed I was doing this until I tasted my blood against my lips. Poor Sean. I'll go back for him; I will!

We pulled up in front of a stone cottage that reminded me of my grandmother's home in Tobernabrone. Except this home was not as neatly kept. The house was set close to the road and was similar to many of the homes in Polrone and Mooncoin. The yard was in need of tending. The stone structure looked like it was growing out from the ivy, blackberry bushes, and other shrubs that surrounded it. Nothing was cut back, and almost the entire cottage was covered in a mess of greenery and thorns.

Through the mass of growth that bordered the place, I could see a short wooden door, a thatched roof, chimney, and windows with wooden shutters. This was the standard design of most Irish homes in the country. Mr. Reagan turned into the yard and drove the auto around to the side of the building. Chickens, birds, and butterflies sprung from the tall grass in front of us as we pulled in.

"Come on then," he ordered me to follow him out of the vehicle and on to the house. I was feeling sick in the stomach after the drive and wondered if Sean had been told yet that I had left. As we walked towards the cottage, thoughts were rolling through my head...what would it be like living here? Would I get on with everyone? What would they expect me to do? How would I get paid? The place didn't look too bad but needed some fixin' up, that's for sure.

As we approached the main door, we had to duck under a line full of fresh washing hanging out to dry. I pushed away the linen and the scent of fresh, clean fabric drew me in. That smell, that glorious smell. My Mum used to hang our garments out to dry after she had washed them. Poor Mother. Sean, Jim, Billy, and I would run in and out of the blankets, my Dad's shirts, and the sheets as they blew in the wind, laughing. Now and then, we pulled something off the line. She never got mad. Well, maybe she did, but she did so in such a way that we knew she still loved us, in way that told me she loved watching us play, and that she loved being our mother. This scent also reminded me of how wonderful it was to snuggle up to her when she wore a fresh apron. What a heavenly scent. Oh, this takes me back.

"O'Keeffe, come along."

When Mr. Reagan called out to me, I realized that I had my eyes shut and was hugging a piece of clothing on the line. I opened my eyes to find Mr. Reagan, not surprisingly, looking at me rather oddly.

"I'm sorry sir, the smell, it..."

Rolling his eyes, he cut me off before I could finish my sentence, "Come along O'Keeffe."

I just shut up and scurried up behind him.

The front entrance to the home was an untidy mess of buckets, table scraps, leather shoes, a pee pot, and a mess of other items. Mr. Reagan tossed his boots off before we entered the house and kicked them to the side of the entry. I followed his lead and left my boots at the doorway as well.

Mr. Reagan was a tall man and had to tilt his head to enter the doorway. I followed him in. Once inside, I saw three women and a man in the home gathered around a wooden table finishing up their afternoon meal. They were eatin' fried eggs and bacon. Jees', it smelt good, and I hoped they'd offer me some.

"This is me Mum, these are my two sisters Katy and Maureen, and this here is Frank. You'll work with 'im and share his room up in the loft," Mr. Reagan announced. They all nodded and kept on with their meal.

Mrs. Reagan was an odd looking woman, quite disfigured with a pronounced, hunched back and crooked fingers. She was dressed in black from her tights to the black shawl around her deformed shoulders. She was obviously in mourning. The two Reagan daughters looked like their older brother, very plump with red veins running through their round cheeks. Both had thinning, red hair and tiny little eyes that reminded me of Aunt Mary. Not at all what you might consider attractive women. Frank was older than me, maybe twenty-five or twenty-six. He was a broad man, quite large, with thick, dark hair like mine. He was handsome and obviously fit. Though he was sitting down, I could still tell he was tall, taller than Jim Reagan, anyway.

"You can put yur' things up there," said Jim as he pointed to a wooden ladder that went up to the loft. "Then come down and Frank will show ya' 'round."

This was a small space for six people to be living in, smaller than our house in Polrone. There appeared to be this one room that tightly fit the eating table, the washbasin, one dresser, and a fireplace. There were linens hanging off the ceiling and pots and pans cluttered on a sideboard that was used for meal preparation. There were two bunks built in under the ladder that went up to the loft, and a small alcove that held two other cots.

I crawled up the ladder into the loft and saw two thin straw mattresses set out on the floor and one wooden stool. It was a narrow space and not tall enough to stand up in. I had to crawl on my hands and knees to get over to the cot that I assumed would be mine. There was one small window in the loft, thank God, or I'd be feeling sick up here for sure. I always got that way in confined spaces.

I climbed back down the ladder, careful not to bump into or step on the crockery stacked beside the fireplace at the foot of the ladder, and still hopeful that they might offer me a bite to eat.

"Come on then," Frank announced as he got up from his seat at the table, "I'll show ya' about." Shit, even though I had filled my belly in the Brothers garden, the smell of bacon was making me hungry. Do I say something or not? No, I'll just let it go for now until I get to know these people better.

It was still daylight as Frank walked me about. He didn't say too much, only what he had to. He told me that the Reagans had two farms. They used one, the one we lived in, as the main house. The other house was used to store wheat. Frank explained that it would be one of my chores to set up the rat traps in the wheat house. Well, I knew I was qualified to do that. The two farms were about three miles apart, and each day I would go between the two carrying out a wide range of chores. The Reagans grew and sold beets, cabbage, and potatoes. They also kept sheep and sold off the wool. It would be my job to help tend the farm, harvest the produce, and keep the sheep. I was also being given the chore of milking the cows and delivering the milk to regular paying customers. All in all, these were jobs I knew I could do, things I had done before. So I felt confident that I would do a good job and earn myself a few pounds. I wanted to ask him when I would get paid but thought I would wait a bit on that.

On our walk, we came to a corral that held just one horse. What a lovely looking mare, she was, tan and white. "This here is Ginger," Frank announced. "Not much good for anything; Reagans are trying to sell her. She's a bit wild, this one is."

"She's beautiful," I said.

"Well, you'll want to stay away from her," he warned. "Reagans acquired her as payment for a debt. Used to be a racehorse, but her lungs are bad and she couldn't race no more. We were going to use her for harvest and hauling, but we just can't calm her down. Not sure what they'll do with her."

I moved in closer to the corral and leaned in on the wooden rail. She was lovely, with strong legs, good form, and she held her head high, as if she knew she was something special. When she caught site of us, she started to dance around as if she was dodging bullets, kicking up a mess of dust. She then began to run full speed around the small, gated pen that held her in. I felt sorry for her. She was locked up and likely had not been taken out for months. Ginger was imprisoned like I had been. The more I watched her, the more I fell in love with her. Finally, she slowed down to a trot and then came to a complete stand still at the opposite side of the corral from where I was leaning. I looked over at her as she stood staring at us. I could calm her down, I thought. My Dad had a way with animals; so did I. I'd come back later and calm her down.

"Lets get going then," Frank called out.

I pushed myself away from the wooden corral fence and started to walk away. I turned back to take another look at Ginger and saw her moving over to the spot where I had been watching her. I knew she was asking me to please come back. "Come on now, we're not done here," she was saying. "We can be great friends, so come on and play with me."

"I'll be back, girl. I'll settle ya' down," I called out to her, then I turned and ran to catch up with Frank.

"So ya' talk to the animals do ya'? Ya' sure Jim didn't pick ya' up from the nuthouse and not the orphanage?" Frank asked, and then he started to laugh. I had hoped that Frank and I might be friends, but he didn't seem too interested.

"Do ya' have any family then, Frank?" I asked him.

"Nope," he replied.

"Are ya' from these parts?" I asked trying to make polite conversation.

"Nope," he announced again, this time in a tone that told me he was annoyed and didn't like small talk. So I shut up.

After being shown where the sheds and the barns were and told how to bag beets and where to stack hay, Frank said he had shown me enough for my first day, and we would get at the real chores in the morning. "Ya' best be in before dark," he said. "We'll be up early and you'll come with me on the milk rounds to learn the route." He then headed into the house and left me on my own.

Here I stood, out in the open, free! Free to roam, explore, do, whatever I wanted. What I really wanted was to head into the house and eat some of that bacon. Instead, I headed back to the corral that housed Ginger. I picked a good handful of wet grass and leaned my body up against the fence railing, letting my arms dangle over the rails as I held out the grass. She stared at me. Then she started running around the corral again, all frantic-like. I think she wanted me to know she was in charge. After a long time of just watching her, I dropped the grass into the corral and pushed myself away from the fence. As I walked back towards the house, I turned to see her nibbling on the grass I had dropped. Aye', she'll warm up to me, she will.

It was getting dark, so I started to head to the main house. I wondered now how Sean was feeling. He would just be going to bed about now and was no doubt confused and angry. I wondered how long it would take to earn enough money to go back for him and set us up on our own.

I was tired; it had been a long day. Only Jim was up when I entered the room. The two sisters were in their bunks, Mrs. Reagan was tucked into one of the cots and I guessed Frank was up in the loft.

"Ya' best head to bed now. Frank will be getting ya' up early," Jim said. Then he headed to his cot to ready himself for bed.

I was still hungry and didn't know if I should ask for something to eat or not. There was a loaf of bread and slab of cheese out on the table. What would happen if I took a slice? Well, lets find out, I thought. I picked up a large knife from the table and started to slice off a piece of cheese. I could see Jim looking at me out the corner of his eye.

"Leave enough for the morning," he called out. Well, at least he didn't say put down the knife. So, I cut myself off a chunk of cheese and a thick slice of bread and headed up to the attic. Frank was already asleep. I savored every crumb as I gazed out into the night from our small attic window. There were no lights from the city, only the light of the moon and the scent of manure as it drifted in on the wind. God, I love that smell.

As I had no night clothes I lay down in what I had on and pulled the blanket that had been left out for me over my body. This wasn't so bad. In fact, this could work out well. The smell of fried bacon was still in the house, and I found it pleasant. I could hear the wind blowing through the grass and small animals, likely rabbits and birds, scurrying about. It was good to hear the sounds of nature again. I missed these sounds while I was at Greenmount. My mind then shifted back to my brother, laying in Greenmount, cold and afraid. Who would look out for him there? I had to get some sleep, but my mind raced, as images of him worrying about me clouded my brain. I supposed I would worry about him every day until we were reunited.

My body was on an automatic wake-up from years of rising early at Greenmount, so I was awake and up before the Reagans or Frank. I made my way down the narrow ladder and out the front door. The night air was sweet and quiet, not like in the city. In Cork, the smell of coal was always in the air, and the sounds of buggies, autos, and bikes racing past the school could always be heard. Inside the school, scurrying of mice or rats, creaking of floors, and the cries and coughs of boys were the sounds that filled the halls. There was never silence in that place.

The silence of this morning was calming and I felt free, even though I was under a new guard. The moon cast a beam that allowed me to see my way around the cluttered yard, and I made my way to the water pump. I held the wooden bucket under the pipe and pumped out a good clean bucket of water. I pulled off my shirt and trousers and dumped the entire bucket over my body. Sheesh, that was cold. My body trembled now, as the cold streams of well water cut through the grime that was embedded in my skin. I rubbed my hands under my arms to try and get rid of the dirt and the smell. I splashed water on my face and rubbed my eyes, behind my ears, and under my chin. I was getting lots of hair on my face now, and it itched all the time. I suppose I'd have to learn how to use a razor fairly soon. As the water dripped down to my lips, I could taste how clean and fresh it was. Jesus, that's good! I pumped out another bucket and then sat on the ground and lifted it to my lips. I drank up a good bit of it then, dumped the rest over my heads. Jees' that felt good. As I pulled my shirt back on and was doing up the buttons, the rooster started to call out and I knew the rest of them would be getting up.

I quickly pulled on my trousers and headed back in. Jim was up now and had started a fire in the hearth. Katy was sitting on her bed, pulling off her nightdress just as I walked in. Her bare breasts were fully exposed. I couldn't move; I had never seen breasts; my eyes were stuck on them. I wanted to look away but I couldn't. When she saw that I had seen her, she gave me a look of disgust and pulled back the white cotton drape that provided her cot with privacy. What do I do? What do I say? Oh God. My eyes were still held on the spot where her breasts had been.

"Don't be such an idiot," Jim said as he whacked me across the head. "Close yur' eyes next time, you fuckin' pervert."

"Jimmy, I don't' like that kind of talk," Mrs. Reagan announced to her son.

"Mr. O'Keeffe, you'll take to announcing yur'self before ya' enter the room now, won't ya'?" Mrs. Reagan asked.

"Yes Ma'am, I'm sorry."

"So did ya' like em?" Katy asked, as she came out from behind the curtain, now fully dressed. I said nothing.

"Don't be acting like a stupid slut now, Katy," Jim told his sister in a loud voice.

"Jimmy, I said I don't want that kind of talk in this house."

"Okay, Mother, calm down now."

I pulled out a chair and sat myself at the table. I knew I was completely red with embarrassment. Frank then came down the ladder.

"What we eatin' then?" he asked, and the breast incident was put aside.

"Grab the sausage will ya', Frank?" asked Mrs. Reagan.

Maureen came out from behind her cot and joined the rest of us at the table. They started passing around a milk jug, a loaf of bread, jam, and butter, and Frank was frying up sausage. But I couldn't get my mind off those breasts. I knew I had to act like it had not affected me. My God, she's not even pretty. I leaned into the center of the table and cut myself a slice of cheese and slice of bread. Katy giggled as she passed me the milk jug. I took the jug but never looked at her. Mmm, fresh milk! I poured myself a full cup and drank it down in two gulps. God almighty, it was delicious, sweet, thick, and rich. I poured another cup and then set the jug on the table.

"Eggs?" Frank asked, as he whacked me on the back of the shoulder to get my attention. "Please, yes. Thank you." Someone was making me breakfast!

"After this, ya' fend fur yur'self, hear?" he announced. I was fine with that. Frank cracked at least a dozen eggs into a blackened iron frying pan and started cooking them up over the fire. I poured myself a third cup of milk and drank down every drop. The rest of them were pulling at the bread loaf, eating jam, and sipping coffee. Frank set a huge piece of smoked meat, ham I think, on the table in front of me. Where had this come from? I didn't care, really. I picked it up with my hands and ate every bit, fat and all. I didn't even bother to cut it up.

"What, they never feed ya' in that place?" asked Maureen. I must have been eating fast and furious because they were all staring at me.

"Sorry," I replied as I slowed down my chewing pace. "This country air must have got to my appetite."

Frank tossed a few runny eggs on a tin plate and set them out in front of me. He then took his place and set down his plate. I watched as he and Jim covered their eggs and meat, and almost their entire plates, with salt. They each took a large slice of bread and dipped it into their eggs. I followed along and did the same. Christ, this was good. I'd never had dippy eggs like these. It felt a bit odd eating like this, with others, and with food within my reach. Odd as it was, I knew I'd get used to it.

Twenty six

SETTLING IN AT THE REAGAN'S

That morning, and for the next week, Frank moved me about from one chore to another. I picked up every task easily. I milked the cows and had the milk route memorized. I packed and sold butter and vegetables and set the rat traps. I knew what had to be done to tend the sheep and the large gardens.

Before long, Frank left my side and I was on my own most of the time. I was now starting and ended each day the same. Before the others woke and before I went to bed, I'd go spend time at the corral observing Ginger. I'd always bring her a treat, a carrot or fresh grass, and stand at the edge of the corral and talk to her. I talked about Josie, Sean, Polrone—anything—to get her comfortable with my presence and the sound of my voice.

After a few weeks, Ginger would run over to the fence to meet me when she saw me coming. Eventually, I was able to get into the pen with her. I'd sit on the ground and stroke her legs, or stand beside her and rub her back. I'd even sing her old Irish tunes. We were becoming great friends. After a few more weeks, I brought in a harness. I just played with it and rubbed it up against her nose. I did this for three days. On the fourth day, I gently slid it on her and led her around the pen, only for a few minutes, then, I took it off. The next day, I did the same thing except for a few minutes longer. Finally, I was able to lead her out of the pen and into the yard. Eventually, I got that horse hooked up and hauling the milk wagon.

Ginger came along on all my deliveries. She knew each house and would stop automatically. Just like the horses that pulled the funeral wagon in Mooncoin, she knew just where to halt. Over time, I was able to ride Ginger with no bridle or saddle. She became my companion, my friend, and my confidant. The love I had for this creature must have been similar to the love my Dad felt when he worked alongside of our Mule, Giny—a companion you could count on, a friend that never lets you down. She listened to my woes and let me talk to her about my dreams. This sweet, gentle, beauty gave me back some of the affection that had been stripped from my life.

Although I was free to move about, I was still held captive by worry and anxiousness. I was a nervous wreck, concerned that at any time I might get sent to another farm. I was obsessed with the idea that I was being watched, and if I didn't do a perfect job for the Reagans, they'd send me back to Greenmount. My mind was a mess of confusing thoughts and images. If I saw a priest or the Gardai I'd start to sweat and put my head down; I was afraid to be seen.

I craved the feeling of absolute freedom, but it never came. I was lonely and longed for my friends at the school, and my family. When I went to sleep at night, my mind raced. Some nights, I'd wake up confused, thinking I had to go down and get the boilers running. Other nights, I'd wake up soaking wet, not from peeing the bed, but from the sweat caused by the constant nightmares I had of Blackie beating me. Images of Sean being whacked and abused wouldn't leave me. I had to forget, I just had to forget. It was too painful reliving those days and the abuse, over and over again.

As part of my route, the Reagans had me collect the money owed to them from the milk customers. As well, they had me sell and collect for vegetables and butter. What a feeling it was to have money in my pocket. The urge to steal it and run off and get Sean was always there, but I never gave in and I never took a penny.

Along my route, I noticed beautiful thick-stemmed mushrooms growing in the fields and in the ditch. I'd often pick a bunch, bring them back to the house, and fry them up.

"What ya' got there, Wattie?" asked Mrs. McDougall, one of my milk customers. She was pointing to a plateful of mushrooms I had on the back of my cart.

"Just mushrooms, I've been picking 'em along the way," I answered.

"Well, they look lovely. I'll give ya' two and a sixpence for a plate of 'em," she offered readily.

"Jesus, that'll be alright," I said, and sold them to her. From that day on,

I continued to pick mushrooms and sell them off the side of my cart. This money I kept in my own pocket. I also collected some odd bits of wood and wire from the farm and made up a set of snares. These I used for catching and then selling rabbits. God, I hated killing those poor creatures. They'd scream when they were caught, ear piercing, high pitched screams like I had never heard. Poor things. I'd whack them with a karate chop on the back of the neck and they'd die instantly. I sold them for two and sixpence as well.

I often heard Mrs. Reagan squabble with Frank over how much money I had been giving her from the rounds, which was significantly more than he turned in. Like me, I'm sure he was tempted to take a little for himself or use the Reagan milk and produce to trade off for other goods and services for himself.

I found this to be true when, on a lovely spring day, I went to the home of Martha, a God-ugly, old woman, wearing colours all over her face, who stank to high heaven, and was almost always half naked. She had me fill her liter milk jug, as well as fill the twelve dishes for her cats. Martha, with her rotten teeth and horrible body odor, moved towards me, pressed her body up against mine, and started fiddling with the buttons on my shirt.

"Listen Wattie, Frank and I had an agreement. He'd give me the milk, and I'd give him something for his trouble." With those words she grabbed me between my legs sending me jumping back at least four or five feet. Holy Christ, Holy Christ, what the fuck was that? I could tell from the look on her face that she was disappointed. I wasn't sure what the agreement was with Frank, but I wasn't about to ask and I hurried off.

In the Reagan house that night, I told them what Martha had done and that I thought she was a bit odd. Frank looked up from his plate and just stared at me.

"Frank, what did she mean that she got milk for female favors?" I asked. I really didn't know. We had learnt nothing about men and women at the school so I was confused.

Frank was pissed off. He stood from the table and came towards me with his fist. What had I done? I jumped to my feet and stopped Frank's fist before it hit my face. Without saying a word, Frank stormed up the ladder, bundled his things, came down, and left.

Jim jumped from the table and ran out after him yelling, "Ya' lying piece of pathetic shit. I knew you were a thief. Get off my God damn property, before I cut yur' dick off."

Although I didn't think kindly of Frank, I hadn't meant to upset him this much but was actually relieved that he was gone. We never saw him again.

I took over all the chores that had been Frank's and also kept doing the tasks assigned to me. The busier I kept myself, the less time there was to let the memories of my past haunt me. If I was occupied, I didn't think about what had happened to me and couldn't worry about what was likely still happening to Sean.

Three or four times a week I was waking up confused, thinking I was still at Greenmont and afraid that I had wet the bed. There were days that I was so pre-occupied thinking about what had happened at Greenmont, that I could actually feel the pain in my ass from Blackie whacking me with his Ash Stick. I prayed that one day these nightmares would end. They didn't.

I could handle every chore they gave me. The only thing I absolutely hated was dumping the rat traps. These rats were worse than the ones at Greenmount. They were wild and savage, not tame and calm like the rodents at the school. I'd set out about six to eight traps every morning. When I returned later in the day, I'd witness the same gruesome site. Rats running around with the traps hanging off their legs. Some chewing off their feet to get away and others eating on the ones who were caught. Jees' it was a horrible site. Poor things. I'd whack them with an ash stick to put them out of their misery. I'd then just pile them up out the back of the barn, and they'd get eaten by their own, stray dogs, or other predators. Other than that, the rest of the chores I did were manageable. Sometimes, there were even benefits.

It was late fall when Ginger and I were coming along the beach, just finishing up our rounds. Over the bank, I could see that a large ship had run aground. The accident must have happened during the night, as there was no one about. I jumped down into the ditch and headed towards the ocean's edge. My trusted companion stayed right at the side of the road where I had left her. On the shore, I saw several large, wooden crates floating in the water bobbing up and down, and some kicking into the sand each time a wave pushed them forward. I grabbed a rock and a large stick, and pried the lid off one of them. Apples! They were crates of apples. My God, what a gift.

I whistled to Ginger and she carefully came down to me with our wagon behind her. Quickly, I moved around picking up as many apples as I could and loaded them on to the wagon. I didn't want to stay around too long, in case someone came by and told me to surrender them all. Once I had as many as I could pack into the back of the wagon, I carefully led Ginger back to the road, and we took off. For the next few days, I took the apples along with me on my route and sold them, pocketing a good amount of money for the day I left Crosshaven and headed back to Mooncoin and Polrone.

Twenty seven

NO ONE TO LOVE

My time with the Reagans can only be described as odd. It was the first week of September, I had been here 13 months, and was coming in from the day's chores. When I entered the house, my eyes were cast upon ten to twelve wailing women in black dresses, holding rosary beads and saying prayers.

"What's goin' on?" I asked Maureen.

"They've seen and heard the Banshee. Sure as Jesus rose from the dead, the Banshee is here to call someone home."

"What ya' mean, they've all heard the banshee, all of 'em?"

"Aye, that's what they say. She's out there now, calling 'em out from behind the barn, foretelling a death soon to be had right here."

For Christ sake, this was crazy. I turned and headed back out towards the barn. They all stopped wailing and ran to the door to see what I was going to do. I did hear something coming from behind the barn but I knew it was not the banshee. I grabbed a rake, just in case I had to whack something over the head, and moved through the tall grass behind the old stone structure.

"Billy, what ya' doing out here?" It was Billy Bryan, a simple fellow who lived down the road. He was completely naked and running about. Poor bastard, he was often seen doing this, running naked in the moonlight yelling and screaming. I pulled him by the arm and dragged him out.

"Here's yur' Banshee, ladies. Not to worry, now. Mrs. Bryan, ya' can take Billy home."

Mrs. Bryan came running from the house and wrapped her son in her black shawl, then sheepishly left the yard. Yes, they and their neighbors were a crazy lot.

Only a few weeks later, in October, the ground on the Reagan property was covered with a blanket of snow. This was unusual, it never snowed this early. Before the snow came, I had warned Jim that we had to get all the sheep indoors as I could smell the snow coming.

"No, I don't want to start feeding 'em hay while there's still grass on the ground. Let 'em eat that until the snow fly's" he said.

Well, the snow flew, and it flew hard. When it did come, it was late in the night, after we had gone to bed. I heard the wind blowing and could feel the chill as it worked its way into every corner of the house. It was impossible to stay warm. I was burrowed down under my blanket in the attic when I heard Jim calling out.

"Christ, Walter. We've got to get 'em sheep indoors. You've got to go out and bring 'em in." The temperature was well below freezing, I had no gloves, no proper boots, or jacket, for this kind of weather, and he wanted me going out in this storm. And I did.

Those poor sheep were trapped everywhere, many of them turned upside down or on their sides unable to get up. For hours, I hauled those animals into the barn, one at a time. My hands were burning, and the sting of the cold on my feet was unbearable, I had to go back into the house to warm up. When I pushed open the door to the house, I looked down and saw that my fingers were purple and blue and could feel that my nostrils had frozen together. The cold felt like it was cutting my arms and legs and my exposed ears were burning, it was excruciating.

"Did ya' get 'em all in then?" Jim demanded.

"No, there's still a couple. I need to warm up first. I can't move."

"You will move, and ya' will go bring those last few sheep in. Do ya' have any idea how much money I will loose on wool if ya' don't get those sheep in that barn?"

"But Jim…" He raised his arm and whacked me upside the head. "You'll go now," he ordered.

I did as he asked and made my way back out into the cold even though it almost killed me. I did get those last two sheep in, but I knew then that I meant nothing to these people. I was just a slave, exactly like I had been at Greenmount. They placed no value on me, or the work I did for them. Jim worried about the few pounds he might loose on the sale of wool, but not that his hardest worker might die out there. I knew then that I had to find a way to make extra money so I could get out of there. I feared Jim like I feared Blackie and wasn't sure how I would ever get away from him.

It was now late fall, and the air was moist and heavy. The snow fall that had come a few weeks before had melted, and the smell of fallen leaves burning was on the breeze. Fall was a time of death and a time for nature to rest. It was also the time for harvest and fall fairs. Jim had told me we would be heading to the Crosshaven Fair to present our beets, cabbage, and sheep, and I was looking forward to going.

On the day of the fair, we rose early to load and ready our wagon. I had hoped Jim would send me on my own, so I could snare a few rabbits and harvest some mushrooms to sell off at the fair. I didn't want him knowing I was collecting extra earnings, so for today the rabbits would run free. Maybe on this trip, I'd ask him about the earnings that were owed to me. I'll see how the day goes and decide if I should.

Even though the Reagans owned an automobile, it was only ever used for long trips and spent most of the time covered up in the yard. Today, we would be taking the wagon. When we left the farm that morning, we were the only ones out on the road, but as we got closer to the Crosshaven Fairgrounds, we slowly became part of a caravan of farmers and families heading in the same direction. Friendship was in the air as old friends waved at each other and children jumped down from their wagons to run alongside the ditches with their cousins. I remember that excitement of going to the fair with my Dad— the people, the food, the sense of connectedness to others. Now, after years of living in that awful school, I was afraid of crowds and groups of people. I wished I wasn't, but, I still kept my head down in an attempt not to be seen.

"Willy how's yur' cabbage this year?" an older gent' with a pipe hanging off his lip called out. "Sweetest crop I've ever brung in Mick. It's gonna' fetch a ribbon sure as the angels sing in heaven," the other fellow called back.

As we drew closer, I caught sight of several tinker caravans. As a child, Sean and I were terrified of the gypsies, as we called them. Now, I found them colorful, interesting, and creative, always displaying an interesting selection of tins, iron-work, baskets, and other items. I loved their caravans painted in reds and yellows with beautiful shapes like stars and moons. These people were free, living free. These people, who I once feared, I now envied.

We set up our spot and organized our goods. Jim was chatting with a group of men so I called out and said, "I'm goin' to have a look around then, Jim."

"Yeah, okay. Don't be too long," he replied.

I tipped my cap forward and tucked my hands in the pockets of my trousers. As I strolled through the crowd, my eyes panned over the colourful collection of people, wagons, and goods for sale. In particular, I was drawn to the young couples that were together, young men and woman holding hands, or wrapped in each others arms.

I wish I had someone to hold and to love. I couldn't imagine how love would ever happen for me. Other than what I'd had with Josie, I had never been close to any other girl except my sisters and the Reagan girls, but they did nothing to stir any emotional or physical reaction in me. I wanted to be loved, to be held, to feel that beautiful warm feeling that had flowed over my entire body the time Josie had kissed me. I was older now, and my body had changed. I thought about girls a lot and thought about Josie differently now, too. I imagined what it might be like to touch her and kiss her and hold her against me. I didn't know how I would meet a girl or talk to one. We had been so isolated in the school and had very little contact with the outside world. I wouldn't know how to act or talk. If I didn't find love with Josie, I didn't think I would ever find it, I wouldn't know how or where.

"What ya' staring at, Mick?" some guy yelled out at me. I must have been staring right at him and his red-haired girlfriend for too long. I quickly looked away and picked up my pace to move into the crowd. I came upon an area where all the games of chance were set up, and a fella' was calling out.

"Three balls for a halfpenny. Come on, Mick, give it a try," he was calling out to me, so I timidly moved in closer to him.

"Give it a try, will ya' then?" he asked. It didn't look so hard. I placed down a halfpenny and took the balls from the fella'. I remembered how I had aimed my musical notes at the Presentation Brothers when we played in the band and thought I would try the same approach here. I pictured Blackie's ugly face on every one of those bottles. I tossed the first ball, and wham! I hit all but one jug. I tossed the second ball and smashed the one remaining bottle.

"Holy shit Mick, where'd ya' learn to throw like that? You've still got one ball left. If ya' can knock down all the bottles set up in the next station, you'll earn this set of dishes here. No one's ever done this before," he said.

I moved over to the next station where there was a fresh grouping of bottles piled up. Again, Blackie's face was on every one of them. I closed my eyes, took in a deep breath, and then wham! I tossed that ball so fuckin' hard my arm almost left the socket, and yes, I knocked every bottled own.

"Holy Christ, Holy Christ, this guy's amazing!" the fella' called out. "Try it again, try it again," he encouraged me.

"No I've got to get back," I replied.

"Well alright then, here ya' go...much luck with yur' baseball career," he chuckled as he passed me the box of china plates I had just won.

My God, how the hell had I done that? I hurried back to our wagon and saw a group huddled around our beets and cabbage.

"Where the fuck ya' been," Jim slapped me across the side of the head as I came rushing up to the wagon.

"I'm sorry, Jim. I won these here china plates; we can bring 'em home to yur' Mum."

"Ya' stupid Paddy, ya' take off like that again, and I'll beat the living day-lights out of ya'."

I tucked the dishes into the wagon and started to help him sell our items. I felt proud of myself and wished I had someone to share my victory with. I also wished I had a family or girl to give these lovely plates too. I hated that they would end up in the Reagan's cupboard.

Twenty eight

GOING TO SEE SEAN

I had now saved quite a few pounds selling rabbits, apples, and mushrooms, but still had not been paid by the Reagans for the year and a half that I had been working for them. Nor had I been given any time off. Christmas had come and gone twice. If they were going to pay me, I thought it might be then. But they hadn't.

I was thinking about Sean all of the time and had saved enough to take a trip up to see him, so, thought it was time to let Jim know that I was planning a visit. I also thought I should ask about my pay.

"Jim, in a couple of weeks I'll be going up to Cork to see my brother and I'll be taking the day off," I informed him as we readied ourselves to go out and feed the sheep one morning.

"Yeah sure, come on now, we've got lots to do today."

"So yur' okay with it then, two Saturdays from today I'll make my arrangements to go up?"

"Yeah, yeah, come on, let's get going."

That wasn't so hard, except I had not been able to ask for my pay. I'd try and do that next week maybe.

As I was always busy at the Reagans, the two weeks before I left to see Sean flew past in no time. I was eager to get going and so on the day I was heading to Cork I was up earlier than usual. I wanted to get the first train into the city so I could spend a good part of the day with Sean, and still have plenty of time to get back before nightfall.

I slid on my cap and tucked my shirt into my trousers. I pulled the bag of coins and paper money I had been saving from its hiding place inside my mattress and placed the bag in the inside pocket of my jacket. I had saved up exactly twelve pounds. I still hadn't the nerve to ask the Reagans for my pay. Before I headed down the ladder, I checked again to make sure the money was still safe in its place. My heart was pounding in my chest and I was fidgety with excitement.

It had been well over a year since I had seen my brother. Maybe he was still mad at me for leaving him there. Maybe he would not want to see me. No, not Sean, he'd happy to see me. Once more I looked around the loft to see if there was anything else I needed to take. I placed my hand over my jacket pocket once more to make sure the bag of money was safely tucked away. It was. I backed down the ladder and as I jumped to the floor below, bumped a pail of cuttings as I hit the floor.

"What the hell are ya' doing rattling around so early fur'?" Jim moaned from his cot.

"Sorry fur waking ya' Jim, I'm going to Cork today to see my brother Sean. I have to get an early start so I can make it back before nightfall."

"Yur' brother?" he questioned, "Yur' not going off to Cork today. I've got ya' loaned out to the O'Donnell farm."

"Well, I won't be able to help 'em today. I'll do it tomorrow if that's okay."

"Its not fuckin' okay. You're not going Cork." He was now up from his cot and standing over me.

"Jim I asked ya' about this two weeks ago, remember? You said it was alright.

"Why would I remember anything a dumb fuck like you says?" His large arm came down and whacked me across the face knocking me to the floor. My face instantly started to burn on the spot where he had struck me.

"I said yur' not going. If ya' don't help out the O'Donnells I won't be able to get 'em to help us. Now get back up 'em stairs and ready yur'self to get over there."

"Alright then," I said and hurried up the ladder. I knelt on my straw mattress only for a moment to collect my thoughts. Taking in a deep breath I quickly started to gather my things. I stuffed my comb and the brown piece of paper with Charlie's Mum's address on it into my pocket. I grabbed the one other shirt I owned and shoved it down my trousers, my extra socks went into my pocket and I pulled my dirty work trousers over top of what I was wearing. I bundled a small stack of drawing I had done and some poems and tucked them under my coat. That was it. This was all I had. Taking in another deep breath, I headed back down the ladder.

"Ya' tell the O'Donnells I'll be along later."

"You'll have to tell 'em yur'self, Jim."

"What the fuck are ya' talking about?"

"I said I'm going to see my brother." And I headed out the door.

"Don't ya' dare. If ya' do, don't you ever come back here."

"Not to worry, Jim. I wasn't planning on coming back," I yelled back at him from halfway across the yard.

He came running out after me in his undershorts screaming his head off. "Ya' dumb shit, get back here. You'll be crawling back to us, and when ya' do I'll kick yur' ass out of here."

"Bye Jim," I called out as I reached Ginger's corral. I pulled the latch on the corral gate and walked up to her. "I love ya', you sweet animal and I'll miss ya'." I kissed her on the nose and then whacked her on the ass and set her free.

I left the yard at a brisk pace that quickly turned into a slow trot. The realization that I had walked away from that Brute was exhilarating. I moved faster and faster. My God, I was free! Now my legs were working as hard as they could to get me as far away from that place as possible. Sweat was pouring from me, and my back was soaking wet in no time. It felt wonderful. My legs just kept moving. My heart was pounding hard inside my chest and the adrenaline was flowing. I was not about to let anything stop me. I was running towards my future, running back to my family. I was in control, nobody else. I was never going back to that farm, those cheap slave-driving bastards. The speed at which I ran was fueled by the anger I felt towards all the people who had taken my life from me: Aunt Mary, the Presentation Brothers, and the Reagans. These people had no right to do what they did to our family; I hated them all. I *had* to run this hard; it was the only way I could release the pent up emotions that were now exploding from every pore of my flesh. I could see where the long stretch of road in front of me ended, and the valley began. Running to the crest of that hill was like running towards the door to my future. On the other side of that crest was the rest of my life.

As I neared the top of the road, I slowed my pace and stopped. I threw up my arms and let out a cry that could be heard echoing across the valley, the same sort of warrior call I had shouted as my fist hit Nacho's face, a cry that told the world I was free. Then, exhausted, my arms fell to my hips and I leaned forward, out of breath. Then another burst of emotion hit me and I started to weep. I was grieving for the life I had lost, the love I had been denied, grieving for the time not spent with my family. I stood hunched over like this for a few moments trying to slow my breathing and trying to stop the tears that were streaming from my eyes. I fell to my knees and let the tears flow. Never had I ever been so overcome with such feeling.

Finally, this surge of emotion settled. I took in deep breaths, and released each one slowly, breath in, breath out. Gradually, I calmed myself and was able to stand and look out at the world in front of me. From this day forward, I was in charge of my life, no one else.

Now I was calm. I stood and gazed out over the magnificent grassy fields protected by large oak and ash trees that were scattered throughout the valley. The sun was now awake and roosters could be heard calling out to let the rest of the world know it was time to wake up. How magical the morning looked. The green pastures set out in front of me were illuminated by the rising sun as its rays reflected off the frozen dew that covered each field. My eyes ran along the edge of the stone wall that lined the road half expecting to see the little people running about. I was free, but was still nervous and emotionally wrecked. It was March 1948. I had worked for those assholes for nineteen months and it was clear I had meant nothing to them.

After walking for a long while, a farmer, an older fella' in a donkey cart, pulled up beside me. "It's cold lad. Where ya' going? Jump in, I'll take ya'." What a gentle looking man he was, thin, and well-aged by the sun. Like most old Irishmen, he had a pipe hanging out the side of his mouth that left a thin trail of smoke behind him.

"I'm heading up to the train station, getting the train to Cork to see my brother."

"Lovely then, I'm heading that way. Come on up, much too cold to be walking."

"Thanks." I jumped in the back of his wagon and sat myself down beside a couple boxes of sheep wool and a few flats of eggs.

"My name's Seamus McQuarry. Where ya' from then?"

"Polrone, just outside Mooncoin."

"Ah yes, lovely there, been to a few fairs down 'dat way." He carried on chatting about this and that and the time passed quickly. Seamus dropped me as near as he could to the station.

"Thank ya' Seamus," I called out as I jumped off the wagon.

"Best of luck to ya' lad, have a good visit wit' yur' brother, now."

"Will do, thanks."

The Irish, we are an odd lot. Some, good as gold like Seamus, others had hearts of stone like Jim Reagan and Blackie. I was no longer worried about Jim Reagan catching up with me. Even if he did, what could he do?

My timing was perfect; the train was in the station. There were lots of people rushing and pushing about, trying to make their way to the ticket wicket and on to the boarding platform. A well-built, short man dressed in black and wearing a navy cap with a yellow rim was hurrying us along. "All aboard, five minutes and we roll." He shouted.

I purchased my ticket and quickly headed towards the long chain of cars and tried to determine which coach I should get on to. I made my way to the nearest one. As I did I came across a middle-aged couple struggling to lift their cases up on to the foot-plate of the coach. As I had nothing to carry, I thought it proper that I help them out. I hoisted myself up on to the coach and then offered them a hand.

"Can I take those for ya' sir?"

"Yes, thank you."

The man had an interesting accent. He and his wife were well-dressed in long dark coats and both in fine felt hats. I could tell they were not from these parts, maybe tourists on their way back from Fountainstown.

I grabbed their three large brown cases. I placed one under my arm, took the handles of the other two in each of my fists, and hauled them through the narrow passage of the coach until I found a vacant compartment.

"Thank you boy, where are you from?" the fella' asked.

"Mooncoin, south of here."

"We're from Australia. It's a lovely place; many young Irish lads like you come over. Would you like to sit with us?"

"Yes, thank you." I replied.

The gentleman slid open the compartment door and the three of us moved in and on to the black leather seats.

The gentleman, his wife and I chatted during our brief trip to Cork. He told me about his homeland and the huge numbers of opportunities available for hard working lads like me. When we got into the station at Cork, I again helped them with their cases. He then handed me a one pound note and a piece of paper with a name, Mr. John Rylund, and an address written on it. "You're a wonderful, young lad Walter. If you ever find your way to Australia, you look me up, and I will find you work."

"Thank you, sir." I had never thought about Australia or any other country, but who knew where I might end up one day? I tucked the paper into my pocket and headed out of the station.

As I moved through the streets of Cork, towards Greenmount, my stomach began to tighten. I hardly noticed my surroundings. I was focused only on seeing Sean. Sweat was again dripping down my back. My hand held its place over the jacket pocket that protected my stash. I must have checked that pocket a hundred times to make sure my money was still there.

The closer I got to that place, the more tense and uneasy I became. Finally, there I was standing in almost the same spot I had been when the three of us stepped out of the Gardai motor car. A wave of emotion rushed over me, humiliation, sorrow, regret, fear, anger, pity, hate, disgust. I felt all these things in one huge surge. The veins on the side of my head began to pound, and a sudden flash of pain hit my temples and eyes. I was overcome with emotion and anxiety. My stomach heaved into my mouth, quickly I ran to the edge of the road and puked up into the hawthorn bushes that had once held me inside this place.

Could I go in? What if they didn't let me out? What if they had heard from the Reagans? Oh Christ, what was I going to do? Shit, I had come all this way, I'm going in, I thought. I walked up the path to the same door Sean, Jim and I had come through when we first entered this hell hole. Again, a swell of anguish came over me. I had to stop once more, before I entered the building, to collect myself. I was shaking and thought I'd burst into tears at any second. Oh Jesus, just do it Walter; ring the God damn bell. I raised my arm, rang the bell, my hand trembling as I did, and waited until I could hear the echoes of footsteps coming to answer it. Being here was strange. The door opened, and a younger looking Brother, who I didn't recognize, greeted me.

"Yes, sir, can I help you?" Imagine that, one of these guys calling me sir.

"Yes, I'm here to visit my brother, Sean O'Keeffe."

"Come in, please."

I followed him in and the smell hit me—that musty, floor wax, incense smell. I'll never forget it. Another rush of memories came over me: of beatings, tears, grief, and loss. I was shaking and angry; my stomach started to swirl about yet again.

"May I get you a glass of water, sir?" the Brother asked.

"Yes please, that would be lovely."

"Please wait here. I'll fetch yur' water and yur' brother."

I took a seat and thought about the years I had spent in this place. My eyes pooled up and my stomach began to rise up into my throat again, but I swallowed the stuff back down. Walter, pull yourself together, I told myself. This place is behind you now. You're here to get Sean and get on with your life. Calm down.

"Here you go, sir," The Brother said handing me a clear glass of water. "Are ya' alight?"

"Yes, I'll be fine…just a little sick from traveling."

"I've sent a boy to fetch yur' brother. He'll be right down."

I nodded as I slowly sipped back the water. I set the glass on my knee, closed my eyes, and took in several deep breaths trying to compose myself. After a few long minutes, I was calm but my head still hurt.

"Wattie?"

A deeper yet familiar voice called out. It was Sean. Instantly, my eyes were flooding my face, and I began to sob. I rose to my feet, my legs still shaking, dropped the glass, and moved towards my brother. I tried to sponge the tears from my eyes with the sleeve of my jacket so I could get a clear look at him, but my eyes just kept filling up. I stood before Sean with dead silence between us for at least five seconds, and then, he collapsed into my arms. The weight of him, and the shaking of my legs, made it difficult to stand.

Sean was shaking uncontrollably as he buried his face into my chest. But he was not crying, just shaking. The scent of sweat, and the well-packed dirt in his flesh, could be smelt while I cradled the back of his head. As I held him, I could feel the huge boils that were embedded in his neck, no doubt causing him pain, this poor kid.

"Sean, they wouldn't let me say goodbye. I wanted to see ya'. I tried, but they wouldn't let me. They sent me to a farm in Crosshaven, and I couldn't get away until now."

Sean pushed himself back from me and stared hard into my eyes. "Wattie, take me out of here. Take me out of this piece of shit hell hole."

"I will Sean, I promise. Let me see ya' then."

I stepped back and looked him over. He was taller but skinny and pale. His entire body was covered in bruises, and a deep cut under his chin indicated he had been in a scrap not too long ago. His sunken, bloodshot eyes had lost their shimmer, were framed by dark circles, and revealed not only a lack of sleep, but the ugliness of what was happening to him in this place. Sean was jittery, and a nervous twitch was making his neck jerk back and forth. He had grown hair on his face, and his facial features had changed; they were hard. This was not the little boy I had left behind. This was the skeleton of a tormented young man whose life was a wreck. What had they done to him?

"Brother, I would like to take Sean out for the day."

"Yes, sir, I'll make the arrangements. You'll have to sign a release form."

"No Wattie, take me out of here forever. I'm not coming back."

"I know Sean; I have a plan. It will be alright."

When the Brother returned, I signed my name and Sean and I headed out the front door. It was cold, and Sean had no jacket, so I pulled off mine and wrapped it around him. As we headed down the street, I put my arm around my brother and kept him close to me. He wrapped both of his arms tightly around his waist and remained hunched over as we walked, as if he was hiding from the world. Sean was different, and it appeared, somewhat disturbed. His general condition could only be described as horribly pathetic. He wasn't a little boy any more; he was a young man in a mental and physical state so bad, it was beyond description. I wasn't sure how to comfort him or what to say to make the inner pain I knew he was in go away. All I could do was try to give him a day to remember.

"Alright, my brother let's feast." We quickened our pace and headed down the road in search of a place to eat.

The squeaky plank boards that covered the floor of the Cross Road Café announced our arrival. As we walked in, a middle-aged, buxom blond in a tight, woolen skirt came to greet us. "Ya' two look like a couple 'a hungry lads. I'm Shannon. Come on, I'll sit ya' down."

She sat us at a small, wooden table near the window. The smell of fried bacon and potatoes filled the room and my stomach began to make sounds.

"Coffee?"

"Yes please," we both replied.

Near the center of the café, a row of elderly gentlemen sat on wooden stools at an eating bar. A halo of blue smoke and a sign that read "Gab, Gossip and Drink" hovered over them. Each one was dressed in a tweed jacket, and all sat facing the same direction like in a pub. The way they were chatting together and getting up and pouring their own coffees, I figured that they must be regulars in the place.

When Shannon returned with the coffee, she brought real cream and a bowl of sugar. Sean poured it all, cream and sugar, into his cup and drank it down in seconds. I had not been hungry while I was at the Reagan's so I let him take it. I knew what it was like to be famished the way he was, and my entire being ached watching him stuff it all down. We ordered up eggs, bacon, pork sausage, and potatoes. I also ordered bread and some cherry-filled cakes. Shannon was attentive and continued to fill up the cream and sugar.

Sean's uneasy eyes roaming the place, the way he was fidgeting and nervously scratching his head each time a fork full of food past his lips, and the way he slouched, were signals that things were not right inside of him. But I didn't know what to say or do. He looked barely alive.

"What's it been like while I've been gone? Have they been horrible to ya'?" I asked my brother.

Sean gazed at me over the rim of his coffee cup like I was an idiot. "It's been a fuckin' holiday camp. I love having those bastards put their hands down my trousers and beating the shit out of me and calling me names and maken' me touch 'em. Fuckin' lovely little place it is." And he carried on eating.

"By the way, little Kenny died of pneumonia," he said as he stuffed an entire sausage into his mouth. "Better that he did. They were tough on him, more than they were on the rest of us. Poor kid lay shaking in his bed for three days before they took him to the infirmary."

Sean had hardened in that place. He was nonchalant about the things that took place there, the abuse, Kenny dying. With the exception of the years spent with our parents, his fifteen years of life had been nothing but miserable.

We talked about other boys, who had been taking away, and about new ones that had arrived. I placed my hand over his. "It's goin' to be okay Sean. You and I are goin' to be okay."

"Wattie, nothing is ever okay. It never has been."

"Don't ya' remember how it was when we were all living in Polrone?" I asked him.

"That's a life I can't remember; it's like a dream that never happened. My life started and ended the day our Dad died. I hardly remember a thing before that."

"Sean, we had a good life."

"Shut the fuck up Wattie. It's never gonna' be like that again. Ya' left me there; Jim left me there. Nobody gives a shit."

He started to anxiously rock back and forth and to scratch his head again. Sean had changed, but I understood his pain.

"Sean, I do give a shit. That's why I'm here. That's why I'm going to get us set up in Polrone and come back for ya'."

"Shut up and let me eat."

He stopped rocking and dove back into his plate. This is not what I had expected. I thought our reunion would have been heartfelt and exciting. I didn't know how to handle this.

When we were done, I wrapped up the extra cakes and bread into a napkin and was stuffing them into my pocket just as Shannon came up to the table. Oh Jees', I've been caught; I felt guilty.

"You've paid for it lad," she quickly reassured. "Here, let me get ya' a sack so it doesn't all go to crumbs." Shannon brought us a small paper sack and some brown paper and carefully wrapped up our extra cakes and bread.

"Thank you."

"Yur' welcome," she replied.

I handed Sean the brown package and told him to tuck it under his shirt. After I was sure Sean had filled up as much as he could, I paid up our bill and we headed out to the street. It was still chilly, but the sky was clear and the sun was bright. I knew that Sean was in emotional pain and I didn't know what to say. So we just walked. Near the end of the road, I saw a cinema sign. Neither of us had ever been in one.

"Shall we go?" I asked.

"Jees', yeah!" For the first time since I had come for him, he smiled.

Sean and I picked up our pace and then sprinted towards the movie house. A big sign showing pictures of Charlie Chaplin stood out in front of the box office. I pulled some coins out of my pocket and set them on the counter.

"Just starting lads, hurry on in," the lady in the box said as she took a few of the coins and pushed the rest back to me.

I knew Sean was glad to be out of Greenmount and lost in what was happening on the big screen in front of us. I looked at Sean more than I looked at the images flickering by, wondering what was going through his head but afraid to ask, wondering how all the suffering of his life had affected him.

Right now, he was having a good time, so I would leave it at that. The clicking of the black and white film running around the reel, and the hum of the machine pulling it, was soothing. Lost here in the dark, where no one could see him, touch him, hurt him, my brother escaped into another world. I wanted to let him stay there for as long as he wanted, so we sat through two showings of the flick and never spoke at all.

When we did come out of the theatre we both squinted, and it took a few moments for our eyes to adjust to the light.

"That was alright, thanks Wattie, thanks for coming back for me."

"Yur' welcome." I threw my arm around Sean's shoulder and headed down the road. I didn't want to send him back to the school empty handed, so took him into a sweet shop and let him load up on peppermints, chocolate, whatever he wanted.

"Ya' sure, Wattie, will ya' have any money left over? I don't want to leave ya' broke."

"Not to worry, I'll just go out and make more. I'm a free man now."

He had settled down and was acting more like the boy I knew. God, I have to get him out of there. I paid the sweet shop owner and counted up how much I had left. There wasn't much, only a couple of pounds, and I still had to make my way back to Polrone.

Here we were. We had nothing, no home, no possessions, no jobs, no education, no proper shoes or clothing—nothing, except the few pounds I had left. God, what was I going to do? I didn't want to take him back there. Maybe we could spend a few nights on the street until I found a job. But what could I do? I feared being around other folk, had no confidence and could barely read or write. Although I knew I had special talents for music and art, after years of being called an idiot, I guess I thought I was good for nothing. As well, Sean looked so bad; he'd never get a job himself. What would he do on the street if I were working? Christ, this was awful.

As we walked down the road, Sean with a mouth full of peppermints and chocolate, I gazed upon the people coming and going, all rushing somewhere. Maybe some were off to work, some rushing home to see their families. Sean and I had nowhere to rush too. As we got closer to the school, that uneasy feeling came over me again, the same feeling I had when I walked up the steps to take Sean out of Greenmount. He's going to hate that I have to leave him here, but it will only be for a short while, I thought.

Before we got to the school, I led Sean into a small open area filled with pigeons and found a black iron bench to sit us on.

"Sean, I know ya' hate Greenmount, but you've got to go back only for a little while. You can do it, and I will come back for ya'."

He said nothing.

"I'm going to find a job, maybe with Mrs. Crowley, and get us set up. At least in Greenmount you'll have a roof over yur' head. We'll tell 'em that I am coming back for ya', and if they touch even one hair on yur' head I'll come back and kill 'em. If they know I'm coming back, that you have family coming to take you home, they won't do anything to you. I promise you Sean I will be back in a month, right after I get things set up in Polrone."

Sean looked at me, disappointed.

"Sean, I promise they will not hurt ya' ever again. If they know I'm coming back, and I am, they won't dare touch ya'.

Sean stared at me for a long time. "Wattie, you're such a dumb fuck. They won't stop doing anything to me, but I don't care. I'm used to it, the beatings, the fags, the work, it's all I know. What would I do out here in the real world? I couldn't do nothing."

God, how he had changed. I knew then I had to get us set up so I could bring him back to Polrone.

"I swear it Sean, on the graves of our mother and father, I swear it. I will be back in less than thirty days to fetch ya'."

We slowly walked back to Greenmount. Sean hardly spoke a word. I felt terrible that I had to leave him there, but I didn't know what else to do. I barely had enough money for one ticket to Mooncoin. Once there, I would try to find work and a room for us and would come back for him. Before we walked back inside the place, I turned my brother towards me and looked him straight in the eyes.

"I swear it, Sean. I will be back. They will not hurt ya' or touch ya'. If they do, I'll bring the Gardai back with me and have 'em arrested."

We stood outside the main door for a long time before we rang the bell. The same Brother greeted us and welcomed Sean back.

"Did you have a good visit, then?"

"Yes. I'll be back before the end of April to fetch my brother and take him to our home in Polrone. I've noticed that he has quite a few cuts and bruises on him. I hope these have healed up before I return."

"I will let Brother Thomas know that you will be returning."

He made a few notes and said they would look forward to seeing me in a month.

I hugged my brother but couldn't bear to look into his disappointed eyes one more time. I kissed the top of his head, again promised I would be back, and then headed out the door. God, I hated to leave him there.

It was now late in the afternoon, and I wanted to make sure I got the bus to Mooncoin before the end of the day. I didn't want to be getting to the Crowley's too late and then have to wake them up. After paying my fare, I had just two shillings left. I didn't care that I had spent almost all I had on Sean. He deserved it, and at least his belly would be full for a couple of days. He would have to hide his sweets if he wanted them to last.

I was tired by the time my bus was ready to load and I stepped on. As much as I wanted to gaze at the sights of the city, my eyes and my emotions were exhausted. I found a spot halfway down the aisle and settled in, letting my head fall against the window. My eyes were heavy, and before long the rumbling of the bus rocked me to sleep.

I drifted off and escaped into my beautiful dream world. My body rose from where I slept on the bus and at rocket speed flew across the sky to my home in Polrone. I could see the River Suir coming into focus. There was my father on his boat. Now, I was running along the banks with my brothers and Josie. I was running towards my mother, who was waiting for my Dad with Prowler, at the anchor where Dad would dock. I ran to my Mum and threw my arms around her. She knelt beside me and hugged me and kissed my forehead. Prowler was licking my face and hands; I loved the tickling sensation I got when he licked me that way. He stank, but I loved the sheep dung smell of that damn dog.

"Yur' almost home Wattie, almost, go back now," my mother said.

"I don't want to leave you," I pleaded with her.

"You'll be alright; you're almost home." She then walked out into the water with Prowler and floated towards my Dad's boat.

"We're still here Wattie," my Dad called out. "Be strong, we're still here," he said, and then they disappeared into the fog.

Twenty nine

GOING HOME

"Can ya' hear me, lad? Wake up, now."

I woke to the gentle nudge of the driver shaking me on the shoulder, letting me know that we had arrived in Mooncoin. My God, where had the time gone? I rubbed my eyes and pulled myself up from the slouched position I had fallen in to. Still confused and not sure if my dream had been real or not, I stared back at the driver for a brief moment. He must have thought I was daft.

"Lad, we're here. Yur' going to Mooncoin, right?"

"Yes." I snapped out of my dozy state and slid out from my seat. "Yes, Mooncoin, thank you."

Dazed and disoriented, I staggered off the bus. What a day this had been. I escaped from the Reagan's, faced the fear of going back to Greenmount, reunited with my brother, went to my first café and cinema, and now had arrived back home. Yes, what a day, and it wasn't over yet.

The bus dropped me off in the same spot Jim and I had been dropped when we came home from Peadmont, outside the sweet shop. It was chilly, and the sun was starting to set. I was home. I sat on the road to wake and pondered what I should do next. The smell and taste of salt on the air was familiar and soothing. I had forgotten how much I loved that scent. The air was fresh and the sky clear as I gazed down the streets and lanes of this quiet humble town that was my home. How peaceful it felt to be back here. The cottages and shops, some that had stood for a hundred years, had meant nothing to me when I was a child. Now, they were familiar and full of fond memories.

As I looked down the roads of our town, I remembered happier times spent with my brothers, sisters, and parents: going to the dairy with my mother and grandmother to buy cheese, the smell in the blacksmith shed when I went with my Dad to buy iron, and going to the tailor and shoemaker's cottages each year for new suits and boots. Even the ditches, hedges, stone-walls, and the large stand of trees that grew inside the churchyard, brought a deluge of fond memories that had been locked away. It was good to be back here; I had to be back here, I thought.

From where I sat I could see the churchyard. This is where I had sat and gobbled up that bag of sweets after my Dad's funeral. I rose from my spot and headed towards the yard where both my parents had been put to rest. The trees were taller, the ivy and other greenery thicker, and the entire yard looked much smaller than I remembered it. Even though this was a place of death, a place where thousands of tears had been shed, it felt safe and comforting. I made my way through the yard to the place where I had remembered my Dad's coffin going into the ground. There were no markers, and it was difficult to figure out which spot was theirs, but I found it. This part of the yard was in need of tending, and I knew I would be back here to tidy it up. I sat on the ground on top of the place where my parents were buried. They were right beneath me. I felt an odd warm wave brush over me. Yes, I had found the right spot.

I never thought I would live long enough to come back to Mooncoin. Seven, maybe eight, years had past. This was the only place I wanted to be right then, so I lay down in the grass and once again drifted off.

When I woke, the sky was pitch black. Glittering little stars were flung across the sheer black sky. What a wonderful sight. I inhaled a few deep breaths. Damn, I better get a move on and see if there are any lights on at the Crowley's. I jumped up, brushed myself off, and headed out down the road. As I passed familiar sights, it struck me that this walk was not as long as I remembered it. As I child, I must have dawdled a lot, taking the longer routes that cut through farms, took time to chase rabbits, pick ivy and violets, and play in the ditch. I always lost track of the time. Being back here now, I was surprised how close Mooncoin and Polrone were and how quickly I made my way to the Crowley home.

When I arrived at the Crowley's, not much had changed. The old stone house was well-tended with all the windows and doorways neatly trimmed in bright, green paint. The water pump had also been repainted the same bright green and stood over a large water trough that was used for washing clothing, children, sheep, vegetables, animals, almost anything. They had also added what looked like a brick barn or chicken house and had replaced their thatched roof with a more modern looking one, wood I think. The garden was tidy and had been nicely tucked in for the winter. Hay protected some shrubs, and it was clear that the garden had been well prepared in the fall before the cold and frost set it.

I was uneasy as I approached the doorway. What if they turn me away or don't remember who I am? I remembered Mrs. Crowley's kind words, and the offer she had made when she came to visit us at Greenmount. I knocked on the door and heard the sounds of chairs push back from the table as the folks inside rushed to see who had come to call. The Irish were always visiting one another, usually to spread gossip, share a pint, or talk about their gardens. I missed that part of life, going to the homes of people we knew, or having friends drop 'round to our house and having a sing-song and whatnot. Mrs. Crowley herself opened the door, one of her boys curiously peering over her shoulder.

"Well Jesus, Mary and Joseph," she called out as she raised her arms into the air. "Walter O'Keeffe, 'tis a splendid eve to see that you've come home." And she flung her arms around me. "Come in boy, come in," and she hustled me in.

Thank God she had recognized me. Inside the house, there were a few lads a little younger than me, a couple older fellas, Mrs. Crowley's daughter, and a couple of black and white, long haired dogs. There were two, half empty, brown glass bottles on the table, and it appeared the group was having a gab and a drink.

"'Tis Walter O'Keeffe, ya' remember 'im Danny? He's one of Ned and Bridgett's boys, was tossed out of 'der house and sent off to Cork to live in the orphanage. Shame what happened ta' ya' all."

They all nodded as if they knew the story of our family, and gathered 'round me like I was a long lost son.

"Jesus boy, we'll all have a drink to welcome ya' home. Tommy, grab Walter a cup dar', boy."

Before I knew it, the Crowley's were throwing me a homecoming. A fiddle was playing, spoons were clapping, and we were all singing lively tunes, and dancing about. After having a cup, or maybe two, of the liquor from the brown bottles I was feeling good, and it is hard to recall all the night's events. I do remember feeling welcomed here in this home. The people were interested in what had happened to me, asked lots of questions, and I felt that they cared. The night ended with me flopping on to a straw mattress on the floor next to one of the Crowley boys. I remember thinking that it was good to be home. Then I was out.

In the morning, I woke to the sounds of a happy home coming to life: brothers and sisters teasing each other, Mrs. Crowley trying to prepare the morning meal, chickens coming and going.

"Walter, you'll be staying with us here, I hope. Like I told ya' when I came to visit, I've got work fur ya' and I'll feed and pay ya'. Now sit down. I know you'll be wanting to hear how the rest of yur' kin are doin'."

Jesus, it was a relief to know I had a place to stay and work. "My God. yes, I'd love to know where my brothers and sisters are and how they're all doing. Are any of 'em back here?"

"Fraid none of 'em are in Polrone, but we've heard that yur' sister Bessie had gone off to London, England and she's been married to an Englishman, Weir's his name. Yur' brother Bill was back a wee bit ago, stayed with the O'Briens and then left to take work at a mine up in Derbyshire, England. Jim 'as also gone to England and was staying with yur' sister Bessie last anyone heard."

This information was coming at me so quickly; I could barely take it all in. All these years I had waited for just a little bit of information, anything. Now, there was so much it was overwhelming.

"Now yur' sister Eileen, she also came home and lived with the O'Briens for a bit. We found out that yur' Aunt Mary had sent her off to work in a farmhouse in Currabalayclay, County Waterford, lots of girls get sent up that way. Wouldn't ya' know it, she became pregnant, had a baby boy she did. She reared that baby, Patrick she called 'im, for two years while she was working on that farm."

Jesus, my sister had a baby. This was too much, but Mrs. Crowley carried on.

"The way we heard it, Eileen was coming in from the fields and saw an auto driving away with her baby boy waving and crying out the back window. He was gone. He'd been fostered out without her knowing. Oh Mary mother of God, the pain of seeing her only wee one drive off like that must 'ave been horrible."

"You've got to slow down. I can't take it all in." I said.

"It's alright, Wattie. I know it's a lot to hear. I'll tell ya' more when yur' ready."

I sat quietly with her and thought about each of them, Bessie, Eileen, Billy, and Jim. What a relief to know they were all alive. All I had to do now was bring Sean home. Jesus, Sean! I had to bring him back here.

"Sean is the last one. He's still in the school and they're horrible to 'im. I've got to get 'im out."

"Like I told yas', you've both got a home here. If ya' want to bring yur' brother back, that's alright, we'll make the room." That woman was a saint. As soon as I could raise the bus fare and a few pounds for shoes and trousers for him, I'd go and bring him back.

It was Sunday and there were no chores to tend to, so Mrs. Crowley encouraged me to visit the town and old friends. "I think ya' should go by and see that Josie Phelan, Walter. I told her you'd been asking about her when I went to visit ya', and she was very interested in hearing all about ya'."

It was unreal to think that Josie still remembered me, or that she would have any interest in me at all. For the past several years, she had been a dream, one that might never come true.

"Yes I might go 'round an' say hello to a few folks and visit my parents' house."

"Yes, and drop by the Phelans like I said."

Mrs. Crowley gave me a clean shirt and told me to make myself at home. I sat outside next to the water pump and watched the life that took place here around her home. This is how it would have been at our home if our parents had still been alive. We would all have been older, but still close, coming and going, doing things families do. I missed my family but the Crowley's made me a part of theirs, and I loved them for that.

After cleaning myself up and combing back my hair, I decided to make the walk to my home, my parents' home. According to Mrs. Crowley, Aunt Mary still lived there, although all of the cousins had left. Somehow, that did not surprise me.

I set out down New Road taking in the sights, sounds, and scents of the area. My eyes drank up the beauty of the countryside as I wandered down familiar pathways, and another flood of childhood memories came rushing in to welcome me home. The cottages, the familiar markers that I had played around as a child, calmed me. As I neared our home, I was at peace. I was not angry and was not afraid. In fact, I thought I might go right up to the door and walk right in.

When I got to the place where I could see our home, I was surprised at how small it appeared. The house was much closer to the road than I remembered, too. The chimney was tipping over; the gate had fallen off and was set up against the stone-fence in front of the home. The yard was overgrown and full of pots, buckets, and other debris. Black smoke came from the chimney so I knew someone was there. The two clothes wires were still strung in the same spot. Only two birds, robins were perched on the line. I sat on the ground at the side of the road looking out towards our home. I imagined all of us running around the front of the house, throwing sticks and laughing as Prowler ran to fetch them. My Mum was taking fresh clothing from the line, and our Dad was kneeling beside his cart fixing the strapping from one of the wheels. What a lovely scene.

I rose, wiped off my bum, and headed towards my house. I walked past the broken gate and up to the front door. Still, I was calm. The door was slightly open so I stuck my head in. It looked small, but not much had changed. My mother's sideboard and crockery were still standing in the same spot.

"Hello," I called out.

My Dad's rusty, iron spade sat next to the hob, and our large, iron pot hung in its place in the hearth.

"Hello," I called out again.

I moved into the room and could see the fire was smoking but no one was there. Perhaps they were out back at the ditch. The cast iron bed that had been my parents', and my father's dresser were in their places, and a few pieces of china that had been my mother's were sitting above the hearth. Although these things were familiar, this place no longer felt like my home. The love I had received here from my parents had been eroded by the anger and unkind heart of our Aunt Mary.

After looking around, I headed outside to see if anyone was about. I didn't see a soul. Maybe they had gone to the neighbors. I had not wanted to see Bill or Mary; I wanted to see my home, and I had. Out across the neighboring field, I could see smoke coming up from the Phelans. This is it; I'm going to go over.

My palms were sweating and my knees began to vibrate. My throat dried up, and I wondered if I'd be able to speak if I saw her. All these years I had dreamt of Josie. Now, I was walking up the path to her home. What if she had a fella'? How would I react? Just act natural, I told myself. I stood at the door wondering what I might say, how I might get the words out, when behind me a voice called out.

"Who've we got there?" I turned quickly and saw Mrs. Phelan coming down the path looking like she was returning from church.

"It's Walter, Wattie, O'Keeffe, Ma'am. I'm not sure if ya' remember me?"

"Oh, for God's sake boy, sure as yur' born I remember ya'. Come, give me a hug." Mrs. Phelan wrapped her arms around me.

"'Twas awful what happened to yas', Wattie. I'm glad yur' alright. Are ya' alright?

"Not too bad," I replied.

"Come on then, tell me all about it," and she pushed me on inside the house.

She looked the same, a few wrinkles and a few strands of gray, but beneath that aging grin and crooked teeth was the beautiful soul I remembered and I was happy to see her.

"I'm all alone here, Walter," she told me.

My chest sunk when she spoke those words. Immediately, I thought I'd missed Josie, that she had gone off to some job or to study in England or got married or...

"Had to leave Josie and her sister in town to pick me up the dairy," she continued. "Then she's going to help the Shea O'Brien's tend their animals and little ones. Not expecting her back 'til supper, but you sit and we'll have a tea and a gab."

What a relief! Josie had not moved; she was still here just like Mrs. Crowley said. It was better that I see her mother first and get an update on her life so I didn't make an ass of myself when I finally did see her.

Mrs. Phelan and I sat for a long time sipping tea, eating Jamison biscuits and remembering the days that our families spent time together. Most of the Phelan children had left home. Josie, her sister and one brother had stayed behind to help with the farm.

"And, she hasn't got a fella' Walter. I know ya' want to ask me, so I'll just tell ya' straight out. She hasn't been going with anyone, so not to worry."

How did she know that was on my mind?

After a pleasant and newsy visit, it was time to head back as I wanted to tend to my parents' graves before the day was over.

"Well, I best be off then. I want to tend to my parents' graves before the day is over. So I'll be up there for a bit I suspect."

"It was wonderful to see ya', Walter. I'll tell Josie you were calling for her."

"Thanks then, and thanks for the tea and biscuits."

"And Wattie, yur' Grandmother Knox, she would love to see yas'. She's still up in Tobernabrone. Shes been down a couple of times wondering if there'd been any news on any of you boys."

"I didn't know she was still alive. That's grand. I'll make the trip up to see her. That'll be lovely, thanks."

Another gift from the Almighty, was my Grandmother. She would have taken us in, but it would have been too hard on her. I was thankful to hear she was still alive and knew I'd be making plans to go up and see her. As I left the Phelan home, I looked back across the field one more time towards our house. I could see old Bill heading in the door. I didn't want to go back there, not now.

I headed back up to Mooncoin, and again was surprised at how quickly I made the trip. How lovely and familiar this countryside was to me: the rolling hills covered in multiple shades of velvety green; unusual stone structures, left behind by our ancestors, sheep dotted the fields; and the smell of the River Suir on the wind. Hmm…if I had been blind, that smell alone would have told me I was home.

I wandered back to the Mooncoin churchyard and found the spot where my parents were buried. I rolled up my sleeves, came to my knees, and carefully started to pull the unkempt grass and weeds growing around their resting place. Having my hands in the earth, gently separating the tall weeds from the ivy, violets, and primroses, settled me. One day, I would come here and make a proper marker. Even after clearing the spot where my parents lay, I carried on clearing the surrounding areas. The earth feeds us and the planet. All things come from the earth and all things go back to the earth, fascinating when you think about it. I was enjoying having my hands in the soil and was lost in thought when my ears tuned into the rattling of a bicycle chain as it came to a stop. I didn't pay much attention, until I heard my name being called out.

"Wattie? Wattie O'Keeffe, is that you?"

I wiped the dirty sleeve of my shirt across my face to clear the sweat that had dripped into my eyes and saw a slim, attractive woman jump off her bike and set it up against the churchyard wall. It was Josie; she was beautiful, a joy to behold.

My throat tightened, and my voice was lost; I couldn't speak. My eyes were stuck on her lovely face. To Josie, I must have looked like a stunned beast. I couldn't take my eyes off of her. My knees felt like jelly, and I thought I might fall to the ground if I tried to stand. As a young boy, I always thought I loved her, but now I knew it was true. I couldn't move and I couldn't get up. Paralyzed by love, I was. My God say something, I thought, but my mouth wouldn't work.

"Wattie, it's me Josie. Don't ya' recognize me. Me Mum told me you'd be here?'

I said nothing.

"Wattie, are ya' alright?"

"Yes, Josie, I do...I mean, hello, how are ya'?" My tongue was tied to my lips, and I couldn't put together an organized thought.

Josie giggled, the same way she had when she had kissed me in the meadow. "Walter, is that how ya' greet a girl you haven't seen for years?"

Slowly, I rose with my knees still trembling and steadied myself. She was beautiful. I extended my arm to shake her hand. Again, she giggled. In my hand was a fist full of weeds that I appeared to be offering her. I dropped the stuff and wiped my hands down the side of my trousers and again extended my arm. Josie grabbed my hand with both of hers. Her lovely, warm, soft fingers cradling mine were amazing, I could feel the warmth of her begin to creep up my arm.

"I'm so happy to see that you've made it home. I've missed ya'; we've all missed ya', she said."

She missed me! My God, she missed me! My head was a mess. I should say something. "I missed ya', too," I answered, still some what tongue-tied.

Josie's thick, sandy-coloured hair was pinned off to the side of her face just like she had worn it when we were young. She wore an ivory coloured blouse with a tiny, green ribbon neatly tied at the top. Her long, woolen skirt outlined the body of the woman she had grown into. She was more beautiful, and even lovelier, than I had imagined she would be. It was hard to hold back the tears that wanted to erupt from me. The emotions I was feeling, including the disbelief that finally I was standing before this angel, overtook me, and I feel to my knees.

"Wattie, are ya' alright?"

"Jees', yes, I wasn't sure I'd ever see ya'; now here you are. I'm not sure what to say or what to do?"

"Sure, you'll be alright. It's a lot that you've been through. Let's sit. Tell me what happened to ya'. You've eight – nine years to catch me up on."

We sat on the grass, and eventually, I was able to make coherent sentences. The nervousness I felt when I first saw her washed away as we sat and talked about our school days, our families, and our lives. We sat for hours catching up on the many years we had been apart. I told her about the year at Peadmont, the years at Greenmont and the Reagan's, she listened intently and showed great concern.

"It's awful what you've been through, but yur home now. Jee's, I best be getting home too," she said. "Me Mum is sure to be worrying about me."

I didn't want this time to end. I had waited too long and wasn't ready to be apart from her again.

"Can I walk ya' home, then?"

"Well, I've got my bike."

"Can I bike ya' home?

"Well, alright then."

We got up from our spot, and I lifted her bike. With Josie sitting on the front handlebars, and me doing the driving we made our way back down the road, the same road we had walked together as children. For the first time in almost nine years, I remembered what it felt like to be happy.

As we coasted down the road, Josie's hair gently blew up against my face as I steered the bike towards her home. The scent of lavender that surrounded her was soothing, and I loved it. I dropped Josie safely at her home and watched as she pushed her bike to the front door.

"Will I see ya' around then, Wattie?"

"Yes, as much as ya' want."

We both waved, and I watched her disappear behind the doorway to the Phelan cottage. The aroma of lavender lingered even though she was gone, and I inhaled a deep breath to capture the scent of her that had been left behind. This is what I had waited for. What a relief to know Josie was still here and that she had missed me.

Over the following weeks, Josie and I spent more time together, and I hated being apart from her. Josie, like most Irish girls was taking in laundry, minding young children, and taking odd jobs at the farms around the county. I was preparing the gardens for the Crowley's, getting ready to plant cabbage and other vegetables, tending the livestock, and fixing things around the place. I was handy I have to say.

In the evenings, when both Josie and I were done with work, we would meet up and spend time together. We'd strolled along the banks of the River Suir reminiscing about the days spent together as children. Some evenings I'd fetch her and we would wander about exploring and rediscovering the Polrone graveyard, our childhood playground; I always felt at home in this place. I felt so blessed to have her, my sweet, sweet, Josie. I was nervous around other people and crowds, being with her nourished my damaged soul. She made me feel special, important and loved. Without her I would have been lonely, lost and not sure how to exist in the world. They taught us nothing in Greenmont. Being away from other people and the outside world made me feel odd and different. I still felt that way.

We were sitting on the grass side by side in the old graveyard, our backs up against one of the ancient headstones, our shoulders touching, gazing out across the field where we used to play, when she put her head on my shoulder.

"It's grand to have ya' back, Wattie. I'd wondered if I would ever see ya' again."

"Me too; I thought about ya' all the time. Yur' memory is what brought me back here."

"Wattie, do ya' remember when I kissed ya' down by the river when we were eight?"

"Could never forget that; it was my first kiss and all."

"Maybe you'd like to kiss me this time," she suggested.

My heart jumped into my chest. I'd been too shy to try and kiss Josie over the past three weeks and wasn't sure if she thought of me that way. Now, I knew she did. Without hesitation, I turned to her, pulled her towards me, and placed my lips on hers. Years I had waited for this second kiss, and it was certainly worth the wait.

Thirty

THE WORST KIND OF A DAY

It was April. Twenty-seven days had past since I had gone to see Sean, and I was making plans to bring him home. I had saved up a good amount selling rabbits, working the farm and doing other odd jobs. I had also arranged work for Sean with both the Crowley and Walsh farms and had made arrangements for him to stay at the Crowley house. He and I would share the attic room. I was anxious and eager to get him out of that hellhole.

Josie walked me to the bus station and waited as I bought my return ticket. "Yur' sure yur' coming back this time, Wattie, and not leaving me fur another nine years?" she asked me.

"Not to worry, I'll be back tonight. See, I've got my return ticket." I kissed her cheek and boarded the bus, anxious to get going, get my brother, and return to Mooncoin.

During the bus ride to Greenmount, my mind was unsettled as memories of the terrible things that had happened to us came flooding back to me. I didn't want to remember; it was too painful. I just wanted to forget that awful time in my life, get Sean, and start our lives over. Looking out the window over the hills and fields of green, I imagined how excited Sean would be to get out, and how much he would enjoy rediscovering the banks of the river and fields around our home in Polrone. I worried about how he had made out these past few weeks and hoped he was looking forward to me coming to get him. They knew I was coming back, so they wouldn't have done a thing to him. If they had, would I really get the Gardai? No, likely not. I just want to get him out of there. If I see that puke Blackie, maybe I'll punch him in the face, I thought. My mind was running wild.

When I walked up the path to Greenmount, I felt sick and started to panic. Oh shit, I didn't know if I could go in that place again. I was not prepared for the anxiousness I felt. I expected to be happy and relieved that I was about to be reunited with my brother once and for all. But I didn't feel that way, I was scared shitless, and I didn't know why. I took in a deep breath and rang the bell. A boy about fifteen opened the door and greeted me.

"I'm here to fetch my brother, Sean O'Keeffe."

"Yes, sir, come in."

I followed the boy in. There it was again—that smell. It seeped back into me and conjured up a flood of memories. God, how odd that a smell could have such an impact on me. The smell of this place messed up my head and my emotions. My stomach tightened, my head began to pound, and my knees started to shake. It was horrible. I took a deep breath and let it out slowly trying to calm myself. After I get Sean out of here, I'm never coming back.

"Wait here, please," said the boy. Then he disappeared, giving me a few minutes to pull myself together. Then I saw him, that fat puke, Blackie, walking in my direction. He was waddling from side to side like a penguin, fatter than when I had last seen his hideous, red, pudgy face. He came towards me walking with an air of arrogance. Sean was not with him.

"Walter O'Keeffe, how nice of you to pay us a visit," he said in a sugary tone.

"I'm here to fetch my brother and take 'im home."

"Well you're just a bit late. He was sent off to a farm in Skibbereen about three weeks ago."

That asshole! "But ya' knew I was coming to take 'im home. Why did ya' send 'im off?"

"I had no correspondence from you indicating such?" Blackie said in an indifferent tone. I wanted to reach out and place my two hands around his fat neck and strangle the life right out of him.

"Give me the address where he's at," I shouted.

"Calm yur'self, boy. I see you're still a bit of a troublemaker are ya'?" Blackie smirked as if he had gotten' the last laugh. I had to work hard to control myself. I felt the blood and heat pumping into my face. I could have killed him. He then pulled out a piece of paper from the sleeve of his robe and handed it to me.

I snatched the paper from him and looked down at it. The paper had the name of the family and the farm Sean had been sent to; Sullivan was their name. I didn't thank him; I said nothing. I turned and marched out of that fucking, miserable place fuming, on the verge of exploding with rage.

What a horrible human being, if you can even call him that. The hundreds and thousands of boys who suffered under his guard, and who were tortured by this demon, would one day get their revenge. The terrible things he did to all of us, I hoped, had secured him a spot in hell right next to Satin himself. I left Greenmount for the last time, not once looking back at that wretched place.

Skibbereen was about six miles away on the west side of Cork, not far really, but I had my return ticket and only enough money to buy a one-way for Sean, so had to get my brother and get back to Mooncoin before day's end. I had no way to get to the Sullivan farm in Skibbereen and no time to wait for the bus, as it would not be coming for well over an hour. Out on the street, I saw a 'Bike for Hire' sign and thought that would do. I paid the operator a pound and headed off. I flew down the road and tried to figure out how I would get both of us back on the bike in time to get the last return bus to Mooncoin. I made my way to Skibbereen in under an hour. After asking a few folks along the way, I had no problem finding the Sullivan farm where Sean was living.

It was a well-kept home that reminded me of our home in Polrone. Like the families in Polrone, I could see that the Sullivans were readying the yard for planting. My eyes scanned the place looking for any sign of my brother. There was no one about. As I walked up to the bright red door, a few chickens scurried by my feet, again reminding me of our home.

A middle-aged woman answered the door; she was dark Irish like me. Two small, blond children ran up behind her and hugged her around the knees. They were about the same age, twins I guess they were. She was well-dressed, and the fancy hat on her head indicated that she was readying herself to go out.

"Afternoon, Ma'am. My name's Walter O'Keeffe. I believe my brother, Sean, might be staying with ya'. I've come to pay 'im a visit." I didn't want to tell her that I was taking him home in case she made a fuss, or she had a husband like that asshole, Jim Reagan.

"Oh Jees', yes, he's talked about ya'. So yur' the big brother. Well, he's all done for today and 'as gone down ta' the River Ilen. 'Said he was going down to paint pictures of the boats. Sometimes, he goes to write poems; today, he was going to paint. I've got some of 'is paintings here in the house, painting all the time he is…"

She was a yappy thing, she was, and I had to cut her off in mid-sentence. "Do ya' think ya' could point me in the right direction, so I could go down and find 'im, please?"

"Sure, sure. Ya' follow along that path there. You'll want to go over the old, stone bridge. That bridge has been there for a thousand years, say our clansmen…"

"Thank you, Ma'am." I had to cut her off again and headed out to find Sean.

As I peddled along, I thought it was interesting that Sean had gone to paint and that he wrote poetry. He and I were alike that way. When I got to the banks of the river, I knew this was a place Sean would love to come to. It would surely have reminded him of our home in Polrone and of the days we watched our Dad fishing. What a lovely spot! I scoured the banks, but he was nowhere in sight. I set the bike down and walked up and down the banks of the river, and in and out of little paths, calling his name. I couldn't see him anywhere.

After searching for close to what felt like an hour, I headed back up to the house to see if he had returned. He hadn't. Again, I wandered about looking for him. I searched the yard, stuck my head into the outbuildings, went around back to the ditch. No sign of him. Damn, it was getting late, and I had to get the bike back and get our bus. I sat for a long while at the edge of the road, hoping he would show up.

After a frustrating wait, I thought I would take one more search around the river to see if Sean was sleeping in the grass, or was on his way back. As I rode over the bumpy path to the river one more time, probably faster than I should have been going, I hit a log and the bike chain fell off. Shit. I rolled up my sleeves and struggled unsuccessfully to get that thing working. The frame had been bent from hitting the log and I was unable to get the chain back on properly. This was a hell of a day.

I pushed the bike up to the house and again knocked on the door. This time, an elderly man opened the door. I explained who I was and asked if I could leave a note for Sean. The old fella' was a bit of a 'pisspot', but got a pencil and paper and said he would pass my note on to Sean. In my note, I told Sean that I would be back in one week to see him.

Shit, I was frustrated. The day had gone nothing like I thought it would. I pushed the bike along the road as fast as I could, hoping a cart might come along and give me a lift. After pushing for a long while, I could hear the sound of a large motor vehicle coming up behind me. It was a bus. I flagged the driver down, and after explaining my situation, the driver allowed me and the bike, on the bus and took us into Cork.

The fella' that had hired me out the bike was not at all pleased with the condition of his bike, but I didn't have the time to argue with him and darted off to the station to catch my ride, while he shouted profanities at me for busting up his property. I made it to the station just in time, but awfully disappointed that I did not have Sean with me.

Mrs. Crowley had made a big supper to welcome Sean home, and Josie was there. Like me, they were all disappointed that my attempts to find Sean and bring him home had failed.

The next week, I set out the same way, except this time I did not get a return ticket, just in case I had to search for Sean as I had done the week before. This time, I had also arranged to take the bus all the way to Skibbereen. When I reached the Sullivan farmhouse, the same woman answered the door.

"Yur' brother's run off. We 'aven't seen 'im since ya' were last here. He must 'ave taken off that same day. Didn't even get to give 'im yur' note. God damn little shit…just up and left, and with all this work we've got to do around here." She continued to babble, but I didn't hear a thing I was so frustrated.

I left the farm without saying goodbye to Mrs. Sullivan. My mind was a mess as I tried to figure out where Sean might have gone. I wondered if he might have tried to find Charlie McFarland. Charlie's mother lived in Cork, and Sean knew that. Maybe he'd gone there. It was worth looking into, so I headed to Cork. The crumpled piece of brown paper was still in my jacket pocket. I unfolded it and gazed down on the faded penciled letters and numbers. After asking a few people where the street number on the paper might be, I made my way to the front of the home of Mrs. Charlotte McFarland.

It was a small, row house, packed tightly between two others just like it. Two steps led up to the door. I tapped the knocker and stepped back down the steps to allow the door to open. Through the screen, I saw an attractive, slim, fair-haired woman coming to answer. She was clad in a housedress and apron, and had obviously been in the middle of meal preparation, as she had bits of flour at the temple of her eye, and on her hands and apron.

"Afternoon, Ma'am, 'name's Walter O'Keeffe. I'd be looking for a chap by the name of Charlie McFarland."

She said nothing and just stood and looked down at me from the door way.

"'Ave I got the wrong flat?" I asked.

"No, Walter, you've come to the right spot." She wiped her hands on the front of her apron and pushed open the screen door.

"Come in, boy."

"Would Charlie be here, then? We had been mates at Greenmount. I'm also looking for my brother, Sean, and thought he might have tried to find Charlie 'imself."

"Come in, Walter. I'll put on some tea. I thought I might see ya' at my door one day." She turned and headed down a tidy narrow hall that led to the back of the flat.

The foyer was neatly packed with jackets on hooks and a bit of fishing tackle. A few buckets, and boots stood in an organized row down the hallway. As I followed her in, I caught a glimpse of the place Charlie had come home to. His photo was displayed here and there amongst others and it gave me great comfort to see his image. The home was sparse but tidy, and nicely decorated with the odd lace doily accenting small pieces of china. In the kitchen, Mrs. McFarland was preparing the kettle.

"Sit down, Walter. I have something to tell ya'."

Mrs. McFarland nervously fumbled to light a smoke. She took in a long puff from it, held her breath and then blew the smoke out.

An uneasy feeling took hold of me. I sat myself on a small stool that stood between the icebox and the rear door.

"Charlie spoke of ya' and yur' brother often. He was very fond of ya' and had always hoped he would see ya' again. We haven't seen yur' brother, I'm sorry to say."

She took another drag from her cigarette, I had a sense now that something awful was about to happen, then blew the smoke up towards the ceiling.

"Walter, we lost our dear boy, Charlie, only a few months ago. He drowned while working in the bog."

"No!" My head fell into my hands. This cannot be right. Maybe I'm at the wrong house. I sat up and quickly drew in a breath to replace the one that had been shocked out of me. Very quickly I became numb. Mrs. McFarland continued to speak and describe how Charlie had lost his life, and how many people had attended his wake. I didn't hear all she had to say as I was still shocked numb. Images of Charlie began streaming through my head: that first beating he had taken for me in our arithmetic class; the strike, when he stood up for everyone in the school; the time he came back after Christmas bearing sweets for Sean and I, memories kept coming.

After a while, the numbness that had taken over all of my emotions began to thaw, and pain and sadness took its place. Tears began to fill my eyes. I was broken. I spent the next few hours with Mrs. McFarland recovering from the terrible news. I felt sorry for her, as my visit had brought back all the pain and agony of losing her only son. She lit smoke after smoke. Together, we sat and talked about Charlie, and I told her what a wonderful friend he had been to me, and how he had protected Sean and I at Greenmount. Mrs. McFarland promised that if Sean came calling, she would take him in until he was able to find his way home to Polrone. I wrote him a note, and she agreed to pass it on if he showed up.

Before I left the McFarland home, Charlie's mother pulled a small, black and white photo from a tiny, wooden frame and handed it to me. It was a photo of Charlie taken shortly after he had left Greenmount. He was happy and looked like he had put on some weight. Seeing the photo allowed me to believe that he had lived the remaining years of his young life well.

I left the McFarland home feeling overcome with disappointment. I had let down my brother and not got him out of that place in time. Charlie had died before I could see him again. What a shitty day! I crossed the road and was heading towards the bus station, when I came within a nose length of being whacked in the face by the large, wooden door on Finnegan's Pub, as a few drunk Irish lads came tumbling out into the street.

I was miserable and not ready to get on the bus, so felt that the door to Finnegan's was my invitation to pause and drown my sorrows in the drink. I entered the watering hole and started my drowning with a few pints of dark ale. I then moved on to whiskey. I have vague memories of singing songs with various strangers throughout the afternoon, and foggy visions of crying into the arms of unfamiliar faces.

I have no idea how I made my way to that bus station. I only know that when I woke, I was crumpled over on a bus seat taking up both spots. My head hurt, the bus was spinning, and I was nauseous. I staggered to the front of the vehicle holding my mouth. Seeing that I was not well, the driver pulled over and quickly opened the door. I stepped off and immediately puked up. I leaned over the stone wall that edged the road and heaved. The driver and other passengers were patient, and waited until I was able to re-board.

"Thanks," I said, as I stepped back on to the bus.

"Rough day, lad?"

"Yes, sir, the worst."

Thirty one

SURPRISE ENCOUNTER

Over the next few months, I waited and hoped that Sean would show up, but he never did. I was haunted with the thought that I had not taken him away from Greenmont. If I had, maybe he would be with me now. I continued to work at the Crowley farm picking cabbage and tending to their livestock. That woman was so good to me. She had taken me in and asked for nothing. Working for the Crowley's provided me with money in my pocket, a roof over my head, and a family.

Josie's affection reduced the anxiety of not knowing what had happened to Sean. She was supportive and believed that Sean would return one day. Josie and I grew closer as time went by. My plan was to save up as much as I could, and then ask her to marry me. We were both almost eighteen, and I hoped that by nineteen we could settle on our own.

As I was returning from town with the Crowley cart, my mind wandered to another time and place—a place in the future when Josie and I had a home, a garden, and a family of our own; a time when I knew the whereabouts of my brothers and sisters, and knew that they were all safe, happy, and living their lives. As my mind wandered, my eyes caught sight of the small frame of a child down the road in front of me. As my wagon drew closer, I could see long, dark hair being blown about by the wind that was coming in off the Suir. The figure of the body indicated that this was a small woman, not a child. Although the shape of the body was not familiar to me, the face was. I didn't think it was possible, but as I got closer, I recognized the softness of the face and the shape of the eyes that were like mine, and that familiar gap in the teeth. This was the smile and the face of my sister, Eileen.

I pulled back the reins and stopped the cart. I stood up and just stared, straining my eyes in disbelief. She must have also recognized me, as she quickened her pace as she moved towards me. I jumped down and quickly ran to meet her. My brisk walk turned into a sprint, and within seconds I was standing before this raven-haired beauty with bright red lips. Neither of us could speak. We cried and held on to each other for a long while. Finally, she pushed me back and placed her hands on my face.

"Wattie, my wee baby brother, it's wonderful to see yur' beautiful face. My God, it's lovely to see ya'."

We sat together at the side of the road and spoke for a long time. I shared with her the horrors of living in Greenmont. She sobbed as I told her about the beatings and the state Sean was in when I had last seen him. I cried as I told her how damn much I wish I had taken Sean with me and never brought him back to that awful place. We spoke about my nightmares, and how even now I was waking up in fear, worried that I would get a beating or miss lighting the fires. What a relief to finally talk to someone about these things. I told her things I was not even able to tell Josie.

My poor sister had been through as much, if not more than, Jim, Sean, Billy and I. She told me tales of her troubled life. When Aunt Mary sent her away, she had been detained to a work farm for girls. One of the men, a farmer, had raped her when she was just 14 years old. She had no idea what he was doing to her. When she was with child she didn't know how it had happened. Like us, the girls sent away were never taught anything about their bodies or babies or relations between men and woman. She desperately missed her baby boy Patrick and was trying to make contact with the people he had been fostered out to. What a hard and horrible life she had lived.

"Wattie, I've been to England and I've seen Bessie and Jim. Bessie has had a baby boy with her new husband, Jim. Bessie has also seen Sean; he's living in London."

My heart stopped. Sean had made it to London. Why had he not come home?

Eileen had also heard that Billy settled in Derbyshire. He was still working in the mines.

Another burst of tears flowed down my face. That was it, then. Every one of us had survived. It was unbelievable. I wanted them all to be with us here, in this moment. I craved each of them more than my next breath. Sharing this moment with Eileen made me ache for the rest of my family. I had to see them.

As the sun began to set, I knew I had to get back to the farm. Eileen was staying at the O'Brien's and would be off in the morning to continue her search for Patrick. I didn't want to let her go. She was my only connection to my family, my parents and the happier times in my life. We sat together at the side of the road and held on to each others for a long time.

"Do ya' remember, Wattie, how we would sing with our Dad?"

"I do."

"I'll take you home again, Kathleen, across the ocean wild and wide
To where your heart has ever been, since you were first my bonnie bride.
The roses all have left your cheek; I've watched them fade away and die.
Your voice is sad when e'er you speak, and tears bedim your loving eyes.
Oh! I will take you back, Kathleen, to where your heart will feel no pain,
And when the fields are fresh and green, I'll take you to your home again."

We sang together with tears in our eyes until we both knew it was time to go. I helped her on to my cart and dropped her at the road leading to the O'Brien's. After a long embrace, I watched as she headed down the road. She turned into the yard, waved, and blew me a kiss. Her white, cotton dress and dark hair then disappeared behind the hedge. I knew it would be years before I saw her again.

Thirty two

NEW HORIZONS

"I've got to go to England, Josie. I've got to find my family. Sean, Bessie, Jim, Billy—they're all there. I was excited and giddy as I brought my sweetheart up to date on my visit with Eileen, and the information she had given me about Sean. "I've got to go, Josie, and I want ya' to come with me."

"I just can't go off to England, Wattie. I've got me Mum and chores."

"Just for a little while, like a holiday, just enough time for me to find Sean and Bessie and Jim. I can't leave ya' behind; I don't want to leave ya' behind. I'll come talk to yur' Mum and ask her if it would be alright."

After a lot of discussion, Mrs. Phelan agreed to allow Josie to come to England with me as long as she stayed with her relatives, and I stayed with mine. I didn't really know how long we would be gone, but I think I may have let Mrs. Phelan believe we would be back in a few weeks.

It was July, 1948. I knew that before Josie and I left, I had to go see my grandmother to bring her up to date on all of us and let her know that we were all alright. Early on the morning before Josie and I were to head off, I made the trip to Tobernabrone to see her. When I arrived to her little stone cottage, there she was out in her garden, talking away to herself. That's what anyone passing by might have thought. However, I knew she was talking to her plants, talking to the birds, and to the sun. She loved nature and could grow anything. Plants, bugs, bees, birds, were her life, and she loved them like children.

She did not see me when I entered the gate. I walked up slowly not to scare her, but to observe her. She had a scarf neatly tied under her chin keeping the sun off the top of her head. She was dressed in a long, black, cotton skirt and a white half-apron with two big pockets in the front. Her plain, white, cotton blouse had turned gray from wear, but she looked lovely.

"Hello Grandmother. Do ya' know who I am?" I called out softly.

"Jesus, ya' scared me halfway to heaven. Who've we got there?" She turned and came closer to me, then her eyes pooled with tears. "Oh, my boy, Wattie, 'tis so good to see ya'." She came up to me and hugged me around the waist. "I've been waiting for ya' to come home safe; I knew ya' would. I've been asking the angels to take care of all of yas'. Come, I've got rhubarb cake." It was unbelievable that she had even recognized me.

I spent most of the afternoon with her. We ate cake, then spent hours walking through her yard as she pointed out every plant and told me the story of how it came to be in her garden. Many plants she had rescued from a ditch or field. Some were cuttings from our home in Polrone. Her yard was full of berries of every kind, and birds, all of which she could name. My love of nature definitely came from her. She had wanted to take us in, but, we all knew it would have been too much for her. I was sorry that I had not come to see her sooner. I wanted to have word about the others before I came, now I did.

"I'll be heading off to England to find Sean, Bessie, and Jim, but I'll be coming back to see ya', I will," I told her.

"That's good, then."

"And when I come back, we'll be having a wedding as I'm going to ask Josie Phelan to marry me."

"That is grand. I'll be looking forward to seeing yas' all together. We'll have a big party, we will."

I was glad I had gone to see her. She reminded me of how much I loved the earth. To this day, I have never seen a garden as grand as my Grandmother Knox's in Tobernabrone.

The day Josie and I were to head off to England had arrived. We would take the bus to Waterford and then get the ferry from Rosslare over to England. Josie's mother came to see us off. We stood outside the sweet shop, with the Mooncoin churchyard in view, while we waited for our bus. I had come and gone from this spot so many times. After my Dad's funeral, when we were sent home from Peadmont, when I returned from the Reagans, going back and forth to find Sean, and here I was again. This spot seemed to signal change coming into my life.

"Wattie, ya' take care of our girl, now. I want ya' both back here safe."

"Ya' know I'll take care and keep a watchful eye over her." I said.

Mrs. Phelan kissed us both goodbye and we boarded the bus. We waved to her for as long as we could see her. I had no idea what was in store for Josie and I. I was just happy that this time, as I left Mooncoin, she was with me.

As the bus moved along, I noticed two small boys sitting across from us, maybe three and five years old. An older woman in a uniform, some sort of guardian I suppose, was sitting behind them. The littlest one had big blue eyes, a runny nose and an angelic, beautiful face. But he looked frightened.

"What's yur' name, then?" I asked.

"I'm Korey."

"That yur' brother?" I asked pointing to the other little fella' beside him.

"Uh huh, he's Ryan," he said as he pointed his finger into his brother's belly.

"Where ya' off to, then?"

"We're going to find our Grandpa?"

"And where's yur' Grandpa at?"

"I don't know, but he's gonna' pwotect us."

"Protect you? from what?"

"Da monsters and da bad guys."

"Korey, leave 'dat man alone," the older one said.

"It's okay. Would you boys like a peppermint?"

They turned to the stern looking woman behind them for the okay. She nodded her head, and so I handed them each a sweet.

"Where's yur' Grandpa?" I asked the older one.

"I'm not sure; we never met 'im; he's waiting fur us; we gonna' go live with 'im. He has a garden, and berries, and a dog."

The older woman cut in, "They've got no parents. We're on our way to St. Joseph's School for Boys, then we find out there's a grandfather. A big waste of my time this is, I tell ya'. They'd be better off in one of them schools for boys, not with some old man in a berry patch."

My heart fell into my stomach. This woman had no idea what she was talking about. I could feel my eyes watering up. Thank God they have someone to take them in. Thank God they would not be subjected to the life my brothers and I had lived. Christ, how many more children were there like them, like me? Hundreds? Thousands? Still being sent to those awful places. I couldn't bear the thought of it.

"Well, I'm glad you have a Grandpa to go to, and he's going to love the two of yous'. What's his name, yur' Grandpa?"

"Grandpa Walter," said Ryan.

"Really? That's my name."

The two of them giggled.

The bus stopped and Ryan and Korey were hustled off the bus by the stern looking, old bag. Just as the youngest one, Korey, stepped off, he turned and called out, "See ya' later, Walter." And they both waved to me.

So many of Ireland's children were taken from the home-towns they knew and tossed into places like Greenmount. Brothers and sisters were torn apart, sent to different schools and different cities. Raped, beaten, starved and neglected. The pain of knowing that children were still being sent to live in these terrible places, and being subjected to the worst kind of abuse, was unbearable. It was horrible thinking about it. I knew I would have to block it from my mind until one day there would be a reason to remember. I pulled Josie closer to me now, relieved that those awful years were behind me.

The ride to Waterford didn't take long. Waterford is the oldest city in Ireland and full of spectacular monuments, old churches, and activity. I had not been here in a long time, and was struck by how much it had grown. About 45 minutes later we arrived at Rosslare ferry-port. When we got to the port, we were both nervous. There were lots of people rushing about, seagulls swooped in and out, and containers of goods headed to England were stacked four and five high. It was an awesome sight and an exciting place to be. Josie hung on to me and barely spoke a word until we had made our way through the ticket line.

"Will we be alright, Wattie?" "Yes darling, we'll be fine. This will be the trip of a lifetime." Neither Josie nor I had ever set foot off of our dear Ireland and we were both scared. I, however, was trying not to show it.

We walked up the long, wooden ramp to the ship, steadying ourselves from time to time on the rope railing that protected us from the rocks and ocean below. The well-worn, wooden planks were faded by the hundreds of boots that had travelled up them and said goodbye to beautiful mother Ireland. Other travellers pushed past us to find a spot on the ship. Once on board, we made our way down the ship's deck and found a wooden bench in a windy corner near the bow. Although we had told Josie's family and our friends we would be back in a few short weeks, something told me that I might not find my way back to Ireland for a long, long time.

With both arms wrapped tightly around Josie, I pulled her into me as we gazed out across the sea. She leaned her head on my chest. My chin rested on the top of her soft, fine, silky hair. The scent of her, her tiny hand resting on my lap, the warmth of her body up against mine, was all I needed. All those years at Peadmont and Greenmount, the memory of Josie and the hope that we might be together one day had carried me and had kept me alive. Day after day, the vision of her was my only hope for a life of love and happiness. For all the love that had come and left my life, this moment made up for it.

I clung to her and for a brief instant, only a few seconds, was worried. Everything I had ever loved had left me. Would she? No, not Josie, I decided. I wouldn't even think that way. I believed that the misery of my life was now behind me. I hoped that the constant nightmares, the fear of authority, my lack of confidence would all vanish now that I was leaving Ireland. I thought that once I was re-united with my family, I would be normal, and feel normal. God I prayed for that. I only wanted to think about the future. I knew that Bessie, Eileen, Billy, Jim, and Sean were all alive. Once I saw them, I knew my mind and soul could rest. Too many tears had been shed over our pain, over our suffering. The tears that filled my eyes now were tears of joy, tears that made me feel alive.

How and why had I survived? I do not know. God must have had other plans for me. I had come to believe that there are no accidents in the universe. Over the years, I had written many prayers, poems, and affirmations to help me survive. The one that came to me now was: "This day will go down with the sun, and the moon will rise with the stars. Yesterday is history, tomorrow is still a mystery, make the best of this day." This poem had a new meaning to me now.

I looked back towards the dock as our ship slowly started to head out. The white waves kicked up against the side of the boat, creating a salty mist that gently fell on my face and lips, as if to kiss me goodbye. The sun was just starting to set and cast multiple shades of pink, orange, and red across the sky of our beautiful, green Ireland. 'Twas lovely, truly a joy to behold.

THE END

END NOTE

The heartache of Walters story continues. Walters quest to find his younger brother and re-unite with his other siblings, is a long and painful journey. His dream of love and a blissful life with Josie is short lived as events unfold that rip them apart for ever. Watch for the tragic and heart wrenching continuation, and conclusion of, the Walter O'Keeffe story in...

"Deliver us from Evil"
by Toni O'Keeffe
Due 2009

FOOT NOTE

On May 11, 1999, the Government of Ireland apologized on behalf of the State to the victims of abuse in Ireland's industrial schools. In September of 2004, after two years of pleading his case, Walter O'Keeffe received a settlement claim from the State for the suffering and abuse he was forced to endure from 1940-1946 while detained in St. Josephs School for Boys – Greenmont.

Epilogue

AUGUST 2006

Hidden behind the tall fir trees wound with dark, Irish ivy, is a wonderful and eccentric collection of spirit poles, leprechauns, Celtic figures, wooden carvings blending nature and humanity together, and an abundance of plants and shrubs, all lovingly cared for by their creator, Walter O'Keeffe. At age 75, O'Keeffe may very well be the best-kept secret in Canadian Folk Art.

When you walk into his studio, situated on the two acre, magical garden where he resides in Surrey, BC, you sense that the magnificent, wooden forms he has created are alive. O'Keeffe says he has developed a deep and loving connection with each one of the more than three hundred pieces of art in his collection. "I don't think I could part with any of 'em. They're like children; they are a part of me," says O'Keeffe in his charming Irish accent. "I know where each piece of wood came from. Some pieces were found in scrap piles, some came from fallen trees, and one of the larger pieces was hauled up from the banks of the Fraser River by my grandson, Ryan, over seventeen years ago."

O'Keeffe says he can see the forms and the faces of his creations in the wood before he carves them. "They are alive in there, waiting for me to release 'em. Caged in and held hostage by the wood around 'em. I free 'em to allow the world to see the beautiful forms that they are."

O'Keeffe's wood sculptures have a unique, Celtic look and feel. All created using only simple hand tools and scraps of wood, each piece was born in the creative mind of this artistic genius. In addition to his wooden sculptures, which all bear the symbol 'WO'K', O'Keeffe has written thousands of passionate, moving poems and hundreds of pieces of music, which he says flow out of him like tears.

His humble and simple surroundings also portray an artist in the truest and purest form. His work is real, raw, emotional, and it is clear that there is no technical or classroom approach to what he does. O'Keeffe was born with a creative brilliance that is rare, and he has put this amazing gift to good work.

O'Keeffe epitomizes the idyllic Irish artist, poet, and musician. Everything about this man—including the soft Irish lilt in his voice; the twinkle in his kind, Irish eyes; the jaunty cap on his head; his green, knitted sweater & well-worn walking stick; and the collection of 'empties' that sit outside his creative retreat—leads one to conclude that this is indeed the creative sanctuary of a good old Irish boy.

REQUIEM TO A ROSE
BY WALTER O'KEEFFE

I have shared this warm, rich earth with my dear friends,
The worms, snails, ants, and honeybees just to name a few,
And I have often wondered why God gave my little friends each a very special job to do,

But me, a rose not able to move around, what can I do when to this earth I am forever bound?

A little butterfly whispered in my ear one summer day; of all the flowers that ever grew, by far you are the most beautiful. So cheer up. God gave you a very special duty to perform—you were meant to look beautiful from the very first day that you were born.

You know, without you little rose, summer would just not be the same.
Oh, little butterfly, I could kiss you. You have given my life so much purpose and reason.

I have seen the sun rise and set now for so many summers, and my weary, old roots are tired; I feel this will be my last summer. Alas, I must die, I must die.

I have had pleasure living on this earth; the wind and the sun were always my friends and were with me every waking hour. The rain always seemed to know when to kiss me with a gentle shower; the wind always knew when to stir my heart for fear I might fall asleep and not do my part. But alas, I must die, I must die.

And now the wind blows the clouds from the sky to make way for the sun to come and say goodbye. I must die, I must die.

Now, in my final hour, the rain kisses me for the last time.

With a gentle shower, the wind reluctantly tears the last petal from my heart, and the sun saps the energy from my soul. I must die, I must die.

I lay naked now in the sun's heat, the green grass still growing at my feet.

I feel myself being lifted from the earth upwards and away from the thorny skeleton that was my home from birth. I must die, I must die.

I thank the wind, the rain, the sun, and the earth for taking care of my every need and now, into whose hands I trust my dying seed.

Free at last, I've played my part.

When summer comes again, will you remember me in your heart?

ACKNOWLEDGMENTS

Dad: Thank you for allowing my hands to be those that wrote this amazing story. Throughout this process, you have been incredibly brave and courageous. I know it was hard for you to go back to those times that were painful and haunting. I hope that through the writing of this book, you have found reconciliation and peace of mind.

Mom: I know that in many ways you have paid a price for the suffering and abuse that was inflicted on our father. Thank you for keeping our family together and strong and, for encouraging and supporting me while I undertook this project. You have been our anchor.

Robert: Thank you for encouraging me to set myself free, for always loving me no matter what I do. Thank you for penguins and campfires, hikes and angels, lattés, laughter and blue topaz anniversaries.

Terri, Suzie, Jacquie, Jeanette, Chris, and Juliette: Through the suffering of our father and the turmoil it has sometimes created in our lives, I love that we have developed a connectedness that is unique. Dad's story is our story and, I think brings understanding to many things we have endured together. I love that we are all strong, happy, and that we can laugh, dance, sing, tickle, and love openly.

My cousins, the sons and daughters of Bessie, Eileen, Billy, and Jim: This book represents only one side of the story, one part of your history. I know that your parents struggled and endured abuse and suffering similar to that of my father. This book is a collection of my Dad's memories as he recalled them. In all my interviews with him, he expressed the deepest love and longing for his brothers and sisters. Throughout his life, he missed them. Thank you to those of you who have stayed in touch with him. In doing so, you have helped to heal a part of his broken soul.

Ryan and Korey: This book represents where you came from. You both swim the same deep well of inner pondering that your Grandpa Walter swims in. He is more a part of each of you than I ever imagined, and I'm glad.

Brendan, Shannon, Nik, Kris, Bridgette, Nicky, Netty, Moira, Bronwyn, Gwen and baby O'Keeffe: You are all my favorites.

Jonas (You rock!), **Stefanie, Don, and Ron**: Thank you for stepping into our lives and sharing this amazing O'Keeffe journey with all of us.

Joe and Sharon Cross: I "leapt" thanks for the push.

I love you all

ABOUT THE AUTHOR

 Toni O'Keeffe grew up in Vancouver, BC. She is the second eldest child of Walter and Monica O'Keeffe. O'Keeffe has been a professional business writer and communicator for over twenty years. She has now put her creative talent to work to carry out a promise she made to her father when she was only five years old, a promise that she would one day tell his story.

"Although my father received an apology from the Irish government for the suffering and abuse he endured as a child, I do not believe he has healed. At 75 years old he is still that small child, wanting to be loved, appreciated and accepted. He is still afraid, hurt, guarded and unable to totally trust, anyone. It is my hope that through the process of telling his story he will be released from the demons that hold him so tightly and that he will find a place of healing. While this is a tale of the worst kind of abuse, this is also a tale of love, hope, courage, fortitude and survival. All the things that I will remember my father as being."

Toni O'Keeffe has two grown sons, Ryan and Korey. She lives with her husband, Robert, in Parksville, BC. She currently works as the Director of Communications and Public Relations at Malaspina University-College on Vancouver Island BC.

ISBN 142510457-6

9 781425 104573